rené
lévesque

Portrait of a Québécois

Design :	PUBLICI INC.
Cover photography :	MICHEL MONTICELLI
Photos :	COLLECTION OF LES EDITIONS LA PRESSE AND THE AUTHOR'S PRIVATE COLLECTION

Originally published in French by
LES EDITIONS LA PRESSE, 1974.

GAGE PUBLISHING LIMITED
© Copyright, 1975

ISBN   7715-9304-X Hardcover
ISBN   7715-9305-8 Softcover

Printed and bound in Canada

rené lévesque

Portrait of a Québécois

by jean provencher

Translated by David Ellis

gage PUBLISHING LIMITED

Acknowledgements

I would like to express my gratitude to the author, Jean Provencher, for his patient and generous co-operation. I wish also to thank my editor, Mark Czarnecki, for his indispensable contribution to this translation.

D.E.

1

A Happy Childhood

The Gaspé in the late twenties — cod fishermen; *Gou-Gou,* the ogress of Bonaventure Island; the Flying Dutchman, a ghost ship that visited Cap-d'Espoir every year; salmon and trout fishing grounds already in private hands — this was the world of Dominique Lévesque, who, in 1929, was on the look-out for French-language radio broadcasts. But his little radio set in New Carlisle, Quebec, would pick up nothing but the station in Charlottetown, Prince Edward Island. Not even the newspapers could be counted on. They invariably arrived three or four days late, unless of course a snowstorm succeeded in stopping the trains and holding up delivery even longer.

Since radio stations at that time had neither relays nor powerful transmitters, Dominique decided to take matters into his own hands. Surrounded by a crowd of curious parents and children, including his son René, he chopped down two of the tallest trees in the neighborhood. Once the trees were lashed together end to end, they made quite an impressive antenna. It was worth the trouble. Now Dominique could pick up not only station CKAC in Montreal, but also several east coast American stations. His wife, Diane, was somewhat less enchanted. The antenna stood right beside the house and swayed menacingly in high winds : if it fell, the sun roof would be demolished. But somehow the shaky structure remained standing.

Dominique Lévesque was a lawyer. In his days as a student he had worked for the law firm of Ernest Lapointe, Prime Minister

7

Mackenzie King's Quebec lieutenant. He met his future wife, Diane Dionne, in his home town of Rivière-du-Loup and moved to New Carlisle after their marriage in October 1920. One of his acquaintances, John Hall Kelly, also a lawyer, had persuaded him to move to the Gaspé and start a law firm with him there.

For a young man who had studied in Quebec City and a young woman who had been raised in Victoriaville, leaving the St. Lawrence Valley and making a new home on the north shore of Chaleur Bay was quite an adventure. Probably no other community in the Province of Quebec had such a high percentage of English-speaking inhabitants as New Carlisle, with its Astles, Caldwells, Chisholms, Flowers, Gallons, Gilkers, Halls, Imhoffs, Mains, Morrisons, Sawyers, Starnes, and Walkers, all descendants of either United Empire Loyalists or British immigrants from the islands of Jersey and Guernsey.

The Era of the Robins

The history of the south shore of the Gaspé Peninsula is to a large extent the history of Charles Robin and his descendants. In 1766, this merchant from Jersey explored the Gulf of St. Lawrence and, although one of his brothers had settled on Cape Breton Island, he himself chose Chaleur Bay. During the next seventeen years Robin operated a chain of stores and warehouses in Grande-Rivière, Percé, and Gaspé from his headquarters in Paspébiac. For many people the name "Robin" soon became synonymous with servitude. As one writer put it, this commercial network symbolized "the iron hand of control that was to rule the lives of the Gaspé fishermen for many years." [1]

In his history of the Gaspé co-operatives, school-teacher Paul LeBlanc carries the analysis further and reveals how this control was exercised :

> The Robin Company gradually took over all the fishing depots — if they were unable to engineer a shady deal, they did not hesitate to use force — and made them part of one large organization. In less than twenty years the Robins had established an out-and-out monopoly over the cod-fishing industry. [. . .] Three principles of operation, all equally pernicious, enabled the Robin Company to maintain its stranglehold on the people of the Gaspé for over one hundred years. First of all, there was the barter system. The Jersey magnates immediately set up

8

general stores throughout the area designed to make the most of the fact that the people were virtually penniless. They started to pay the fishermen half in cash, half in goods bartered in exchange for fish. The meagre half-salary quickly found its way back into the company coffers with interest, since the stores charged exorbitant prices for their goods. During the summer, this system barely kept the fishermen from starving; but in the off-season, from November to April, they were forced to live on credit from the local store. By continually mortgaging away next season's catch, these fishermen forged the chains of perpetual bondage to the system. The people of the Gaspé had only one immediate means of escape from this brutal exploitation: cultivation of the land. But the cunning Robins foresaw this possibility and left nothing to chance. Backed by their considerable influence in high places, they made certain that their serfs could not own an allotment of land exceeding a maximum of ten *arpents.* * Throughout the nineteenth century, this edict effectively prevented the cod fishermen from supplementing their insufficient means of livelihood by tilling the soil. All they could manage was a small garden, a hayfield, and some pasturage. The third and final principle — no schools, no education of any kind for the people of the Gaspé! [...] An insidious and continual propaganda campaign perpetrated by the Robins led the fishermen to believe that formal education would not make them any better at fishing. [2]

That is what life was like under the Robin dynasty, and when the Lévesque family came to live in New Carlisle, many talked bitterly about that era. The company was still thriving in 1920, but the ownership had changed hands, and business was now conducted under the name of *Robin, Jones and Whitman Ltd.* Its hold on the economic life of the Gaspé remained strong, but the fishermen were thinking of organizing themselves. In 1923, with the help of the government and the Bishop of Gaspé, François-Xavier Ross, an organization of fishermen's unions was established. Although the initial steps in this co-operative movement were difficult, the Gaspé fishermen had found the means that, twenty years later, would enable them to replace the Robin dynasty as the major economic force in the Gaspé.

In the early 1920's, a sizeable proportion of the white-collar

---

* Roughly equivalent to ten acres. (All notes appearing at the bottom of the page are the translator's, unless otherwise indicated.)

9

workers in Bonaventure County lived in the village of New Carlisle, whose population numbered about 1100. Here were located the district law courts, the county jail, the registry office, several banks, and a number of law offices. The village was virtually the private domain of its English-speaking, middle-class inhabitants.

Four miles away was its blue-collar, French-speaking counterpart, the village of Paspébiac (population 2700), which supplied by far the greatest number of working fishermen in Bonaventure County. Apart from fishing, the principal local industries were agriculture, dairy-farming, and lumber. And so, although it appeared somewhat remote and provincial, the Gaspé was in fact a microcosm of Quebec society at that time. It was here that René Lévesque was born on August 24, 1922.

In Quebec City, Taschereau was well entrenched as head of the provincial government and, when not busy opening new bridges, he was testing out some of the earliest provisions of the social welfare laws. These, too, were the days when the *Confédération des Travailleurs catholiques du Canada,* the future *CSN,* * and the *Coopérative fédérée* † were making their start. Quebec's population was then around two and a half million. In Ottawa, meanwhile, the Liberals had formed a minority government under William Lyon Mackenzie King.

Elsewhere, in France for example, Raymond Poincaré, who served as President of the Republic during the First World War, had again been named Prime Minister. In Rome, the new pope, elected after the death of Benedict XV, chose to be called Pius XI. He would soon have to come to terms with a political leader who was the idol of the Italan masses : Benito Mussolini. Egypt was enjoying her freedom now that she was no longer a protectorate of Great Britain. In Russia, the October Revolution was five years old, Stalin had become the Secretary of the Communist Party, and the GPU had succeeded the Cheka as the Soviet secret police.

Life in the province of Quebec, let alone the Gaspé, experienced no such great upheavals. But Dominique and Diane Lévesque, for

---

* The CTCC (Confederation of Catholic Workers of Canada) was founded by the Church in 1921 to stem union radicalism. Forty years later it was secularized and its name was changed to *Confédération des Syndicats Nationaux* (CSN) or Confederation of National Trade Unions (CNTU).

† The *Coopérative fédérée* was also founded in 1921, with the specific aim of helping Quebec's agricultural producers. Today the CF and the *Mouvement Desjardins* are the two largest co-operative movements in the province.

their part, were overjoyed by the arrival of René, especially since their first son had died at birth the year before.

Dominique Lévesque had never fully recovered from a bout of Spanish flu contracted during the great epidemic of 1918. Frustrated by his inability to endure physical effort for any length of time, he applied himself to his law practice with a devotion that earned him a place as one of the best lawyers in the lower St. Lawrence region.

His professional interests were closely allied with his favorite pastime—reading. He devoured everything he could lay his hands on; he bought books in New Carlisle itself or ordered them by mail. Dominique Lévesque eventually built up a collection of several thousand volumes, not including his law books. It is important to remember that, for many professional men living in rural areas at this time, reading was often the only entertainment. Cultural centres, musical and theatrical tours, and the now ubiquitous television set were unknown. Reading was indeed one of their few means of relaxation.

René Lévesque ransacked this well-stocked library "like a fiend." "Not surprisingly," he adds, "since that's what my father did. It was simply a case of follow the leader." So he imitated his father who read for hours on end.

Nothing could have pleased his father more. As soon as the youngster could listen to a story without fidgeting, Dominique Lévesque read him La Fontaine's *Fables*. René listened attentively to his father's words and watched all his gestures.

Then the boy bent over the book himself and tried to decipher the hieroglyphics confronting him. It's true that there were some pictures, but they didn't tell the whole story. Was there something hidden in all those funny black squiggles? His father didn't help much by telling him that the squiggles were called letters. Further questioning revealed that each letter had a name, and all the letters that looked alike had the same name. Well, that provided some kind of explanation, even for a four-year-old. One letter had a name that was particularly difficult to pronounce — "double u." At least that made it easier to remember than the others. And what about those others? Well, they could be strung together in groups of different lengths, called words. Take this word for example : w-o-l-f, wolf. Of course — that must be a wolf!

His father gave him the clues that eventually solved the whole puzzle. "He taught me French from an illustrated edition of La Fontaine's *Fables*," René Lévesque explained to journalist Hélène

Pilotte. "I only realized later that the story of the wolf and the stork, which I still remember, was a masterpiece." [3] In an interview with the author he added, "We had one of those large old editions of La Fontaine's *Fables* — it had a red cover and was beautifully illustrated. My father used to read us the stories. Gradually I began to decipher them as he taught me the alphabet and things like that. It was only much later I realized that they were classics. They were just stories to me then." [4]

After René had learned to read, he was asked at the age of four or five what he wanted to be when he grew up. He did not, like other boys, reply that he wanted to be a driver, a garbageman, or a fisherman, seduced by the power of big machines or by the romance of putting out to sea. René's answer was always the same : all he ever wanted to do was to write. He had already unconsciously felt the power of the written word; he could only guess how marvellous it would be to be able to write.

In September 1928, Dominique Lévesque took his son René to the primary school in New Carlisle. Rain or shine, the youngster walked the mile and a half between home and school, more often than not, four times daily. "It was fun walking this mile and a half to school," René adds, "and even more fun walking home again."

The New Carlisle primary school was like any other rural primary school. According to Lévesque, it was "a typical *one-room schoolhouse,* * with six grades all together in the one room." Since there were a lot of Irish in New Carlisle, all the Catholic children had been placed in the same school, whether they spoke English or French. Lévesque adds that the teacher "usually spoke better English than French because it was a bilingual school."

Lionel Allard has given us this picture of a Gaspé primary school :

> In the wintertime, the big cast-iron stove roasted those pupils who by chance or merit (your standing in the class sometimes determined where you sat) found themselves close to it, while those who had the misfortune to sit by the draughty windows shivered in the cold; the water bucket had to be filled every recess at a neighboring house or in a nearby stream; during the winter we found the ink frozen in the inkwells every Monday morning; the outhouse that stank in the summer turned into an icebox once the snow came; we had to take turns sweeping the knotty spruce floor with damp sawdust. [5]

---

* In English in the original. Words or phrases that occur in English in the original are italicized or set off in quotation marks.

12

About 1930.
A young lad in
his sailor suit.

In an age of school buses and community colleges, such a description comes as a bit of a shock, but Lévesque confirms its accuracy :

> That's just how it was. I remember the stove; we left our clothing beside it to dry because we used to arrive covered in snow. But to tell the truth there was only one thing that really mattered; as long as your family wasn't badly off — and some of the families were quite poor — it was an easy life and nothing to make a fuss over. The schoolhouse wasn't the nicest place around, but we had a good time. It wasn't the end of the world. [6]

The Catholics of New Carlisle had their *one-room schoolhouse;* the Protestants had their *high school.* * Lévesque elaborated on his school days :

> It was fun being a kid in New Carlisle. We used to walk to school and if you got there late, or didn't show up at all, the teacher tended to be pleased, because that meant one less pupil to deal with. Sometimes I was late for school and I often didn't do things the way I was expected to, so people took to calling me *triste.* That was an expression they used in the Gaspé to mean that someone was a bit strange. † Every morning I walked past the big, shiny, modern English *high school* — it looked much bigger to me than it actually was because I was so small. [7]

This *high school* became a symbol for Lévesque.

> Whenever I go back there, I think I see everything in its proper perspective — everything except that *high school.* In fact, it seems to get bigger and bigger as the years go by. Looking back on it, I realize now that it was the symbol of our whole co-existence with the English. New Carlisle was initially settled by Loyalists who entrenched themselves there and they had all the power. They weren't evil people: they simply treated the French Canadians the same way that the white Rhodesians treat their blacks. They don't do them any deliberate harm, but they have all the money and therefore the nice homes and the good schools. [. . .] It's very difficult for people to catch up on an education they've missed earlier in life. That fine English *high school* with its senior grades gave its graduates the opportunity to go on to McGill University. My own school, the one for French Canadians, with one teacher for four or five grades, led nowhere. It was that simple. [8]

The division along ethnic lines within the educational system was also evident outside the classroom. It was not just a case of French-speaking kids and English-speaking kids engaging in friendly competition. On the contrary — their games turned into racial struggles, French against English. Naturally there was a lot of scuffling, and a general brawl had usually broken out before the game was even off the ground. It was out-and-out warfare, with neither side ever able to claim lasting victory. "There was a running

---

* In English in the original.
† Literally, *triste* means "sad."

14

battle on," explained Lévesque, "between gangs of French-Canadian and English-Canadian kids. We had fistfights. They called us 'pea-soupers,' and for some unknown reason we called them 'crawfish.' It was all very colorful, and I don't feel any resentment towards the English as a result. It all seemed quite natural, just part of growing up." [9]

At one point tempers ran so high that Dominique Lévesque had to act as his son's bodyguard and walk him past a particularly dangerous corner. "We had to do it that way, otherwise I would never have been able to get to school and probably would have got myself into real trouble." He adds : "It's funny, but these aren't unhappy memories for me. We have a tendency to over-dramatize such events when we're describing them to other people. But you have to have grown up in an environment like that to under-stand how you can leave it behind — or at least how I left it behind — and not feel any bitterness. In fact, I think these experiences gave me a much deeper understanding of the whole problem."

Once René had experienced some formal education, reading became all the more appealing, and he would lose himself in a book for hours at a time. At first this mania pleased his parents, but soon they realized he was not getting enough fresh air. They eventually had to force him to go outside. "My life revolved around two centres, so to speak : orgies of reading and orgies of playing by the sea or just gallivanting around. These activities always prompted one of two extreme reactions : 'He's simply got to get out of the house,' or 'Where's he gone now ? Isn't he back yet ?' "

But when he went off to the seashore, René did not play the serious student, strolling pensively along a Gaspé beach — he joined in the fun along with everybody else : "Every now and then they would kick me out of the house because the weather was nice. Once you were out there, you realized how nice it really was. I wasn't the thoughtful type, because at that age you're always too full of energy. Back then we played all kinds of games outdoors. It's sad that so many children today are raised in big cities, cut off from nature. They get to be three or four years old and they've never even laid eyes on a cow or a pig." [10]

The seashore and the gallivanting around meant fights with the English kids, skipping pebbles along the water, diving from a boat because it was five feet higher than the wharf, and many hours spent gazing at the ships in the harbor. They also liked teasing Antoine Delarosbille, the fisherman from Paspébiac who was "the best known fishmonger in the area." Delarosbille made his rounds every morning and talked to his customers in *paspéyâ* * : "Fresh cod this marnin', Mrs. Lévesque? Fresh cod?" Although the accent was endearing, the youngsters invariably burst out laughing. Antoine Delarosbille — one more memory from a happy childhood...

In 1933, it seemed as if the economic depression in the Gaspé would never end : "Our hopes had never been so low, our fishing industry was in ruins, and the fishermen at the end of their tether." [11] But even this crisis left few bad memories with Lévesque, who was eleven then, and, apparently, others shared this feeling as well.

> We weren't really that affected by it. The kind of thing you heard from people was "we won't be able to buy a new car for two or three years." You got the feeling that times were rough at home and elsewhere. Nobody talked much about spending money. But it wasn't that terrible for us, and it wasn't that terrible for people we knew. What I mean is that where we were things were pretty bad, but not nearly so bad as I later learned they had been in the cities. Back home there was enough to go around and, besides, we were all in the same boat. We suffered a bit, but everybody was used to suffering and we endured it happily in a way. The thing about being poor is that it really hurts when you compare yourself with other people. But during those few years we were all poor and we didn't have a chance to compare ourselves with anyone else. What can I say? We were in our own little neck of the woods and.... No, I wouldn't say the depression had a catastrophic effect on the people back home — nothing like the effect it had on those in the cities. [12]

He added later : "Basically, we were all poor, but very happy. We set traps in the forest, and all we had to do to go swimming in Chaleur Bay was follow the railroad tracks to the beach in Paspébiac." [13]

College

In 1933, after five years in primary school, René Lévesque entered *Eléments latins* at the seminary in the town of Gaspé, an event of much greater importance to him at the time than the Depression. †
The seminary in Gaspé had been founded in 1926 and, since there was a shortage of lay instructors, a number of Jesuits had been

---

* Dialect of the inhabitants of Paspébiac.
† *Eléments latins* was part of a course of studies at the seminary known as the *"cours classique."* Before the educational reforms of the sixties,

brought in from Montreal to teach in the school. Because the town of Gaspé was 115 miles from New Carlisle, René had to become a boarder at the seminary.

Fourteen years later, Lévesque wrote this description of the journey between his home and the seminary :

> Clickety-clack, clickety-clack, clickety-clack ... The train from Chaleur Bay is "heading down" to Gaspé. [...] even though it's continually out of breath from climbing up yet another steep hill ; but that's how the saying goes — you always go "down" to Gaspé.... There have been a lot of changes on the miniature convoy which we used to flag down at the curve ; we didn't have to hurry, since it was never less than half an hour late. Inside the decrepit coaches, the seats were covered with plaited yellow straw or equally dirty green velours. The passengers' only relief during the voyage was the rasping voice of the vendor shouting "Chocolate, sandwiches, cigars, cigarettes, tobacco, matches !" [...] Fortunately, something of the past still remains : the train still proceeds at a snail's pace, jerkily grinding to a halt here and there for no particular reason at all. I remember the rough wooden shacks, darkened and weather-beaten, the sickly-looking cows, the chickens all skin and bones, and the wan, undernourished kids straddling the fences. [...] At the foot of a multi-colored promontory, a long, sandy triangular beach tapering to a fine point, a wharf, a number of big barges, some old red and white buildings and the ever-present smell of cod — fresh, salted, or pressed into oil .... This is the fishing centre of Paspébiac, headquarters of the acknowledged champion of evil on the Gaspé coast — Robin, Jones and Whitman Ltd., or as they are known locally, "the Robins."
>
> Not long ago, the whole area through which we're travelling, all the way to the tip of the peninsula, was part of the Robins' empire. Quite a few of their stores remain, staffed by loyal clerks from Jersey, and their annual turn-over is still impressive. But their rule is over : their subjects revolted and toppled the dynasty some years ago. In desperation the fishermen finally found the only effective solution — unionization and co-oper-

---

a student leaving primary school in Quebec had three options before him: the "general" course, the "scientific" course, and the "classical" course. The latter two qualified a student for university. The classical course was eight years long and the eight levels were named as follows : *Eléments latins, Syntaxe, Méthode, Versification, Belles-Lettres, Rhétorique, Philosophie I,* and *Philosophie II.* A heavy emphasis was placed on languages (French, English, Latin, Greek), as well as history and philosophy.

ative effort. [...] In these harbors sheltered by tongues of land and zigzagging breakwaters — Hope, Saint-Godfroi, Port-Daniel — the Robins, still pretenders to their lost throne, stand face to face with the burgeoning fishing co-operatives.... Farther along, past the cloud of smoke that indicates the town of Chandler with its enormous pulp mill, we find more peaceful little hamlets, their rows of look-alike houses reminiscent of building blocks a child might leave behind on the beach. On we go, heading "down" to Gaspé.... But wait a minute — there's Percé! Percé — incomparable, indescribable, unbelievable.... Long ago Champlain and his men came here, and now countless thousands of wide-eyed Yankee tourists come back year after year.... Percé is well worth a day's visit. [...]

Don't worry, it's all right, that's how we go in — through the freight yards. The little station, its red paint well camouflaged with dust, is situated on the edge of a thick forest. [...] At the end of the platform, men in overalls are dropping piles of sacks and crates marked "Fragile! Handle with Care!" * out of the boxcar: carrots, turnips, juicy tomatoes, big green cabbages, and even eggs (A-1, if you please).... Each one is stamped "Saint-Jacques Market, Montreal." At first glance this seems completely absurd — to send fresh produce at great expense to the country from a city 600 miles away! But the Gaspé just isn't suitable for farming. I remember the ragged lettuce and wormy radishes my poor father used to harvest whenever he fancied himself in the role of gentleman-farmer.... The strongest chemical fertilizers and the most conscientious weedings seemed to have no effect whatsoever. The land isn't a barren desert by any means, but it isn't exactly the promised land either. Oh, there are a few farms of course. Some of the locals have cultivated the *idea* of getting back to the land, but not much else....

Percé is the glory of the Gaspé Peninsula. Cannes has its *Croisette,* Nice its *Promenade des Anglais,* Mont St-Michel its *La Merveille,* Naples and Capri their Blue Grotto — all are wonderful places whose beauty has been celebrated by writers of genius! But if Europe did not have thirty centuries of history, twenty empires, thousands of illustrious heroes and precious ruins, then surely Percé would be the place to see.... Be that as it may, it is difficult to understand why many Québécois go out of their way to see Banff or California and yet overlook Percé. [14]

---

* In English in the original.

Lévesque lingers at Percé. But he can not linger too long, because the little train from Chaleur Bay is about to set off again, this time for Gaspé. Once the train arrives there in the evening, its daily run is over — five hours have elapsed since it stopped at New Carlisle. But Gaspé lacks the romance of Percé.

> The feeble lamps inside the station cast an uncertain light on the uncovered platforms and set a few vague shadows dancing ; the yellow eye of a car headlight flashes briefly in a sea-green puddle .... The world really seems to end here. The taxi bounces and groans along the narrow streets. [...] Gaspé never had a chance. Things look even worse in broad daylight, if that's possible — an overgrown village pretending to be a city. It has spread out so disjointedly around the spacious bay that it seems to have lost touch with itself. [...] On one side of the bay stands the hospital, where it is always over-crowded and there are never enough doctors to keep up with the work ; on the other side, the Ursuline convent and the little seminary. [15]

The seminary at last — his *alma mater*. A pretty exciting place for a boy of eleven, thrown in with some eighty other boys. A far cry of course from the *Collège d'enseignement général et professionnel* * *de Gaspé,* which, forty years later, would have over one thousand students. But the prospect of living there as a boarder, a kind of recluse, in a place where even recreation periods were regimented, was not pleasant, especially for a boy who had gone pretty much his own way, with his orgies of reading and gallivanting around. First they stuffed you with Latin, then, two years later, with Greek. As if that were not enough, they had monitors on patrol during study periods. Gone were the days of the schoolmistress who was glad to have one pupil less to worry about.

But you had to adjust. And René did adjust ... in his own way. Along with the other boys, he quickly learned how to get around the monitors. Because the seminary was under-staffed, the task of overseeing the younger pupils had to be delegated to senior students, who of course did not have the authority of a priest or an abbot. Nevertheless, since for many of them this was their first taste of power, they often tended to be even stricter than the college authorities themselves. The youngest boys soon took to calling the seniors "ass-lickers" and "sons-of-bitches."

But the monitors did not count for much in René Lévesque's school life. Far more important was his acquaintance with Father

---

* "CEGEP," popular acronym for community colleges in Quebec.

Alphonse Hamel, the rector of the college, who transformed his studies into a "great adventure." Lévesque explains :

> He was a pretty amazing guy. He was called late in life, which happens among the Jesuits, and to others I suppose, but basically he was very mechanically minded. He served in the navy during the First World War and, if my memory serves me correctly, it was about the time of some important developments in modern physics and navigation, and when the younger generation was searching for meaning in life. He was mad about radio, photography, things like that, and he had a lot of scientific *hobbies*. * I was one of the smallest boys in the college when I arrived, and he was looking for someone to do his donkey work. So I ended up being his darkroom assistant. Almost without my realizing it, he provided me with some interesting recreation and a break from my studies. He was a pretty amazing guy. [16]

Alphonse Hamel, for his part, came to know his young pupil well. He later told René's mother that her son's smile and some of his ideas occasionally reminded him of a two-year-old child, while at other times, René seemed to reason "like a forty-year-old man."

Now that he was a serious student, the young Lévesque was confronted with a whole new set of problems — politics, nationhood, the language question, etc. Like other boys his age, he was aware of the changing intellectual currents of the day. In this respect, the province of Quebec during the thirties was already experiencing a veritable "quiet revolution." Philippe Hamel, a dental surgeon from Quebec City, was one of a number of individuals trying to convince the people of the province that nationalization of the hydro-electric industry would be beneficial for Quebec. "This," he said, "is the only way we can hope to overcome the dictatorship of the hydro-electric monopolies." In 1933, a group of Jesuits from the *Ecole sociale populaire* † in Montreal, in collaboration with a number of laymen, published their *Programme de restauration sociale* [Program for social re-organization], in which they demanded government intervention to put an end to "economic dictatorship" and ensure "a more equitable distribution of wealth."

In July 1934, Philippe Hamel's followers in Quebec and several

---

* In English in the original.
† A movement founded by left-wing Catholics in response to the economic hardships of the period.

young progressive activists founded the *Action libérale nationale* [National Liberal Action Party]. In its manifesto, inspired to a great extent by the *Programme de restauration sociale,* the new provincial party declared that "the jurisdictional disputes between the municipal, provincial, and federal levels of government, the blind faith placed by some of our leaders in solutions whose potential hazards have become clear in the present crisis, the pernicious influence of campaign contributions, the lack of co-operation between our politicians and our economists, and the confusion of our civil administration, are all conspiring to postpone indefinitely the implementation of key measures and the formulation of comprehensive planning, which is a prerequisite to remedying the situation as it now stands."

Since the other two parties were more or less offshoots of the national Liberal and Conservative parties, the newly-formed *Action libérale nationale* constituted the only real provincial party. During the next eighteen months, they took Quebec by storm : 119 election rallies were organized and 37 talks were broadcast. The theme of social and economic liberation for French Canadians was on everyone's lips.

Young people began to organize themselves. In 1932, the *Jeune-Canada* [Young Canada] movement grew out of a *Manifeste de la jeune génération* [Manifesto of the young generation], published by the University of Montreal student association, and called for a rejection of the older generation's values. There was soon talk of a "revolution against capitalism." From 1933 to 1938, the *Association catholique de la Jeunesse canadienne* [Catholic Association of Canadian Youth], made up mostly of young French-speaking Québécois, multiplied its membership ten times over, to a total of 50,000, in more than one thousand cells across the province. The *Jeunes Patriotes* [Young Patriots], who felt that too few Québécois held important posts in the province's industries, denounced the economic domination of foreign capital and rejected Confederation. All these youth movements led a foreign observer to state that "youth played an important role in the political battles of 1935 and 1936, battles which made French Canada conscious once again of its vitality and power."

Some young people organized, others wrote. The magazine *Vivre,* edited by Jean-Louis Gagnon, also condemned capitalism. In 1936, Rodolphe Dubé published *Leur inquiétude* under the pseudonym of François Hertel. His book was both an attempt to explain the unrest among youth and an appeal to the young people themselves, urging them on to greater efforts. Hertel was thirty-one at the time, and independence for Quebec seemed to him inevitable :

> Although the province of Quebec enjoys a nominal independence from the rest of the Dominion, its natural development is in fact shackled by that unfortunate political arrangement we call Confederation. Why is Quebec always crawling on all fours ? Because of Ottawa. [. . .] In my opinion, as long as the federal system keeps Quebec under Ottawa's wing, we will never accomplish anything. Whichever political party saves us will have to present as the first and most important part of its program withdrawal from Confederation. This is what the young are beginning to understand. And if they are turning to the *Action libérale nationale,* it is because they believe this party will offer them more support in their struggle for autonomy. [17]

For Hertel, the youth of Quebec provided another argument for the inevitability of withdrawal from Confederation.

> Another reason, and a very compelling one, for considering separation inevitable is the renewed spirit of nationalism (now virtually taken for granted) among the younger generation in Quebec. And in the natural course of events can we not expect this awakening to continue growing, so that soon our whole province will be hostile to the very idea of Confederation ? Once today's young people are in power, perhaps fifteen years from now, they will actively seek and demand separation ; they will see clearly what a farce Confederation has been at our expense and they will realize that they have absolutely nothing more to gain from it. [18]

But as he wrote these lines, Hertel could not have foreseen the designs of Maurice Duplessis. The cunning Duplessis had anticipated the probable political success of the *Action libérale nationale* (ALN). Soon after Duplessis and his party had formed an election coalition with the ALN he broke up the coalition with much fanfare and managed to win the majority of the ALN sympathizers over to his side. The ALN was finished as a political force. Duplessis' new party, the Union Nationale, scored a resounding victory in the August '36 elections by reaping the fruits of the ALN campaign. There were those who saw in the election results the beginnings of real liberation. But then Hamel and his supporters, who had left the ALN to follow Duplessis, were stunned to learn that the new premier was not going to nationalize the hydro-electric industry after all. He was too convinced of the virtues of private enterprise to entertain such a notion. Duplessis' rise to power therefore spelled political disaster for this first "quiet revolution."

The students at the seminary in Gaspé were as aware of these issues as the intellectuals in Montreal, 600 miles away. The reason for this was simple, as Lévesque explains :

> The Jesuits who ran the seminary were for the most part from Montreal or Quebec City. They were therefore in touch with what Abbé Groulx * or Hamel and his followers were up to at the time. My first Latin teacher, for example, Father Dubé, happened to be the brother or first cousin of Rodolphe Dubé, alias François Hertel. At that point Hertel, who was just beginning his career with the Jesuits, had finished writing, or was completing, *Leur inquiétude,* a book of the "youth-of-the-province-unite" sort, which basically tried to define and explain the Quebec situation. The book soon fell into our hands. In addition, we always had teachers who were acquainted with the latest ideas. Every year there was a rotation of staff : some would leave and others would arrive from Montreal to take their place. Ironically, we were probably in even closer touch with the changing climate of opinion than the "in-between" students in Rimouski, Rivière-du-Loup, etc., simply because of our teachers. In other words, we felt pretty much in the swim of things . . . from a distance, of course. [19]

While at the seminary in Gaspé René Lévesque learned about the province of Quebec for the first time. "I began discovering there was such a thing as French Canada and I began to learn about its problems. It was quite a shock for a boy from New Carlisle." [20] It was a feeling he would never forget.

In 1960, when the provincial Liberal Party's program was undergoing re-examination, Lévesque recalled the platform of the *Action libérale nationale.* Two years later, the policies of Dr. Philippe Hamel surfaced again, virtually intact, and it is sometimes difficult to distinguish the separatist thinking of the thirties from Lévesque's political stance in the sixties. Beyond a doubt he was deeply influenced by the intellectual and political ferment that stirred Quebec during the 1930's.

---

* The nationalism of Abbé Lionel Groulx exerted a strong influence on the political thinking of Quebec students in the thirties and forties. He was one of the founders of the *Association catholique de la Jeunesse canadienne* (see p. 21).

First Works

Young Lévesque still dreamed of becoming a writer. His wishes were finally fulfilled at the seminary, where, for the first time, he was able to write for a readership that extended beyond his teachers and his parents. In his third year he was asked to write for *L'Envol,* a small, cheaply-produced student paper of ten to twelve pages. One of his first pieces was printed in December 1935. It was a Christmas story entitled *Le Noël du Chamelier* [The Camel-Driver's Christmas]. Writing in the style of a neuwspaper reporter, he describes a young camel-driver's journey to the manger where Christ was born :

> We are in Bethlehem ; the year is 749 on the Roman calendar ; Octavius Augustus is Emperor. The cold December night has driven all the inhabitants of the village indoors. The streets are deserted. A light mantle of snow has fallen, covering the golden domes of the sumptuous palaces and the roof of the synagogue. Here and there the pale, cold light of a crescent moon flecks this immaculate carpet with red. Passing on to the outskirts of the village through the eastern gate, not far from the wall, we find a caravan of camels kneeling in the snow, fast asleep. These animals have Arabian blood : they are a rare breed and very costly in Palestine. Who might be the owner of these superb beasts ? Some rich Arabian or Egyptian emir, no doubt. Not a Jew in any case, because they are not harnassed in the Jewish manner. But what are those little shadows huddled between the sleeping camels ? Let's move closer. Ah, that's what they are — three of the caravan's young camel-drivers, asleep in the snow beside their animals. Poor things ! They are Arabs most likely, and are probably accustomed to harsh life and cruel treatment ! Their master has left them to sleep on the ground, so here they lie, chilled by the cold snow.

One of the camel-drivers wakes up, and Lévesque, still telling the story as if he were a reporter, invites us to follow the young man to the manger. He stops in front of a tumble-down stable :

> Our guide does not enter, but slips in behind the stable. He finds a crack in the wall, quickly bends over and looks inside, curious. Let's creep up behind him and take a look over his shoulder. Inside we see one of those dirty cramped rooms which Jews today often abandon, just as their ancestors did nineteen centuries ago ; a smoky torch casts a dim light over the chilly

lodgings ; the holes in the walls are so numerous that the cold penetrates everywhere. A cow and a donkey lie sprawled on the hay in the middle of the floor, breathing gently on something or someone hidden from view by their massive bodies, an object that seems to have brought great happiness to the man and woman seated close by. The man looks old and a bit worn-out. He has a grey beard and his long robe gives him a dignified air. His face is serious but kindly. His young companion is beautiful, divinely beautiful, and rather small. She has a self-contained, modest look about her. Her gaze remains fixed on the spot hidden from sight which is the centre of attention of all those present. [21]

René Lévesque was then only thirteen, but his gift for narrative enabled him to lend an air of suspense to this familiar story.

His second story, printed in March 1936, was about the wreck of a schooner during a storm at sea. [22] His third piece was the imaginary history of a grandfather clock, supposedly built by one Franz Schwartz in 1663, which witnessed the splendors of Louis XIV's reign before ending up in the Gaspé. [23] These stories were all quite clearly the work of a boy who had read a great deal, and his extensive vocabulary allowed him to write with considerable subtlety.

Although he spent a lot of time writing, reading was still one of René's greatest pleasures. Raymond Bourget, a classmate, wrote a little satire in which he went to heaven in the year 2010 to visit his old friends, and found them working away at their favorite occupations. He comes to René Lévesque : "You're still the same — you just love books, don't you ? So now of course you're reading *The Divine Comedy !*" [24] He would spend hours and hours reading everything under the sun.

During vacations and study breaks, he went home to his parents in New Carlisle. The Lévesque family now included four children : René, Fernand, André, and Alice. Their father Dominique always took a great interest in his children's intellectual development, and since René was the oldest, he was the first to benefit from it. An important challenge was presented by the crossword puzzle in the *Standard*, the weekly supplement to the *Montreal Star*. Lévesque explains :

The story of the *Standard* crossword puzzles was typical. My father learned English very late in life and, although he had a very large vocabulary, his accent was atrocious. You could barely understand what he was saying. It's hard to get the accent right when you learn late. I liked to tease him about his accent, because I spoke English very well. I had no trouble at all — I had learned it almost without thinking. So I thought I was pretty smart. But when the *Standard* arrived each week there was always a contest to see who could finish the crossword first. That's why we took two copies. It was a humbling experience — I thought I was so clever, but my father would always beat me because his vocabulary was much bigger than mine. [25]

Dominique Lévesque also had a passion for geography. He would often get the children together and organize a geography quiz. "What's the capital of . . . ? How many inhabitants ? Where's such-and-such a city ? In what country ? What kind of government does it have ? . . ." Lévesque adds : "I tended to be a bit more successful at that kind of game." In this way he acquired a multitude of facts about geography which later stood him in good stead. His father's passion is easily explained : "He always wanted to travel, but like many people whose health is poor, he didn't have much chance to. Perhaps it's understandable when you live in the Gaspé — in a remote place like that, geography can easily become an obsession. And besides, you're right by the sea — that's sure to make you dream of far-away places." [26]

What, in fact, does René Lévesque himself prefer — the Gaspé of the sea or the Gaspé of the forest ?

> For me, it's definitely the sea ; I'm not at home in the forest. I've got nothing against it mind you — I like a walk through the woods as much as anyone else. But that's about it. I was never interested in hunting — or even fishing, for that matter. To tell the truth, I've just seen too much of it. Being the oldest, I was my father's drudge, so that every time he went fishing and needed a hand, I ended up going with him. I didn't mind it ; but you always had to be so quiet, especially when you were trying to pin-point a good feeding ground. I love the sea just by itself. For me, it's the best thing about the Gaspé. I'd be happy as a king if by some chance Montreal had been built on the ocean. I think a city by the sea is a really fantastic place. [27]

For a long time, the political loyalties of the Québécois had been sharply divided between two opposing factions : the supporters of Wilfrid Laurier and the supporters of Henri Bourassa. The hatred for one was proportionate to the love for the other. Author Jean

26

Hamelin, describing his childhood in Montreal's east end during the thirties, recalls this polarization :

> It didn't matter that certain federal prime ministers, such as Borden and Meighen, were the most unprepossessing individuals imaginable (of course, they would have been maligned even if they had looked like angels) — they were just the lowly hangmen of the aristocratic, the refined, the charming, the legendary, the superhuman Sir Wilfrid Laurier, that extravagant, almost unbelievable apotheosis of French-Canadian urbanity. And what of the hatred for the thick moustache and grey beard of Henri Bourassa, that proud and rebellious spirit, who had impugned the great man's integrity and, so the story goes, even made him *cry* ? [28]

Dominique Lévesque was possessed by this kind of unqualified admiration for Laurier. Lévesque describes his father's brush with politics :

> A year after the fall of the Taschereau régime, my father was approached by the Liberal Party. He was a great admirer, a fanatical disciple even, of Laurier. Since he had never been involved in politics before, his reputation was spotless. At first he turned them down because he had nothing good to say about the régime. * But eventually he agreed to work with them, provided he did not have to speak in public, and he consented to do a fifteen-minute radio talk. He left for the broadcast feeling quite mortified, because the party was so corrupt at the time that he still hadn't managed to find anything good to say about it. We were sitting around the kitchen table, all ears. He finally ended up praising the virtues of Laurier, who had been dead for seventeen years, throughout the entire fifteen minutes of his talk. That wasn't exactly what they wanted, but it was quite funny. [29]

In the spring of 1937, tragedy struck the Lévesque family. Dominique Lévesque died of a heart ailment at the age of forty-eight, leaving the children without the father who had been such an important influence on their development. The author gave Lévesque his own impression of what the man must have been like : "It seems that your father presented you with a very high ideal of what a man ought to be, but this ideal wasn't so formidable that you would later be condemned to live in your father's shadow." Lévesque replied :

* In the spring of 1936 an inquiry into the handling of public funds allowed Maurice Duplessis to bring to light certain scandals at the highest levels of the Liberal administration, which had held power in Quebec for forty years. [Author's note.]

I think he was an extraordinary guy. Many people who knew him have said the same thing. Since I was only fourteen when he died, it's obviously difficult for me to pass judgment on him. All I can really say is that what you've said is true. I never felt there was anything either petty or authoritarian about him, in the sense that he would run roughshod over the children or anyone less fortunate than himself — and there were plenty of men like that in the Gaspé. He respected other people without reservation, whether they were children, poor people, or business competitors. In other words, I'd say he was basically very human, very tolerant, yet capable when necessary of giving guidance, which you really need when you're young and foolish, especially living in the country like that, where you could do pretty well as you pleased. But you were never left with the feeling that he was acting arbitrarily. In other words, you could really understand him. [30]

René Lévesque had lost a father and a friend. But Dominique Lévesque had shown him that his devotion to reading and writing could make him independent, and René was soon able to stand on his own two feet. In the summer of 1937, he was taken on as an announcer and news editor at radio station CHNC in New Carlisle. In July, he won the Parker Prize. *L'Action Catholique* reported :

> The seminaries in Three Rivers and Gaspé were honored today when Father Emile Beaudry announced the results of the competition for the Parker Prize. First prize went to Mr. Lionel Dessureault of the Three Rivers seminary, and second prize to Mr. René Lévesque of the Gaspé seminary. The Parker Prizes are awarded in an inter-collegiate competition to those students who have composed the best essay in the area of Canadian history and, more specifically, on a subject relating to the Canadian Jesuit Martyrs. The prizes were endowed by Lord Gilbert Parker, who was deeply impressed during a visit to the province of Quebec by the tragic and sublime history of our holy martyrs.

But the work at CHNC was only a summer job. There was no question of abandoning his education ; in September 1937, Lévesque went back to the seminary in Gaspé and enrolled in *Belles-Lettres*. * However, this was his last year in Gaspé : his mother liquidated his father's estate and moved the family to Quebec City in the summer of 1938.

---

* "Humanities," *i.e.*, fifth year. See note on p. 16.

New Horizons : the Old Capital

In September 1938, René Lévesque enrolled at Garnier College, which was run by the Jesuits. Why the Jesuits again ? Several people explained to the author, only half tongue-in-cheek, that "Lévesque wasn't an easy pupil to manage and the Jesuits were the only ones who would put up with him." In any event, a month and a half after his arrival, he wrote his first article for *Le Garnier,* the college student newspaper, in which he attempted to enlighten these ignorant city folk about the Gaspé. First of all he described his arrival in the city :

> On September 6, a young man from the Gaspé got off the train in Champlain's old city feeling quite nervous and strangely out of his element.... His previous visits to Quebec, all very brief, had inspired him (as they would any self-respecting country dweller) with a holy dread of this chaotic Babel they call the Big City. The poor guy began to worry about just how long he would last in a place like that. A month and a half has gone by.... Bit by bit the *rusticus* [yokel] has calmed down.... Without wishing to sound ingratiating (like a "browner," as the students put it), he would like to say that the warm welcome accorded him has had a lot to do with his successful adjustment. [31]

Lévesque wrote a short piece in the same issue featuring "Benes, Adolf, Polack, Magyar, John Bull and Edouard." The article satirized European politics and revealed the keen interest on the part of the author in international affairs. By December he had become a regular contributor to the paper. Pierre Boucher was the editor, and his staff included Jean Boucher, Jean Bernier, Gilles Pion, François Cloutier, Saint-Denys Prévost... and René Lévesque.

Lévesque worked for the paper throughout the '38-'39 academic year. Although many of his colleagues on the staff took their position seriously, Lévesque made light of just about everything. He discussed the seven hours of detention he had been penalized, during which he chalked up "30 lines of Cicero, 30 of Latin composition, 28 of Greek translation, and 11 second degree quadratic equations." He managed to get an exclusive interview in heaven with Mr. Jean Racine on the occasion of his 300th birthday. He ridiculed his classmates' mania for organizing parties at the drop of a hat.

In June 1939, however, he published a much more serious work. Here he was at the age of sixteen expounding a philosophy of life and social action that is astonishing in its maturity. The article in question was entitled *L'esprit sportif dans la vie* [The Sporting Spirit

29

1938.
In the sixth year
of his classical
course at Garnier
College in
Quebec City.

in Life]. Lévesque first explained what he meant by the sporting spirit, quoting by way of definition these words by Emile Maussat : "The religion of fighting without hatred, losing without bitterness, and winning without pride."

He went on :

> A fighting spirit is a prerequisite if you really want to win the game, especially the game of life .... You must fight to live. [. . .] You cannot be prepared to fight well unless you are completely realistic and practical and can see things as they are — the problems, the chances of success, the means of achieving your goals .... Dreamers with their heads in the clouds and utopian philosophers invariably miss the mark. [. . .] Misplaced idealism can be just as dangerous as none at

all . . . . Take, for example, the befuddled intellectuals who see themselves as the guiding lights of our so-called patriotic movements. (No, my friend, I'm not naming any names.) High-sounding, sincere phrases, stirring calls to arms . . . And then, nothing — no action, nothing concrete ; just idle chit-chat, well-meant perhaps, but ineffectual all the same . . . We hear visionaries beating the drum of patriotism, but not men of action, men with tangible constructive proposals . . . . Does this mean that practical idealism is only a myth ? Do you really think so ? Hopefully not . . .

These few lines written at the age of sixteen state a philosophy of life which has not changed substantially since then, and anyone interested in understanding René Lévesque's ideas would do well to start with this article. In what follows, we see Lévesque forging his own political philosophy from the nationalist tradition to which he had been exposed :

It's a fact that many people are shamefully ignorant of History . . . . But there are many more (and they are in the majority) who know it but don't understand it, which is probably worse . . . . What a lot of chest-beating and gibberish we have to endure each year for Saint-Jean-Baptiste * and Dollard des Ormeaux ! † (Please note that it's the gibberish I'm objecting to and not the holidays themselves.) As Arthur Buies ‡ put it : "Because of our obsession with that sacred catch-phrase, which we have seen inscribed in a thousand places : 'our institutions, our religion, the laws of our fathers,' because we wanted to live only in the past, we have become lost, blind to the present, oblivious to the future . . . ." If in years gone by your ancestors had lapsed into the passivity displayed by all these dotards who worship them so much, how would they have performed the miracles we admire so much today ? . . . They did not waste words on their high ideal of spreading the Gospel and the glory of France ; instead they made their ideal live with every blow of the axe, every furrow of the plough, and every thrust of the sword . . . . Undistracted by idle adulation of their own ancestors, they strode across the continent hoping that their descendants . . . . What a naïve heroic lot ! . . .

---

* The patron saint of French Canada; Saint-Jean-Baptiste Day (June 24) is Quebec's national day.

† Dollard des Ormeaux distinguished himself in the French colonists' struggle against the Iroquois. The traditional Dollard holiday referred to here falls on May 24.

‡ Arthur Buies (1840-1901), a prominent writer, journalist, pamphleteer, and anti-clerical.

But why should we disappoint them ? ... Let your own ideals give meaning and direction to your life and let our history serve as an example, a source of consolation, or a handbook filled with lessons gained from experience, but never as a shackle that will break your spirit and keep you enslaved.... And so to work, on into battle ! ... Turn away from the Past .... Come down to earth .... Feet firmly on the ground, face to face with reality ... mind focussed on the present ... hands grappling with the here and now ... one eye fixed on the present, the other on the future (without going cross-eyed, mind you ...). Instead of being the victim of History you will become its master ....

Lévesque then sums up this philosophy of life and relates it to the French-Canadian community :

Remember that whether you are fortunate or unfortunate you must exercise self-restraint : the victor cannot lord it over his defeated rival and crush him underfoot ; it is not the victory that arouses bitter hatred, but rather arrogance on the part of the victor .... Only moderation will win other people's approval and make them applaud a brilliant victory. [...] Exercise this love of battle and of calm, persistent striving towards a truly practical goal ; learn how to gain strength from defeat and temper your victories with tact and moderation .... If you have higher goals than your own personal success, do not forget that you are a French Canadian, that your people have been mired in lassitude for generations and that if the masses do not act, this nation — your nation — is lost ! [...] There's no use saying : "Bah ! What difference does it make — one person more or less ?" or "That's none of my business !" ... Imagine what would happen if everyone sloughed off responsibility onto the next fellow's shoulders .... Let's have none of that ! ... Everyone has got to pitch in. "Every descendant of the 60,000 defeated in 1760 must stand up and be counted !" The future is in the hands of young people like yourself. This is no Saint-Jean-Baptiste Day rhetoric : the truth is self-evident and it affects you deeply, for you are, let me say it once again.... Ah ! but you've had enough .... You're yawning, all you want is to fall asleep in your armchair .... Go ahead, then, go to sleep, and in your dreams repeat to yourself these words of Clemenceau which adapt themselves so well to our situation .... Say them to yourself over and over again : "French Canadians will get the French Canada they deserve !" [32]

In September 1939, René Lévesque enrolled in the first year of the "Philosophy" program. * A month later he succeeded Pierre Boucher as editor of the school paper. Like all student newspaper editors, Lévesque was forced to appeal to his reading public for more contributions. The staff included Bernier, Cloutier, and Pion from the previous year ; they were joined by Lucien Côté, André Dechène, and Yves Pratte. But they were still too few and Lévesque often had to write two articles in the same issue.

The *Académie Sciences-Arts* [Arts and Sciences Academy] of Garnier College was founded on November 6. The first executive council included Pierre Boucher, president, René Lévesque, vice-president, François Cloutier, secretary, and Guy Dorion, treasurer. On the agenda of the Academy's first semi-public meeting was a debate between Humanities [*Belles-Lettres*] and Philosophy I. † The speakers had to argue the question : "Was Napoléon beneficial to France and to Europe ?" Paul Legendre, the secretary on this occasion, has left us the following account of the proceedings :

> It took some daring for the humanists to do battle with the philosophers, but François Cloutier and Christian Hardy, the standard bearers for the humanities, were equal to the task. Their opening speeches, formally composed, fully documented, and delivered in a forthright manner accentuated with gestures that were a little melodramatic but effective, established that Napoleon had been of no use at all to France or to Europe. Then came the reply, scathing and incisive. Jacques Roy's cold logic, René Lévesque's exhaustive documentation and irrepressible energy, his brilliantly improvised elucidation of the subtlest arguments, complete with names, places, and dates, all transformed the debate into a display of impassioned oratory. In the twenty minutes allowed for rebuttal, the two sides exploited every possible weakness, clarified points that had been misconstrued, and further substantiated their claims. Jean Bernier, who presided over the judges, brought the debate to a close and announced the results : René Lévesque, Philosophy I, was voted best speaker, but the students from Humanities were declared the winners. [33]

This was a new feather in Lévesque's cap. But he did not enjoy his success for very long : by January 1940, he was no longer in charge of the newspaper, and Pierre Boucher was in fact obliged to reassume his former position. What had happened ? The Christmas examinations had been a turning point for Lévesque. He explains :

---

* See note on p. 16.
† See note on p. 16.

In those days, Philosophy I had been stormed and nearly taken over by higher mathematics. Because of the teaching methods and my own dislike for it at the time, I flunked. I showed up at the exams having done no work during the term and I got exactly 1%, if I remember correctly. I carefully copied out all the questions and then didn't answer a single one! The rector called me in and said in a fatherly manner that he had been following my progress. You know they do that, these damned Jesuits. He had been following my progress carefully and, in his opinion, it would be best if I left the college. [34]

Lévesque did leave Garnier and enrolled in the Faculty of Arts at the Quebec City seminary for the second term. "As a result I found myself among the black sheep in the Faculty of Arts. That is, we were day students — the seminary included both day students and boarders." When it came time for the *baccalauréat ès Arts* examinations, * Lévesque passed with flying colors : "Strangely enough, I got 19.5 out of 20 in mathematics. I had learned my lesson, and I realized that I could do just as well as anybody else. I even beat Jacques Roy, who was nicknamed Oedipus. He was the genius of the math class. I beat him, and for a long time he couldn't bring himself to forgive me, because I was supposed to be the class dunce." [35]

Day students were not allowed to take part in the boarders' extra-curricular activities. But even though René Lévesque had enjoyed his brief spell with the *Académie Sciences-Arts* at Garnier College, he probably would not have found the debates of the *Académie Saint-Denys* at the seminary quite as stimulating. When he arrived there, the Academy was holding its 154th solemn session. Among the subjects discussed were "the beatitudes," "alcoholism and the Church," "our worldly knowledge," "living is a victory over our animal nature," "quantity," "the act of knowing as an immanent action," "nature and art," and, finally, "logic in the true sense of the word is the mathematics of thought."

In the June 1940 examinations, Lévesque came out twenty-first in a class of sixty with an average of 69.5%. If good marks are any indication at all of genuine interest, Lévesque must have been mad about astronomy and the history of philosophy.

In September 1940, still a day student, he enrolled in Philosophy II at the seminary. The first term proved uneventful, except that he "forgot" to show up for the physics examination in December.

---

* The *baccalauréat* was the diploma granted upon successful completion of the *cours classique*. This "BA" allowed the student to enter university ; not to be confused with the BA conferred by English-speaking universities.

34

Fortunately, he obtained sixteen out of twenty on the supplemental examination in January. The second term was much harder going. The priests noticed that his performance in class was excellent, but that he was often absent. In June, he "forgot" once again to show up for his theology and physics examinations. But after successfully completing the supplementals in August, he finally received his *baccalauréat* from the Faculty of Arts at Laval University. His high school education was finished, and not a moment too soon.

But a high school diploma without any other qualifications does not open the door to many jobs or professional careers. Further studies at university were inevitable, and in September 1941, Lévesque enrolled — without much conviction — in the Faculty of Law at Laval University. His fellow students included Jean Bernier and Pierre Boucher, both of whom had been with him at Garnier College, as well as Robert Cliche, Fernand Jolicoeur, Doris Lussier, Jean Marchand, François Lajoie, Louis-Philippe Bonneau, and Gaston Cholette. One day, Jean Bernier, who supervised the arts page of the student newspaper *Le Carabin*, * asked him to write something for them. Lévesque described the encounter :

> 48 minutes, 50 seconds past 3 o'clock . . . Sitting glumly in the student's union, finishing off my before-lecture Coke. Suddenly, a ray of sunshine : my friend Bernier rushes up, dragging his briefcase . . . . His manner is almost too obliging and his tone so saccharine, that I suspect something right away. I'm not mistaken. Mr. Bernier says to me, in so many words : "Hello there, old buddy. Did you know that the next wonderful issue of *Le Carabin* will soon be out ? They've put me in charge of the arts page — and it's no cinch, believe me ! . . . I've been having such an awful time with it . . . . Now you're a talented young man (free publicity), couldn't you just whip off a little something for me ? . . ." Honey-coated words and histrionics. He stops at nothing — what a con artist ! Metternich, Dale Carnegie, and the fox talking to the crow couldn't have put it better in such a short space of time . . . . How could I refuse ? [36]

Needless to say, Lévesque became a regular contributor. On October 25 he wrote an article along with Robert Cliche and Jean Bernier, in which he attacked the French-Canadian propensity for bestowing honors indiscriminately, especially when the persons involved were often totally undeserving. After discussing poet X and novelist Y, he turned to politician Z :

---

* Canadian French for a university student.

Z . . . launched his campaign. He made eleven magnificent speeches, all written by his secretary . . . . A generous sowing of election promises, enriched with *caribou*, * and handouts of cigarettes and sugar, yielded a harvest of votes (thanks to the majority vote assured him by his uncle the returning officer) sufficient to win him a comfortable seat in Parliament. Now he answers only to the title of "Honorable Member from the lovely county of . . . ." And so he takes his place with the others, decked in patriotic glory. One day our great man may be heard to exclaim : "What have Churchill and Roosevelt got that I haven't ?" — "You'd be surprised !" reads the writing on the wall . . . . But he only shuts his eyes and dreams of the bridge he'll try to wheedle out of the Minister.

And Lévesque concludes :

How many others are of the same stripe ? . . . What a happy country we have ! . . . In French Canada, honor is a salable commodity, graded A, B, or C like eggs or pears, according to the magazine, newspaper, or learned society which doles it out . . . . Our patriotic heroes swarm over the land like grasshoppers in the harvest ; everywhere you look there's another famous man . . . . We have been stuffed to bursting with great men ; it's a wonder there are any ordinary men left at all ! [37]

As part of the university tradition, a run-off "debate" was held in Convocation Hall on October 23. The speakers and their subjects were :

Charles-Henri Beaupré : Trade unions ;
Marcel Bélanger : Annexation ;
Raynald Bélanger : Canada's French-speaking minorities ;
Pierre Boucher : Pan-American civilization ;
Jean-Louis Boulet : Did war change your way of living.? ; †
Jean-Paul Chartrain : Quebec, province of untold agricultural wealth ;
Robert Cliche : Individualism ;
François Lajoie : The Statute of Westminster ;
Léo-Paul Lévesque : Racial inequality ;
Louis-Joseph Marcotte : Post-War adjustment ;
Donat Quimper : Providence and war ;
Emilien Simard : The two faces of France.

Lévesque went to the "debate" and, having treated himself to this display of oratory, came away very disappointed. He explained

---

* A French-Canadian drink consisting of wine spiked with whiskey.
† In English in the original.

his feelings in an open letter to Jean Sirois, President of the Debating Society, a close friend who had worked with him on the Garnier College paper :

> The word "debate" basically implies the idea of a struggle, a dispute, an argument. As I listened to the various speakers, I detected no trace of contentiousness in that jumble of well-turned phrases .... Here they are, twelve or fifteen subjects as varied as the ladies' hats at Sunday high mass .... One speaker takes the stage to deliver a laborious eight-minute treatise on certain aspects of potato cultivation in the province of Quebec ; then we are presented with the two faces of France, individualism, and a comparison of Hitler with Napoleon .... With this hodge-podge before them, the judges (and you, Mr. President) soon gently nod their heads, drift away, and take a blissful nap, leaving their guardian angels to pass judgment on the poor contestants .... The audience, having been set such a distinguished example, doesn't hesitate to catch a sneak preview of their upcoming dreams .... Meanwhile, up on stage, the last speaker desperately flails his arms, his vocabulary, and his flagging spirit in an attempt to revive his discourse on pan-American civilization .... Some of these chatty little lectures were pleasant, but debates they were not ! Why not take five or six of the most interesting topics submitted, choose two speakers for each topic and pit these teams against each other in a real debate ? This system would not involve any more time, would require less indulgence on the part of both the judges and the audience, and would be far more worthwhile for the participants. Moreover, the feeling of a contest, of coming to grips with an argument, of a *debate*, would allow a much more precise evaluation of the contestants as speakers, as *debaters*, than this jumbled mosaic of pretty little speeches which are about as eloquent as the election promises of a political candidate, whether his color is blue, yellow, red, or green .... * Otherwise, don't call the performance a "debate," but *Pot-pourri éliminatoire* [Grab-bag run-offs], *Les pavots d'éloquence* [The Opiates of eloquence], or *Les grands chanteurs Laval* [The Laval songsters] ! [38]

This somewhat violent attack probably did not endear Lévesque to the debaters or the president of the society.

---

* The Tories and Reformists of Lower Canada and their successors, the Union Nationale, were traditionally known as *les Bleus* (the "Blues"), while their more left-wing opponents, those who later formed the Quebec Liberal Party, were known as *les Rouges* (the "Reds"). Lévesque is being ironic when he refers here to yellow and green as political colors.

An honest man loves the truth, and if anything made René Lévesque fly off the handle, it was someone who did not tell the truth. He had already ridiculed poet X, novelist Y, and politician Z ; on November 22 came the turn of Cornichon, * that pillar of the writing establishment who never revealed the sources of his quotations.

> Lucky Cornichon ! To all intents and purposes, he holds an extended lease on the works of a dozen great writers, even though he himself has not been graced with even the smallest flickering spark of talent. This arrangement insures his reputation and his prospects : he passes the barbs and criticisms on to his sources ; but in the name of the talents with which he has so abundantly supplied himself (to make up for the Creator's negligence), like the honest pirate he is he treasures for himself alone the bouquets strewn before his protean personality by a handful of easy dupes ! . . . There are so many Cornichons both great and small. They would be quite amusing if they weren't so pitiable. No, on second thought, they are simply of no consequence since they have no life of their own . . . . They are only capable of living through others, like inmates in an asylum who wake up one fine day thinking they are Napoleon, win an Austerlitz a week, and repudiate Josephine twice a month. [39]

This was the last article Lévesque wrote during the '41-'42 academic year. He hardly had time for writing, not to mention his law courses. For the past five months he had been working as an announcer at CKCV, a radio station in Quebec City. More out of sheer interest than for the money, he climbed up to the second floor of the Capitol Cinema in Youville Square every evening to go on the air. In the summer of '42, he left CKCV to go to CBV, the CBC's local French-language station, whose studios were located in the Chateau Frontenac.

Lévesque loved the medium of radio, which was then coming into its own thanks to the Second World War. The young law student became a great promoter for the medium, particularly in front of his colleagues :

> Radio, the celebrated prodigy, with its countless tentacles reaching out to rooftop antennas everywhere, curling over speeding cars, encircling our shrinking planet, transporting the bright lights of Broadway, the bistros of Montmartre, and the tom-

* Slang for "dolt" or "idiot."

toms of the jungle to the peaceful countryside of Saint-François and the birchbark canoe works of Loretteville ! A magic carpet upon which Yvon Horte, Gaspé fisherman, can fly in an instant over the moors and processions of his ancestral Brittany . . . . The blood of the legendary *coureurs de bois* stirs in Jacques Laroche, and the magic carpet whisks him off to the poppyfields of fabulous Cathay or the banks of the Ganges, where the descendants of the crocodiles who once sharpened their teeth on Gengis Khan's soldiers wallow in the mud . . . .

Further on in the same article, Lévesque introduces Valérien, an endlessly complaining Don Quixote, for whom "the radio, like the cinema, the airplane, and the twentieth century itself, figures importantly among his windmills." He is fed up :

If you keep on shrinking poor Mother Earth like this, you'll eliminate all national characteristics and eradicate every trace of distinctive culture. Thanks to your wretched Progress, we soon won't be able to tell one human being from another. You force-feed us a mess of syncopated jazz and caterwauling country-and-western guitars, then you rush us from Barbados to Kamchatka. Once we've digested this mish-mash, we aren't ourselves anymore, but a patchwork of every race and culture on earth !

Lévesque replies :

Patchwork ? Why patchwork, when in the final analysis all cultures are one ? Culture is the cultivation of intellectual soil, whether yellow, black, or white, and the entire harvest we reap as a result. Shakespeare offers us the fruits of his labor equally with those of Racine or Molière ; Bizet keeps company with Wagner and Verdi, Goethe and Victor Hugo, Balzac and Tolstoy ; each works the field of human experience in his own way, according to his personal vision. This does not mean, however, that the field will always yield the same harvest. The Franco-Graeco-Latin-Canadian apple just isn't the same as the Slavic or the Anglo-Saxon variety — and that's how the Supreme Gardener meant it to be. Yet the basic rules of working, tilling, and irrigating remain everywhere the same. That is what we mean by culture in a practical sense.

The devil's advocate does not give up.

In Europe, centuries of experience lie behind each well-worn stone, each received opinion. The European stands at the head of a long line of imposing figures who stretch out behind him

39

like the procession of ghosts in *Macbeth*. But we are Americans and therefore young ; we lack this tradition.

Lévesque does not agree with this view :

> On the contrary, we have inherited a rich legacy from France and hence from Rome and Athens. However, like any heir burdened with a huge, unearned inheritance, we must be very careful not to make ourselves hated by recklessly squandering it. We must work at this inheritance, shape it, make it grow, and leave our mark upon it. Until this time, we only had books ; today the radio has come to fill a specific need — after the eye, the ear now has its own tool . . . .

But Valérien does not give up so easily. For him, the radio, like so much else about the twentieth century, only tends to encourage laziness and a line-of-least-resistance philosophy. Lévesque counters once again :

> So you have a grudge against the laziness of our age. Nevertheless, my poor Valérien, man has never been any different in this respect. He has always liked his creature comforts. A complete study on this very subject would be fascinating : "The Search for the line of least resistance through the ages." Adam walked, Charlemagne rode on horseback, your grandfather cranked, your father turns a key and speeds off, we can fly, and your children will probably take a spaceship to the moon for the weekend . . . . When printing was invented, Gutenberg's greatest admirers were undoubtedly the poor monks who had ruined their eyes reading and worn their fingers to the bone copying manuscripts. Radio is just another step along the way, that's all. But watch out, because soon television will take us another leap forward. And so it goes. For most people, leafing through a book and trying to understand it — much less copying it — is too much trouble ; but just to listen without any effort and immediately understand, that suits congenital laziness just fine ! For most people, radio has taken the place of books.

Valérien is clever. He has noticed that certain stations have developed their programming along the lines of the Hollywood philosophy, "quantity before quality." But for Lévesque, this is no reason to do away with radio. He replies :

> Nonsense ! The fact that some people cannot or will not rise above the lowest common denominator shouldn't prevent *you* from expanding your horizons ! Who is forcing you to accept

as psychological gospel the nonsense set down in the advice-to-the-lovelorn columns ? Even eggheads should be very grateful to the late Mr. Marconi — without him their front row seats at the Metropolitan Opera would cost not pennies but five dollars, not to mention travel expenses !

But Don Quixote tilts on. He alludes to the flood of advertising that degrades the best programs, especially on the commercial stations, since the CBC did not allow more than two minutes of advertising per hour of broadcast time and privately-sponsored broadcasts on their French network represented no more than one fifth of their total programming. In any case, Lévesque adopts a moderate position, refusing to play the purist :

> Why should our performers live in dire poverty on bread and water ? They couldn't even if they wanted to. They have to eat, just like everyone else. As long as society won't foot their bills for them, they'll sell their services to the highest bidder .... It's the old story of supply and demand .... And don't think that this only started yesterday. When St. Augustine was a professor *artis dicendi* [rhetoric] he let his friends and students be his publicity agents. And didn't Le Brun have to count on a little material encouragement from his patron Colbert before he could finish his paintings ? I would be willing to bet that in the year 2242, Roger Baulu's Campbell's soups and Jacques Desbaillets' *Barsalou* * will be considered part of our folk culture, just like the seventeenth-century mountebanks who dispensed their nostrums and rejuvenating waters to the passers-by on the Pont-Neuf.

"But if the radio mongers fob off crass, stupid programs on us," points out Valérien, "then this junk will lower artistic and intellectual standards."

Lévesque agrees :

> Of course, Valérien ! There's junk around and plenty of it. One word of caution, though : light food isn't necessarily dishwater, so you don't have to call on Aristotle and the Church Fathers when you want to do in Tino Rossi. † In any case, a little variety never hurt anybody. After a fireside chat with Roosevelt I don't see why I shouldn't abandon international politics for a quarter of an hour and have a little fun listening

---

* An allusion to two radio commercials read by Montreal announcers Roger Baulu and Jacques Desbaillets.
† Tino Rossi, a Corsican vocalist now in his seventies, was a very popular interpreter of French love songs.

to Jovette. * I acknowledge the need for a little relaxation between two fine symphony concerts, so I hang up my top hat, ease into a pipe-and-slippers frame of mind and let Ray Ventura entertain me at the expense of soldier Lebrun . . . . †
On that note, I leave you with a slew of incoherent, badly prepared, badly presented, perfectly awful programs — but let me remind you that to get your revenge, all you have to do is turn the dial . . . a bit like sending a shady lawyer or a quack doctor to Coventry . . . .

Valérien ends up unconvinced that radio is worth very much. But Lévesque has the last word :

The medium of radio, like the cinema, the submarine, the airplane, and the Electrolux, will stand on its own two feet without my support until man's next leap forward. Meanwhile the Earth keeps on turning, deaf to the buzzing of gadflies like ourselves, laughing up her millennial sleeve at the calculations of Ptolemy and all the Inquisitions, past and future . . . . I shrug my shoulders philosophically, light a cigarette, settle down in my overstuffed armchair, and after cheering on the clever Séraphin as he strikes another blow for thrift, I take a ride in the fat doctor's sleigh as he heads for bashful, blushing Angélique's . . . . ‡ Life in the twentieth century isn't so had after all ! [40]

This was the only article Lévesque wrote for *Le Carabin* during the school year, and he kept himself just as busy as the year before. Early in September 1943, he began his third year of law school. In December of that year, a few weeks before the end-of-term examinations, he was caught smoking by one of his professors, Louis-Philippe Pigeon. Smoking in the classrooms was strictly forbidden. "He was forced to leave the room at once and not return until such time as his deportment improved and he was ready to apologize." [41] Lévesque left the university and never went back. A few days later, the rector appealed to his mother. "Your son is much too talented to let him do this ; see if you can persuade him to come back." But there was nothing his mother could do. All Lévesque said was : "Listen. I'm not interested in passing those

---

* Jovette Bernier was a Montrealer who wrote popular sketches for radio.
† Ray Ventura was a Quebec country-and-western singer, many of his songs were about men going off to war.
‡ Séraphin, the doctor, and Angélique are characters from the novel *Un Homme et son Péché* by Henri Grignon. Written in the thirties, it became so popular that it was serialized on both radio and television for 30 years.

exams, because I'll never practise law. All I want to do in life is write, nothing else."

For quite some time, in fact, his heart had not been in his studies. In retrospect, it seems that, as a student, Lévesque found his courses distasteful because they had little social relevance. When the author put this idea to Lévesque, he replied : "That's a pretty shaky *post facto* judgment because you can't really tell what it was like then. What you say may be true — all I know is that I felt less and less involved in what they were teaching me and in my studies. I felt less and less interested. I don't think I could really look back and say that the work was irrelevant. That would be a bit pretentious." [42]

But we pursued the point, because it appeared to be a valid estimate of the situation : "Granted — but the student who doesn't show up for certain exams, especially when he has already proven his ability to pass them, isn't doing so because he's afraid he's going to fail, is he ?" Lévesque still refused to make any *post facto* judgments :

> I just lost interest. It's as simple as that. But there was something else which really bothered me, because I was the oldest and my father had died. You mustn't forget that our good French-Canadian families have a long-standing obsession with regard to professional careers. Since my father was a lawyer, the oldest son was destined to follow in his footsteps. In addition, there was always a feeling that I shouldn't let my father down. An office had even been rented in the Gaspé just in case.... So of course you feel trapped in circumstances that are beyond your control, but the more I looked at law the way it was then — you had to collect bills for I don't know how many years right from the time you started — the more I saw it was to all intents and purposes simply a matter of going into those offices and collecting any way you could. So the more I got to know it, the less I liked it. I think that played a large part too.

His total lack of interest in such a "business-like" profession and the thought of being caught in that system for many years had encouraged Lévesque to think more and more about quitting his law studies and becoming a *drop-out,* * so to speak. But what would he do if he quit ? "I was beginning to get interested in journalism," he explains, "but I was all mixed up." [43]

---

* In English in the original.

Chapter 1 — References

1. Antoine Bernard, *La Gaspésie au soleil* (Montreal, 1925), p. 181.
2. Paul LeBlanc, *La Gaspésie avant et après la coopération* (Montreal : Institut Carillon, May 1945), pp. 13-15.
3. Hélène Pilotte, *Châtelaine*, April 1966, p. 94.
4. Interview with René Lévesque, 25 May, 1972.
5. Lionel Allard, "L'éducation en Gaspésie en 1925," *Revue d'histoire de la Gaspésie*, April-June, 1964, pp. 103-104.
6. Interview with R.L., 25 May, 1972.
7. Pilotte.   8. Ibid.
9. Jacques Guay, "Comment René Lévesque est devenu indépendantiste," *Le Maclean*, February 1969, p. 25.
10. Interview with R.L., 25 May, 1972.
11. G. Guité, *A pleines voiles,* pamphlet quoted by Romuald Minville in "25 ans en arrière," *Revue d'histoire de la Gaspésie,* January-March 1965, p. 32, note.
12. Interview with R.L., 25 May, 1972.
13. Guay.
14. René Lévesque, "Gaspésie, pays du passé, pays d'avenir," II, III, *Le Canada*, 3 and 4 September, 1947.
15. Ibid., IV, 5 September, 1947.
16. Interview with R.L., 25 May, 1972.
17. François Hertel, *Leur inquiétude* (Editions "Jeunesse" — ACJC, and Editions Albert Lévesque, 1936), pp. 106-110.
18. Ibid., pp. 143-144.
19. Interview with R.L., 25 May, 1972.
20. Claude Hénault, *Montreal Gazette,* 14 October, 1967.
21. René Lévesque, *L'Envol,* no. 3, 20 December, 1935, pp. 3-6.
22. Ibid., no. 5, 30 March, 1936, pp. 6-7, 9.
23. Ibid., no. 6, 12 April, 1936, pp. 5-9.
24. Ibid., p. 11.
25. Interview with R.L., 25 May, 1972.
26. Ibid.   27. Ibid.
28. Jean Hamelin, *Les rumeurs d'Hochelaga* (Editions Hurtubise HMH, 1971), p. 56.
29. Pilotte, p. 96.
30. Interview with R.L., 25 May, 1972.
31. René Lévesque, "Ma Gaspésie," *Le Garnier,* vol. 2, no. 2, November 1939, p. 4.
32. René Lévesque, "L'esprit sportif dans la vie," *Le Garnier,* vol. 2, no. 6, June 1938, p. 8.
33. Paul Legendre, "Académie Sciences-Arts," *Le Garnier,* vol. 3, no. 2, December 1939, p. 5.
34. Interview with R.L., 25 May, 1972.   35. Ibid.
36. René Lévesque, "Le jeu de l'inspiration," *Le Carabin,* 11 October, 1941.
37. René Lévesque, "Célébrités," *Le Carabin,* 25 October, 1941.
38. René Lévesque, "Débat ou pot-pourri," *Le Carabin,* 8 November, 1941.
39. René Lévesque, "Les deux habits mais . . . non le moine," *Le Carabin,* 22 November, 1941.
40. René Lévesque, "Propos en ondes," *Le Carabin,* 14 November, 1942.
41. Michèle Tremblay, "Ce que j'ai en lui, c'est sa profonde honnêteté," *Le Nouveau Samedi,* 24 December, 1972.
42. Interview with R.L., 25 May, 1972.   43. Ibid.

2

The War in Europe

René Lévesque's decision to abandon his law studies came in December 1943. But he did not remain a *drop-out* for long ; his imagination had been captured by the Second World War. Then only twenty-one years of age, he decided to become involved in the war not by carrying a gun, but through the medium of radio. Why at so young an age did he choose to go to war ?

> You really had to be there to understand what it was like. Even from our remote vantage point, it was quite obviously the most important upheaval of our time — a war like that involves almost every nation in the world. So over here we felt far from the major event of modern history. And there was another factor in addition to that. I said to myself : "Conscription is just around the corner. I don't feel like dodging it, because that would be far more trouble than going along with it." I had no desire whatsoever to be in the Canadian armed forces, for all kinds of reasons. It just didn't appeal to me at all. [1]

In December 1943, Lévesque ran into some American friends, who introduced him to a certain Mr. Robb, head of the Office of War Information [OWI] branch in Montreal. The Americans, who were already in the early stages of planning a full-scale invasion of Europe, had no intentions of relying on outside help and were recruiting their own bilingual support staff. Lévesque decided to try his luck and went to Robb's office for a preliminary interview. When he saw how fluently Lévesque spoke both languages, Robb told him : "If you want the job, it's yours."

Lévesque then went to New York to meet Pierre Lazareff, a French Jew who had escaped to the United States and was in charge of the French-language division at the Office of War Information. After Lévesque had passed tests examining his writing skills and his knowledge of radio, Lazareff told him : "If you're ready to leave, take your physical and wait until we get in touch with you." All these goings-on had a certain air of intrigue about them, since there was always the danger of infiltration by German spies.

Pleased with his interview in New York, Lévesque returned to Quebec City to take his physical and break the news to his family. His mother's only wish was that she would never see him set sail for Europe. The long, two-month waiting period gladdened Mrs Pelletier * and frustrated her son. Finally, early in May 1944, the OWI ordered him to report to Montreal and to sever all contact with his family from that moment on. "My mother nearly died," recalls Lévesque.

Noah's Ark

In Montreal, I hung around the hotel for a couple of days, then suddenly one morning they told me, "Go to pier no. 9 — a French ship is waiting for you there." It was there all right, a little French ship called the *Indochinois* [Indochinese]. The strangest collection of people was on board, sort of like Noah's Ark, and even more got on at Halifax. Among them were a dozen English children who had been evacuated during the blitz in 1940 when they were quite young. Now that they had reached the ripe age of seventeen or eighteen, they were considered old enough to go back. There were also all kinds of technical people, like myself, off to serve on various support teams — electricians, cameramen, signals corps specialists. And a French crew to top it all off. It was quite a mixture. [2]

So the "Ark" weighed anchor for Halifax, the assembly point for the cargo ships which made up the convoys. At the beginning of the war the cargo ships crossed the Atlantic unescorted, but the German submarines wreaked havoc among them, and many Allied vessels never reached their destination. The intensity of these attacks, which

---

* Lévesque's mother had remarried ; her second husband's name was Albert Pelletier. [Author's note.]

often took place at night, led to the creation of convoys — groups of cargo ships with destroyer escorts. In May 1944, the memory of a catastrophe which had occurred a year before was still very much alive. The previous May, two escorted convoys came under attack from German submarines : seventy-seven vessels had left Halifax and thirty-three were missing by the time the convoys reached Liverpool. Nevertheless, the *Indochinois* dropped anchor in the port of Halifax and waited to join a convoy.

> Well, the funniest thing happened once we got there. At that point the submarine warfare was almost over, but it was terrible because ships were still being sunk all over the place. The captain of the *Indochinois* was an irritable old Frenchman, a big guy who did exactly what he pleased and considered the boat his private property. He had apparently been squabbling with the convoy administration in Halifax. We never did find out what it was about. In any case, he turned up suddenly in his motor launch, climbed on board and said, in French of course : "We're leaving ! Get ready to weigh anchor right away. We're going alone — without a convoy. God damn their convoys anyway, the more rules they make, the better our chances of going down. We're leaving unescorted !" It took a few minutes before his message was translated into English. I remember there was a guy from Brooklyn called Cooney and a friend of his — the Americans had put them on board. About five minutes later Cooney came back up on deck with his bags, sweating like a stuck pig, and announced : "If there's no convoy, I'm getting off !" But unfortunately he couldn't, because our departure wouldn't have been a secret any more. The Germans had agents all over Halifax and they would have found out for sure, so two big sailors grabbed Cooney and dragged him back down to his cabin.

So on May 7, 1944, the captain of the *Indochinois* decided to leave Halifax without destroyer protection. In spite of his blustering, he must have been as nervous as his passengers during the crossing. Lévesque describes it :

> We did in fact make the trip all alone. I don't think I took my trousers off once during that voyage. Every night, whenever the boat creaked, you'd think to yourself, "This is it !" It was a long trip and the boat wasn't fast ; it must have taken a good eight or ten days. At night you tried to distract yourself playing cards, reading, anything at all. Those nights were awful ! When morning came, you said to yourself, "Well, we're good for another day." And then you'd try to get a little sleep. [3]

47

London during the Blitz

On May 17, the young Québécois, twenty-one years of age, landed in Great Britain. A week later he was finally able to send word back to his family. He wrote to his mother, carefully avoiding any reference to the nights spent on the *Indochinois* :

> Our journey was wonderful. Fine weather, a few people sea-sick — not me though . . . . Our boat was French, and since the other passengers were either English or American, I was more or less the official interpreter, which made me feel pretty important ! There were only twenty-four passengers, including me : twelve from the O W I, three or four older Englishmen, and a group of young English refugees who were returning home. During the crossing I sunbathed and played cards, so I arrived with a tan, just like in the old days in New Carlisle, and $38.00 richer = not bad ! [4]

Then, the first impressions of a tourist in a new land :

> London is a very big city, very spread out because the buildings aren't more than five or six stories high. You can see the scars of the blitz here and there, but the raids are so rare now you'd hardly know there was a war going on. The weather's beautiful, sunny, and very hot. I haven't seen any sign yet of the famous London fog. Food is pretty expensive, but there's enough of it. I wouldn't say it's as good as the food at the *Kerhulu,* * but it isn't bad. Lots of vegetables, and always mountains of noodles. Meat isn't too hard to come by, but there isn't much in the way of desserts. The worst thing about the restaurants is that most of them are so dirty. I've never seen such filthy table linen ! In fact, London gives you the impression that the whole city is waiting for the end of the war before fixing itself up and doing a proper house-cleaning. There aren't any streetcars here, just buses with two decks, and the routes are so numerous and complicated they have me completely baffled ! I haven't once ended up in the place I originally set out for ! The newspapers, with very few exceptions, only come in a war format of four pages : it's quite amazing ! No social page, no comics, and very few sports. Hyde Park is the only interesting place I've seen so far. It's huge, well laid out, and full of people, especially on weekends. Real oddballs get up on old crates and hold forth on every subject imaginable. I even heard a Hindu with a long, long

---

* A restaurant in Quebec City renowned at the time for its cuisine.

beard railing about the inevitable downfall of the British Empire! That's really the utmost in freedom of speech! [5]

The letter must have been reassuring to a mother with visions of her son on the battlefield.

After the Allied forces had been driven from the Continent by Germany, England became a refuge for European nationals who looked forward to the day when they would recapture their homelands. In the heart of London the English found themselves living side by side with Belgians, Frenchmen, Americans, etc. Lévesque described to his family the attitude of the Englishman who suddenly found his country "occupied" by so many military personnel : "The English have gone up in my estimation," he wrote. "They have very unselfishly resigned themselves to the great influx of troops being assembled here for the second front . . . . The average Englishman isn't particularly talkative or brilliant but he is obliging and courteous and does a good job of minding his own business."

His opinion of the first Frenchmen he met in London was much less complimentary.

> I've met a number of different people in the French section who strike me as very odd. There's Pierre Lazareff, the director — I told you about him when I came back from New York. And then some other Frenchmen who are hardly worth describing in detail . . . . If I didn't know that the French weren't all like that, I'd say France was in big trouble and that we Canadians don't have to go into raptures over the *real* French from France! All in all, even in terms of *writing,* I think we run them a very close second . . . . The only thing is, they have more of a knack for blowing their own horn . . . . For example, there's a complete idiot registered here under the name of "Laferre," who insists, *believe it or not* * on calling himself "De La Fère" (after Dumas' Athos?) ! [6]

In spite of these first impressions which make him sound like a vacationing tourist, Lévesque had in fact wasted no time in getting down to work : "I've been working just about continuously up to now. I'm busy *newswriting* † (editing news items and other announcements) and reading various broadcasts addressed to the . . . ahem . . . *People of France.*" He worked in the French-language radio section of the American Broadcasting Station in Europe (AB SE), part of the United States Office of War Information. Lévesque

---

* In English in the original.
† In English in the original.

described his functions during this period : "I put in several months as an announcer on American radio. We were part of an international team that wrote and broadcast different items for occupied France — news, propaganda, and coded messages, like 'A friend is coming tonight'." [7]

In an age of spy satellites, it is difficult to appreciate the importance of radio in those days. As we mentioned before, CBC radio came into its own during the Second World War. Many Québécois had begun tuning in to shortwave broadcasts so that they could keep on top of events in Europe. In London, wartime radio became an instrument of liberation. Its task was to support the French Forces of the Interior (F F I), who normally worked in the open, and the clandestine organizations, who were concerned with the distribution of leaflets, with sabotage, subversion, and the gathering of intelligence. One French observer, J. L. Crémieux-Brilhac, gave as an example General de Gaulle's speech broadcast over London radio on June 18, 1940 :

> The fact that this history-making rejection of defeat took the form of a radio address transmitted, moreover, via the national facilities of a foreign network, and the fact that France still acknowledges, quite rightly, that this broadcast of June 18, 1940, marked the beginning of the French Resistance, sufficiently underscore the unprecedented importance of the radio medium during the Second World War. [8]

When Lévesque arrived to take up his duties in London, use of the medium had reached an advanced level. Communications between London and the resistance fighters on French soil were perfectly synchronized. "In June, July, and August, 1944," Crémieux-Brilhac observed,

> the BBC was truly part of the war machine, in the full sense of the word. Although underground receivers and transmitters exchanged the secret messages that focussed the strategy of national insurrection on specific objectives, information intended for the French people as a whole came from the BBC. It announced the accomplishments of the FFI, broadcast the news items periodically gathered by the Resistance, and helped transform the FFI fighting arm into a genuine source of concern for the Germans. [9]

In 1944, London radio was broadcasting all kinds of information intended for both Allied and enemy ears, as well as secret messages.

This was the job of Lévesque and his fellow announcers. But how did the senders and receivers of these messages manage to understand each other ? Crémieux-Brilhac explains :

Most of the "personal messages" were designed to confirm or call off clandestine operations involving parachute drops, landings, or shipments planned for that night. They were broadcast at the beginning of the 9 : 15 pm program, and were usually composed by the staff of the *Bureau central de Renseignements et d'Action* [BCRA, Central office of information and action]. The messages were then sent over for verification and approval to English liaison, who finally passed them on to a special section of the BBC. Messages had been relayed beforehand to the resistance groups involved by coded telegrams, which confirmed details of the operation and its code name, as well as the position of the word in the message to be broadcast and the letter in the word which, according to its numerical position in the alphabet, specified the date of the operation. For example, the message already agreed upon would establish the code name of the operation as *"le Canari"* [Canary], to take place on the nineteenth. The letter "s" appearing as the third letter in the second word of the broadcast message after the code word would confirm this. The corresponding message given out by the BBC might then have been : *"Le Canari picore des graines"* [The Canary is picking at some seeds], confirming that the operation would take place on the nineteenth. If the operation scheduled for the nineteenth could not take place for some reason, then a message was made up incorporating the code "Canary" and using a word in the *third* position whose *second* letter was "T" (the twentieth letter of the alphabet). This would indicate that the operation was to take place on the twentieth ; a "u" in that position would indicate the twenty-first, etc. [10]

In June 1944, the Allied forces landed in Normandy. The Germans bombed England repeatedly to show that they had no intentions of giving ground. But the English had learned to live with these sudden changes of mood. Lévesque told his family about the bombings in a letter written on August 3 : "There they are again, those damned sirens. Houououou ... houououou ... houououou ... like blowing into a whistle and not letting the sound completely fade away before blowing again. That moaning is by far the most hateful sound I've ever heard. It's been going on now for seven weeks. Seriously ... I'm beginning to wish I was in Normandy." [11]

The wail of the sirens followed the detection of enemy bombers and preceded the actual bombardments. Most lights were extinguished and many Londoners took shelter in the subways. Lévesque continued his letter, and a few lines later he wrote :

Here comes the first *flying-bomb* * of the evening. It's close by ("close by" means "off target") — the kind of racket a big truck might make that had lost its way, gone flying through the air, and smashed into the roof instead of the walls ! ... The motor has stopped, close enough to make me lift my pen from the page for a moment. Then bang ! ... The window sill shakes for a second and the air trembles ... so do I. I'm used to it now. During the day, when you're at work, you don't even think about it. And once I'm in bed at night, I count five or six of them — like sheep — and then I sleep like a log !

You'll probably read some alarming figures taken from Churchill's speech yesterday — the number of casualties, the property damage, etc. It all seems much worse from a distance. Here, you hardly notice the recent damage compared to what happened in the real *blitz.* † As for myself, all I've suffered is three shattered window panes, which took me an hour to sweep up the next morning. I didn't much like the idea of crawling around on all fours in the middle of the night. And it allowed me to play the part of a *bombed-out* ‡ casualty and miss half a day's work ! [12]

Lévesque has a good sense of humor, and many of these passages from his letters show this quite clearly. During the war, it became necessary to censor all mail to North America, for fear that German spies might glean useful information from it and endanger a military operation. Lévesque's letters were no exception and certain paragraphs were deleted from time to time. His mother had promised to send him food as soon as he arrived in London, but by August he still had not received any. "So far I haven't received either of the parcels you mention. Please don't send any more until I tell you that I've received one, or else explained the delay. It would be crazy to keep feeding either His Majesty's or Mr. King's government, or even the sharks for that matter ...." For the censor's benefit he added in English : "Censor : please note this is only *hunger,* not treason !" [13]

---

* In English in the original.
† A reference to the devastating German raids of 1940. [Author's note.]
‡ In English in the original.

On November 8, 1944, the American Broadcasting Station in Europe organized all-night coverage of the American presidential elections as part of the "battle of the airwaves." Lévesque was one of the three announcers on the program. The *London Star* had this to say about the program, under the three-column headline, "Europe *listens* to freedom via London radio."

> Three young Americans, speaking from London, today fought a major action in the Allies' psychological warfare against Hitler. They are announcers of the American Broadcasting Station in Europe, who kept a sleepless vigil to ensure that Germany, the countries still occupied, and those recently liberated, should have a supreme example of a great nation exercising its Democratic right. Each was typical of millions of their countrymen who are fighting the battle of freedom. Eldest was Tys Teowey, aged 34, of Dutch ancestry, who spoke in English, and the youngest was Rene Levesque, 22, who originally came from Canada and spoke in the French of his forefathers. The third, who spoke in German, was Alfred Puhan, born in Germany 31 years ago. Reception is known to have been good, and Europe heard the sounds and a description of the scenes in the Republican and Democratic headquarters, the voices of thousands of New Yorkers in Timessquare, and the election atmosphere in the villages of the west coast, the south and the middle west. [14]

Lévesque sent the clipping from the *Star* to his mother and took the opportunity to tease his two brothers: "The enclosed clipping is from the *Star,* one of the biggest, most *exclusive,* etc., etc. newspapers in London. Show it to Fernand and André and let them *suffer* : you-ve got to swim four miles and *win* before you even get a mention in the papers here. Paper is rationed in England, and unless you're Winston Churchill or *somebody just as famous* — you don't get into the papers !" [15]

Several other topics in this letter were treated in a humorous vein, including the food package, which had finally surfaced :

> As you can see, I received the food parcel post-haste .... I spent three-quarters of an hour carefully unpacking each item — the liver pâté, the *relish,* * the fudge .... Only the biscuits suffered minor injuries. When I spotted the crumbs at the bottom of the box, I thought for a moment that someone was

---

* In English in the original.

sending the poor exile a handful of Canadian soil to comfort him in his loneliness .... Alas ! Nobody understands my poetic soul. Many thanks. I'll think of you all every time I make a sandwich ... and every time I get indigestion !

The London climate also prompted a few remarks. "Apparently England is a country where snow is unknown. It rains a mere twelve hours a day instead; the other twelve it's dark and lights aren't allowed .... When I get back I'll write a book called *More Fairy Tales from Sunny London.*"

He made fun of his own absent-mindedness :

> I lost my *trench coat* * (or I should say, somebody in a restaurant lost it for me). Fortunately the *quartermaster* † had some more. I also lost my rubbers : the *quartermaster* had more of those too .... Then I lost my cigarette case : the *quartermaster* doesn't carry cigarette cases. At least I won't be able to lose another one .... I also lost my black wallet, but I had two to start with and there was hardly anything in it anyway. But since I'm so careful with my things, I haven't lost anything else. [16]

In his letters, Lévesque told his family very little about his daily routine. On the first day of 1945, however, he slipped in a few remarks that foreshadowed the style of *Point de Mire* : ‡

> On certain days I have to put together the *commentary,* as succinct a summary as possible of the military situation. Most of the time, I'm busy writing *Images du monde en guerre* [Pictures of the world at war], dramatizations of the most important events, personalities, and places. [...] Thursday I'm to do a ten-minute piece on Canada ; I've already done several like it before. When I get back I'll ask Ottawa for a medal !

Despite the young journalist's witticisms, the days had gone very slowly. He had been almost eight months in London, and the Allies had long since begun their invasion of Europe. Having spent day after day describing the advance of the Allied forces, Lévesque was very anxious to "cover the ground" himself. He continued in his letter : "I'm just living on hope at the moment .... After taking a three-week training course, I'm one of the correspondents slated

---

* In English in the original.
† In English in the original.
‡ The public affairs program that made Lévesque famous. See pp. 92 ff.

to leave next. Where ? I don't know and I don't give a damn . . . .
When ? Sometime in 1945 I hope !" [17]

Three weeks later, Lévesque was very happy to hear that he
was to join up with the American troops at the beginning of February. His joy was more than evident in the brief letter he sent
home to announce the latest news :

> Greetings, comrades ! How is everybody ? Everything's just
> fine with me, as long as the Russians don't reach Berlin in the
> next few weeks ! I'm finally getting a chance to observe what's
> going on and although, of course, I don't want the atrocities
> to continue, I wouldn't miss a minute of the action. I'm leaving
> in two weeks — for sure this time. I 'm just waiting for one of
> our writers to get back before packing my bags. I won't miss
> being away from London and this winter weather for a while,
> even though they say that Paris and the front aren't very well
> equipped with central heating either . . . . In any case, these
> past nine months weren't all in preparation for my departure.
> The delay was caused by the shortage of transport facilities,
> which were tied up with the evacuation of wounded servicemen
> and the return of high-ranking officials . . . . But in about two
> months, when I've done my stint abroad, I should be entitled
> to some holidays *in America.* * I'll see when the time comes.
> Right now I'm off to bed, because it's one o'clock in the
> morning, and even Stalin should be through for the night.
> Goodbye. Say hello to everybody for me. [18]

Bubbling over with good spirits, he signed himself "Vladimir-René."
But there were times when his family could not help worrying about
him.

Interlude in Alsace

During the first week of February, a new team of correspondents
arrived to relieve those who had been in Alsace for nearly three
months. As a member of the group, Lévesque was assigned to the
US Third Army, led by General Patton, and was temporarily
billeted in Saverne. It was here that Lévesque's voice acquired the
husky quality which later became his trademark :

> Yes, I actually lost my voice in Alsace that winter. It happened
> once, then again, then a third time. But it wasn't anything

---

* In English in the original.

serious and you didn't go bothering the military hospitals with silly complaints like that. So it was a matter of just waiting until spring. More often than not we camped in the basements of bombed-out houses where it was always terribly damp. We were on the outskirts of Saverne, right at the foot of the Vosges. Needless to say it was always drizzling, or else a light snow would fall which melted as soon as it hit the ground. By the time spring came, my voice was gone.

But this did not pose any problems when it came to recording his reports :

The guys I worked with just weren't that interested in quality. In any case, a lot of our work, even the recorded material, ended up in the American army newspapers. That was how the various units kept up to date on one another's activities. Lucky for me, they weren't looking for a Roger Baulu. * [19]

But Lévesque was not gathering news just for the Americans. He was also using his mother tongue, French, to help the people of France :

I was with the troops at the front. My job on the team, so to speak, was to provide a running commentary in French — in English too, because sometimes I'd be covering an assignment by myself — on what was happening, so that the French public would be kept informed. The French were at a serious disadvantage because they were badly informed. Their radio was full of lies, and more or less all of their newspapers had collaborated. There was a period when if they hadn't been getting information from us, they would have had nothing but German propaganda. [20]

The Rhine Offensive

This stay in Alsace lasted a few weeks, long enough for the Allied generals to mount the great Rhine offensive. The Canadian and English commanders, Crerar and Dempsey respectively, deployed their forces to the north of the Rhine, while the Americans, Simpson and Hodges, took up positions to the south. General Patton's army left Alsace and headed towards Mayence. Lévesque stayed in Haguenau for a few days with Patton, then left for Kaiserslautern to join General Patch's US Seventh Army as Senior Correspondent.

---

* A well-known Montreal announcer. See p. 41.

Since the French First Army under General de Lattre de Tassigny had joined Patch's American troops for the campaign in the Rhine Palatinate, Lévesque was responsible for reporting the activities of both the French and the American armies.

By early March 1945, the Allied forces had taken up their positions west of the Rhine, while the German troops massed on the east bank of the river. On March 7, the US First Army stormed the bridge at Remagen and crossed the river, an assault which has gone down in history. On March 23, Patton and the three Allied armies to the north crossed the Rhine. On March 26, they were followed by the US Seventh Army and, five days later, by Lattre de Tassigny and the French First Army. Following the destruction of the Ruhr industrial complex, the Allied crossing of the Rhine signified the beginning of the end for the Third Reich. The first two phases in the huge offensive, namely, the destruction of the German forces west of the Rhine and the occupation of the east bank, had now been accomplished. The final stage — the advance through Germany to meet the Russians — was to take place in April.

The Nuremberg *Hillbilly* *

General Patch's troops, having crossed the Rhine between Ludwigshafen and Speyer, immediately occupied the town of Heidelberg. But Germany did not give in so easily. In Nuremberg, large numbers of Hitler Youth resisted with a courage born of despair. Lévesque had several close calls there :

> Nuremberg was sacred to the Nazis because of Hitler's enormous stadium and the big Nazi Party rallies. Since their armies were short of manpower, the Germans had mobilized detachments of Hitler Youth — girls and boys about twelve years old and up — in the outskirts of the city and especially in the area around the stadium. They were young but they could kill just as well as anyone else. They used to hide in ditches and jump you with their bazookas and grenades. I remember a girl, about thirteen or fourteen, with the face of an angel — we managed to grab her just as she was about to blow us up with two or three grenades she had pinned under her skirt. It was no joke. And what could you do to them — they were just kids. The operation lasted several days, and they fought like fiends.

---

* In English in the original.

But there was more to come.

In the big cities, scout patrols were often used. This was the
procedure in Nuremberg, which was a pretty large town. One
day I went out with a sniper and his assistant. A sniper was a
kind of scout, usually attached to a regular unit, who went on
ahead of the others. He was often a *hillbilly* from somewhere
like Tennessee, which meant he had sharp eyes from shooting
squirrels and what not. They tended to be good shots, but
they were pretty unruly — just the kind of guy you needed
in a messy situation like the one in Nuremberg. The sniper was
always on the lookout five or six streets ahead of the main
detachment, to make sure the sky didn't fall in on us. Because
I was attached to the army, I didn't normally have the same
freedom of movement as a civilian correspondent, and I was
anxious to go out with one of these snipers and see some of
the action first hand. Any guy who could survive two years
at that kind of job had to be lucky, so I went off with this
sniper and his partner. In a little while we heard gunfire, but it
was behind us. We had gone too far and lost contact with
our unit. Our sniper climbed on top of a bombed-out house
and came back to inform us, "There's Germans behind us
all right, and in front of us too — we're surrounded!" Immediately the three of us — not one at a time or two at a time,
but all three at once — jumped through a ground-level
window and found ourselves in the basement. We broke the
window-frame, but not so that it was really noticeable. In the
meantime our unit had retreated, as often happens on both
sides in the give-and-take of street fighting. We must have
spent two days in there, watching the Germans go back and
forth along the street. The battle wasn't over any too soon
as far as we were concerned. [21]

If any Germans had been living in the house these three American
lives would certainly have been worth very little.

The Horror of Dachau

The battle of Nuremberg lasted five days, from April 16 to April
21. After the American victory, Lévesque was assigned to cover
the activities of the French First Army in Stuttgart. The French
had just won a painful victory in the Black Forest : it took them
eighteen days to battle their way from Karlsruhe to Stuttgart, a
distance of about fifty miles. For a few days Lévesque served as
liaison officer between different units commanded by Lattre de

Tassigny and General Patch respectively. But he was soon ordered to return for duty with General Patch's troops, who were now making their way from Nuremberg to Munich via Ingolstadt and Augsburg.

Some ten miles from the centre of Munich lay Dachau. Lévesque was in one of the first jeeps to enter the camp grounds. An inmate describes it :

> Our camp was about 400 metres long and 250 metres wide. It was surrounded by an electrified wire fence and flanked by numerous watch-towers, each with two machine guns on top. You passed in under an arch which opened directly onto a huge parade ground where the roll was called and where, regardless of the weather, winter or summer, in the snow, the rain, or the icy wind that blew down from the Tyrol, we were compelled to stand in rows for many long, painful hours. On the south side stood an enormous, u-shaped building which housed the clothing and shoe stores, the kitchen, the showers, and other stores. Running north from the middle of the square was a wide road called the *Lagerstrasse* [Camp-street], which was about 300 metres long and lined with poplars. [22]

On either side of the road and at right angles to it were the barracks, all of them numbered. The buildings with the odd numbers served as infirmaries and "quarantine" areas; the even-numbered buildings housed the "well-behaved" prisoners. Building 30 was the end of the line : the only exit led directly to the ovens.

Lévesque talked about his experiences there :

> I was among those who arrived the first day, and it wasn't a pretty sight. I remember trying to interview two or three of the prisoners, but they were completely incoherent. Your first reaction was that everything was in chaos, turned upside-down. First of all, there was the sheer horror of it ; then the fact that you were looking at animals — it isn't true at all that human beings pushed to the limits of pain and suffering become ennobled. Just the opposite. It turns them into animals. These people we had liberated tried to rob us and grab anything they could lay their hands on, and you couldn't blame them. The whole situation was so crazy and confused. I remember it took three men to hold back the American general in command of our unit, because he went completely berserk when he saw what the camp was like. He pulled out his revolver and started looking for a German to kill on the spot. "If

1944.
Lévesque
served as an
American war
correspondent
with General
Patch's Seventh
Army in Europe.

there are any Germans around here I'll shoot the lot of them."
That's what it had come to.

Were there, in fact, any Germans around ? According to Lévesque,

The remaining German units had cleared out an hour or two
before our arrival. A few tried to hide by mingling with the
20,000 to 30,000 inmates. But the inmates, knowing they
were now free, joined hands and went around looking for
Germans. Once they'd spotted one in the crowd and singled
him out, he was finished. That's all there was to it: not a single
German got out alive. It was their turn to be torn apart. [23]

Lévesque recalls meeting a Breton who knew Quebec :

I arrived at Dachau, which was literally a death factory, and
among the half-starved inmates who surrounded us when we

60

arrived was a guy, a Breton I think, who began to talk to me about Quebec. "Are you Canadian?" he asked. At that time of course, people over there didn't know about Quebec as such. That was long before de Gaulle made us famous. Anyhow, he asked if I was a Canadian, so I said, "Yes." Seeing that I spoke French, he said, "I know it very well." I think it was Montreal that he had visited. Quite a strange coincidence. But I soon lost track of him, because he was among those who had been less badly treated, so he was evacuated right away. The dying were looked after first when the concentration camps were liberated, because the Germans had left the inmates in pretty poor condition, and a lot of them were about to die. The others were all inoculated for typhus and other diseases to prevent the outbreak of epidemics and then quarantined for a day or two, sometimes longer. None of this had been started when we arrived, of course, because the Germans were running out one end of the camp as we came in the other. But we immediately moved the inmates to new camps, so that they could be cleaned, deloused, inoculated, and so forth. [24]

The physical and psychological condition of these half-starved prisoners shocked the American soldiers, who had never seen anything like it. But the worst was to come — the discovery of the cremating ovens. Since this was the first camp to be liberated, Lévesque made a tape about the ovens, describing to the outside world a scene which is by now familiar to us:

The sight of the crematoria themselves was bad enough, but the *stockroom* .... * They didn't have the time to burn all their "stock" at Dachau, because they'd run short of fuel. So they left behind perhaps a week's worth of unburned bodies. They had yellowed and gave off a strong smell. Women, children, all piled together.... They'd cut off the women's hair, because they could always use it. They'd torn out all the gold teeth, because they were useful too. Doing the tape wasn't easy, because we didn't have portable machines. Our recorder ran off a big diesel unit and the machine itself weighed about 25 lbs. We needed a jeep to move them around. There was a French cameraman working with us who belonged to the FFI. He began to do some shooting in the worst parts of the camp and I think I saw him vomit three times before he was able to finish his roll of film. It was a

---

* In English in the original.

heartrending experience, one that really stuck with you. You'd wash your hands days later and think to yourself, "I can still smell those corpses." And at first, you know, nobody would believe us. [25]

For a long time Lévesque could not understand the incredulity of those in the West who refused to consider the reports about the crematoria as anything but American propaganda. Lévesque commented to a journalist : "There were no words to describe the horror of it. If those fine people who thought it was all nothing but anti-German propaganda had been with us, they would have understood." [26]

The author asked Lévesque, as a first-hand witness, whether in his opinion the ordinary German citizen knew about the ovens, but he could not say definitely one way or the other :

> I've never been able to get a valid answer to that question. I suppose when people are that close to something so horrible, there comes a time when they stop asking questions and just don't want to know. At one point we were in Munich itself, which is twenty miles, maybe only ten, from Dachau, and had to ask some German civilians for directions to Dachau. The contrast between the two places is amazing, because Bavaria is very Catholic ; many of the houses have niches with statues of the saints. It's very much like Sainte-Anne-de-Beaupré in certain respects. * So we asked these ladies standing on their doorsteps. "Which way, to the camp at Dachau ?" "Ah yes ! they said, "That way, that way." It was as if we were talking about some tourist attraction. They always maintained that they knew there was a concentration camp there, but that they thought it was a penitentiary, not a crematorium. I guess that's not completely out of the question. People are very good at turning a deaf ear when they don't want to know about something. [27]

The Itter Incident

From the moment the Allies crossed the Rhine, Germany's defeat was only a matter of time, particularly since the Russians were also advancing from the east. General Patch brought the military operations in the south to a successful conclusion at Nuremberg. Munich and Dachau were taken virtually without opposition. "After-

---

* Sainte-Anne-de-Beaupré, a village 20 miles from Quebec City, is a much-frequented place of pilgrimage.

wards, all that remained," explained Lévesque, "was a mopping-up operation — chasing down the last few German units that were still on the loose." He left Munich to rejoin the French army near Lake Constance, where another concentration camp, exclusively for women, was discovered. Then he returned to his post with the Americans in Garmisch-Partenkirchen before witnessing the capture of the "Eagle's Nest" near Berchtesgaden.

But there were more surprises still to come, including, for example, the adventure of Itter Castle. The setting would have been ideal for a vampire film or the love story of a prince and his mistress. "This fantastic castle was perched high on a cliff in the middle of the valley which joins Wörgl and Salzburg, in what was once Austrian territory. The whole area was quite unreal. [. . .] a great square fortress, surrounded by wooded mountains and green meadows, thrusting into the sky and dotted with arched windows." In 1532, the castle was the scene of a love affair between Archbishop Wolf Dietrich von Raitenau and the beautiful Salome. One hundred years later, Barbara Gudenhauser, an alleged witch, was burned at the stake for having slept with the devil, so the story went, and numerous men. With her dying breath she confessed that the only man she had refused was her denouncer, the parish priest of Söllen. Some time later, a "rich and powerful nobleman" imprisoned the daughter of a peasant in the castle dungeons because she had refused to marry him. In 1884, the castle was purchased by Sophie Mender, a virtuoso pianist and friend of Franz Liszt. Her guests at one time or another included Wagner, Sebelnikow, Wolf, Liszt himself, and Tchaikovsky, who actually composed his sixth symphony while staying at the castle.

In April 1945, the musicians were gone. Twelve people lived in the castle, which had been converted into a Tyrolian Bastille complete with bars, bolts, and locks. The distinguished prisoners in Itter Castle were under the supervision of Hauptsturmführer Wimmer. They included :

Lieutenant-General Tadeusz bor-Komorowski, 50, Polish officer and leader of the resistance in the Krakow area in 1940. Taken prisoner in 1944 while leading the Warsaw uprising.

Jean Borotra, 47, tennis champion famous both in France and abroad. From 1940 to 1942 he was Commissioner-General of Education and Sports. Arrested in November 1942, for "anti-collaborationist activities."

Edouard Daladier, 61, deputy in the French National Assembly since 1919, Prime Minister, Minister of National Defence, and then Minister of War in 1939 and 1940. Arrested and imprisoned in May 1941.

General Maurice Gustave Gamelin, 73 ; French officer, graduate of the military academy at Saint-Cyr, Commander-in-Chief of the French armed forces from September 1939, to May 1940, when he was succeeded by General Weygand. Arrested and imprisoned after the French defeat in 1941.

Léon Jouhaux, 66, French union leader, Secretary General of the *Confédération générale du Travail* [General Federation of Labor] since 1909. Imprisoned in 1941.

Francesco Saverio Nitti, 77, Italian economist and politician, Prime Minister and Minister of the Interior in 1919 and 1920. He was forced to leave Italy after the fascist rise to power and was arrested in Paris by the Gestapo in 1942.

Paul Reynaud, 67, Minister of Justice, then Minister of Finance in the Daladier cabinet from April 1938, to March 1940 ; Prime Minister in March 1940. Two months later he replaced General Gamelin with General Weygand as Commander-in-Chief of the French armed forces. Arrested and imprisoned in 1940.

General Maxime Weygand, 78, French officer, graduate of the military academy at Saint-Cyr, member of the *Académie française* since 1932, Commander-in-Chief of the French armed forces in May and June 1940, Minister of National Defense in the Pétain government from June to September 1940. Arrested in 1942.

Apart from these notables the group included an Italian banker named Georgini, who had been arrested in Paris by the Gestapo ; a Frenchman named Granger ; a Madame Brucklein, secretary to Jouhaux and "an excellent cook" ; and Christiane Mabire, Paul Reynaud's private secretary.

No matter what purpose it served, Itter was a summer resort compared to Dachau. One of the prisoners, André François-Poncet, a former French ambassador to Berlin, described an incident involving several inmates from Dachau :

> For three days now, four wretched political prisoners from Dachau have been repairing a section of wall which crumbled away in the rain. Two Austrians and two Poles, one a high-school teacher from Warsaw — they are pale and haggard, and look pitiable in their blue-striped convicts' trousers. We try to pass them cigarettes and sugar without attracting the

attention of their guards. One of the Austrians is a communist. Compared to them we have a glorious fate ; we are more than privileged, we are virtually demi-gods. Let us pity them and learn not to pity ourselves ! [28]

The prisoners in Itter were certainly deprived of their freedom, but in return they enjoyed sunshine, deck-tennis, card games, comfortable armchairs, and legs of mutton with kidney beans. At one point François-Poncet received a small parcel of foodstuffs from his wife and wrote in his journal : "She assumes I am starving and does not realize that in certain respects we are eating better here than we would in France. She is unaware that our life here is a complete paradox, with bolts, bars, and prison guards on the one hand, and all the comforts of a residential hotel on the other !" [29]

These prisoners, most of them prominent political or military leaders, were not subjected to any physical hardships except the hardship created by putting such disparate, often conflicting, personalities together at close quarters for three years. Friction was inevitable. General Gamelin, obsessed with the French defeat and the scorn he endured because of it, was forever absolving himself of blame. Nitti dreamed of seeing once again the Italy he had been forced to leave behind twenty-five years earlier. Jouhaux saw only one solution to the social and political ills of the day — placing power in the hands of the people. Paul Reynaud, like Nitti, believed that no attempt should have been made to appease Germany.

It is therefore not surprising to find François-Poncet, who spent three months at Itter, noting in his journal that "relations between certain members of our group are strained," and "my companions in captivity here at Itter are not always easy to live with. They are a strange mixture of highly idiosyncratic people, whose personalities and ideas are at odds with one another." [30] And the ex-ambassador added : "The best man of them all in spirit is certainly Borotra. A whim of the Nazis threw him in here, but his background and his character are so different that he has nothing in common with them at all."

By the end of April 1945, they felt certain that their days in prison were coming to an end. The signs were unmistakable : the enigmatic pronouncements on German radio, the groups of refugees on the Austrian roads, and the German officers exchanging their uniforms for peasant clothing. It seems that Jean Borotra had got wind of the US Seventh Army's arrival in Austria and rumor had it that there were a number of National Socialist Party members in the area. The prisoners were afraid that they might be overlooked, held for ransom, or simply mistaken by the Allies for the enemy. All were possible risks in an area far removed from the front where the hostilities could not be depended upon to end in an orderly fashion.

With these dangers in mind, or simply because he wanted to finish his days in prison as soon as possible, Borotra decided to meet the Americans before they reached the castle :

> Borotra arrived just as German opposition was collapsing. He had run five, perhaps ten miles to get to us : the guy was still in good shape, despite his 47 years. He told us about this bunch of aged celebrities not far away. So a group of us left in two or three vehicles, because we had to bring them all back somehow. Soon we found ourselves at the castle. [31]

Lévesque was therefore the first journalist to meet and interview these "celebrities." He thinks it is probable that the Germans shut them all up together "just to make them suffer," so that they might tear one another apart :

> I was the first one to interview them all, and it was a very funny experience. Daladier, for example, insisted on being interviewed alone, but he didn't have much to say. What could you expect ? All he said was "I've been here for two and a half years and I don't really know what's been going on." So I said to him, "Yes, but you've been with Reynaud, haven't you ?" "Yes," he replied, "but what I have to say about him and the others will have to wait until I leave and get down to writing !" Then I went to see Reynaud and he said, "Yes, well, you see, I've been confined here in the company of people with whom I don't really get along. But I'll be writing about it before very long and then people will sit up and take notice." It was funny how all those Frenchmen basically said the same thing — every one of them had a book to write. [32]

Kesselring's Army Surrenders

The US Seventh Army left Itter and the end of the war found them at Innsbruck, "the loveliest spot you could imagine for finishing off a war," as Lévesque put it. But he hadn't packed his bags yet. Curiosity prompted him to push ahead towards Italy, where he witnessed the surrender at the Brenner Pass of the last main German army, commanded by Kesselring. This general had acquired a reputation as a military genius and matchless tactician ; in Italy he had managed to keep both the American and the British armies at bay for some time. But Kesselring himself was not present when Lévesque arrived at the Brenner Pass : a month and a half earlier Hitler had recalled him and made him commander of the German forces on the Western front. Lévesque described the surrender :

> It was incredible ! I didn't see the actual surrender — that is, I didn't see Kesselring himself surrender. His army had been marching north out of Italy and when they got to the Brenner Pass they couldn't go any farther because we were blocking the way into Austria and other Allied troops were pressing them from the rear. So their only choice was to surrender or die. They surrendered. You know, the Germans had an amazingly well-disciplined army : when they surrendered, they really surrendered. You felt safer, more secure, in the middle of a bunch of German soldiers who had just surrendered than you would in a public place where some civilian might have tried to pick a fight. You know how that happens, sometimes. But the really incredible thing was that the Brenner Pass at that time was just a narrow two-lane highway, with sheer cliffs very close to either side of the road. And there were all those German soldiers surrendering by the hundreds ; the war was over, and they'd lost everything. But they still maintained their ranks along the side of the road. Their guns, their tents — everything was in order. You'd see just the remains of a company or a batallion, but the men would still be in formation. And they stayed like that until they were told where to go. It was an amazing sight to see. [33]

From there Lévesque headed south into Italy :

> Here he had one of his most unforgettable experiences. In the village near Lake Como where Mussolini had met an ignominious death after being virtually deified by his people, René Lévesque saw the Duce's almost unrecognizable body hanging by its feet, covered with bruises, spittle, and filth ; beside it, hanging from the same gasoline pump, was the body of Claretta Petacci. He saw them with his own eyes .... [34]

On April 29, 1945, as one eye-witness put it, "an entire nation gave itself over to a sadistic frenzy before that body hanging by its feet, a frenzy completely unbecoming to civilized people." [35] When the author questioned Lévesque about this event, he was noticeably reluctant to discuss it :

> I did see it, yes, from some distance away. I saw it from a distance because the behavior of the crowd was revolting and the sight of those corpses kept you away. They looked like two slabs of meat. You didn't want to get any closer ; there was no point in trying even if you'd wanted to. The delirium we saw didn't give a very good impression of the Italian people, in any case. It's all very well to say : "The guy . . ." Anyway . . . what can you say about a thing like that ? It was there to see, just about 500 feet away. [36]

Journalist Odette Oligny describes the rest of Lévesque's stay in Italy :

> Continuing his journey through Italy, he found himself in Florence, which had suffered extensive damage and where only a single bridge remained standing over the Arno. He then passed through Rome, on his way to Naples and spent a few days on Capri, which at that time had not yet become a tourist haven.

She then alludes to one of his television appearances :

> Recently you may have seen René Lévesque on the television program *Ciné-Club,* delivering a commentary on the film *Païsa.* He was well-qualified for the job because he was there in Italy when its people, caught in the miserable aftermath of the war, suffered the humiliation of defeat perhaps worse than any other nation. For the Italians, liberation was merely a kind of occupation, and their poverty forced them to go begging to the Americans, who had large supplies of food and clothing. It was the era of the *sciuscià.* * [37]

The First Interview with Goering

After Hitler's death in Berlin on April 30, he was succeeded by Admiral Karl Dönitz. The task facing him was not easy : he was charged with negotiating the best possible conditions for Germany's capitulation. [38] At the beginning of May, Hermann Wilhelm Goering, who had long been Hitler's right-hand man but had lost his chance of assuming power through personal indiscretions and inner-circle rivalry, tried once and for all to reassert his authority. His biographers describe how he undertook negotiations with the Americans :

---

* Literally "shoeshine boys." The war created such hardship in Italy that many youngsters took to the streets as shoeshine boys in order to earn a little money.

On May 7 he despatched his chief A.D.C., von Brauchitsch, to the nearest American headquarters, bearing letters to General Eisenhower, in which he requested an interview with the Allied Commander-in-Chief. After encountering considerable difficulties, since all roads were choked with traffic of one sort or another, von Brauchitsch delivered his letters at the headquarters of a Texan division and was ordered to return to his master with instructions that he should proceed to Fischhorn Castle, where he would be placed under American protection. When on May 8 General Stack reached Fischhorn with thirty men to take charge of the distinguished prisoner, he was annoyed to find that Goering had not arrived. He could still not make up his mind, but this time the Americans made it up for him. A sharp order from General Stack brought him hurrying from Mauterndorf, and after a long and tiresome delay in a traffic block, from which he had to be extricated by American troops, Goering stood at last face to face with an enemy General. [39]

Immediately following his meeting with General Stack at Fischhorn, Goering held a press conference for four or five journalists who had heard about his arrest, among them Lévesque, who had just returned from Italy :

Goering had left Berlin because he'd had enough. This was before Hitler died in the bunker. He left, so the story went, in order to take charge of what was supposed to be the "underground." Rumors to this effect flew around until the very last minute, even though they were often contradictory, but the Allied soldiers were scared to death of this alleged underground. The Russians had their underground and the French their Resistance ; why shouldn't the Germans have one too ? They were supposedly called the "Werewolves," and everybody was afraid they might appear at any moment. They said Goering had left Berlin to take command of the remaining troops and these "Werewolves" in southern Germany, which was where we were. Of course there weren't any "Werewolves" and there weren't any more troops. It soon became obvious that Goering had left Berlin to get himself ready for the end of the war and try to save his own skin. That's why he went to the Americans. He arrived about half an hour before we did, to turn himself over to them. I saw him wearing his pearl-grey uniform — he was one of the Reich's fashion plates — but someone, maybe he himself, had ripped off his epaulets, his decorations, and all that kind of stuff. His uniform was really stripped bare. He sat under a weeping willow in a huge armchair because he was quite fat. They had treated him well but he knew his life wasn't worth much. Needless to say, he was under heavy guard. So he held a small press conference — there weren't many of us, maybe four or five. Later on, journalists started pouring in from the other fronts, but that first time there were only four or five of us. You had to hand it to him : he did carry it off with dignity. He didn't harangue Hitler or the régime ; all he said was, "It's all over," and "I ask the German people ... ," and so on. You know, at the end he tried to make himself out to be a kind of savior, just like the others. But he did it with an air of dignity, knowing full well his life wasn't worth a dime. We didn't press the interview with him too far, because all we were interested in was whether he would say something to try to save his skin. That was about it. [40]

Nuremberg, Dachau, Itter ... Kesselring, Mussolini, Goering, and many other prominent figures ... the war itself ... the twenty-two-year-old American war correspondent from Quebec had certainly seen his share of the great events. On May 9, Lévesque took time out to write a quick note to his family from Rosenheim, near Munich :

No more bullets, no more explosions. It's almost too quiet. People must be dancing in the streets over there ; here, it's very peaceful. No more noise. We've had the feeling it's all over for quite some time. I've run around like a madman for the last month : Nuremberg, Munich, Tyrol, Brenner ... Reynaud, Daladier, Weygand, Kesselring, Goering, etc.... I'm spending another week in the Tyrol, then on to the Swiss frontier, then Paris, then home as soon as transport is available. See you soon. Sorry to rush this, but I've got to go. It's 9:25 am and the jeep leaves at 9:30.

He added a postscript :

No stamps ! Hope this gets there anyway ! [41]

The war was over. After the Tyrol and Switzerland, Lévesque went to Paris, but his job was not over yet. He was ordered to go south to the French Riviera where convoys of American ships from Germany were docking in Marseille before sailing on "to fight the war against Japan." Lévesque arrived and acted as an interpreter for the Americans in their dealings with the French.

However, the troops never had the chance to set sail for Japan ; the atomic bomb saved them the journey.

Lévesque took advantage of the peace to travel around at his leisure for a few weeks, without the pressure of military duties. He could easily afford to since he had several thousand dollars in his pocket. He explains :

> We were among the most highly paid men in the army. At first I had an "assimilated" rank of lieutenant, and by the end I think I was a captain. I wasn't in charge of a unit, but I held the equivalent rank, which the Americans called "assimilated." They paid well, but there was nowhere to spend it, of course. The black market was so bad that money was not nearly as acceptable as a pack of cigarettes or a box of rations. The war had left Europe in a state of virtual famine. [42]

Before returning to Quebec, Lévesque stopped by the headquarters of the Office of War Information in London and said goodbye to Pierre Lazareff :

> Lazareff was our top man in London and already a distinguished journalist. While still very young he had been editor-in-chief of *Paris-Soir*. Throughout the war, *Paris-Soir,* like most other French papers, was forced to collaborate and publish German propaganda. After Paris was liberated and things returned to normal, the writers for many of the papers were shaken down and a kind of commission or board decided who was fit to take over these papers under the new free régime. Lazareff was well known and also on the side of the angels — he was, after all, a Jew who had fought with the Allies throughout the war. So he thought to himself, "If I go back to Paris now, I'm bound to look good to everybody. I might even get my hands on a paper." He knew what he was doing, all right. I remember one day when I was in London, he was making the rounds of the office and borrowing all the money he could, because he was really broke at the time. I gave him five pounds ; other people gave him what they could. Lazareff collected enough money to get to Paris and keep himself for a few days. I passed through Paris about a month later and I think that by then old Lazareff had already landed himself a newspaper.

Lévesque added :

> He never did remember to return my five pounds ; but then, I never remembered to ask him. [43]

71

Chapter 2 — References

1. Interview with R.L., 25 May, 1972.
2. Ibid.
3. Ibid.
4. Letter from R.L. to his mother, London, 24 May, 1944.
5. Ibid.
6. Ibid.
7. Interview with R.L., 25 May, 1972.
8. J.-L. Crémieux-Brilhac, "Les émissions françaises à la BBC pendant la guerre," *Revue d'histoire de la deuxième guerre mondiale*, November 1950, p. 73.
9. Ibid., p. 94.
10. Ibid.
11. Letter from R.L. to his mother, 3 August, 1944.
12. Ibid.
13. Ibid.
14. *London Star*, 8 November, 1944.
15. Letter from R.L. to his mother, London, 17 November, 1944.
16. Ibid.
17. Letter from R.L. to his family, London, 1 January, 1945.
18. Letter from R.L. to his family, London, 24 January, 1945.
19. Interview with R.L., 21 March, 1973.
20. Interview with R.L., 25 May, 1972.
21. Interview with R.L., 21 March, 1973.
22. Olga Wormser and Henri Michel, eds., *Tragédie de la déportation, 1940-1945* (Hachette, 1955), pp. 73-74.
23. Interview with R.L., 25 May, 1972.
24. Interview with R.L., 21 March, 1973.
25. Interview with R.L., 25 May, 1972.
26. Odette Oligny, "René Lévesque, journaliste de l'air," *Le Samedi*, 7 December, 1957.
27. Interview with R.L., 25 May, 1972.
28. André François-Poncet, *Carnets d'un captif* (Arthème Fayard, 1952), p. 59.
29. Ibid., p. 51.
30. Ibid., p. 77.
31. Interview with R.L., 21 March, 1973.
32. Ibid.
33. Interview with R.L., 21 March, 1973.
34. Oligny.
35. Charles Ewald, "Comment mourut Mussolini, le Duce d'Italie, il y a un an," *Le Canada*, 27 April, 1946.
36. Interview with R.L., 21 March, 1973.
37. Oligny.
38. See Marlis-G. Steinert, *Les derniers jours du IIIe Reich : Le gouvernement Dönitz* (Casterman, 1971).
39. Ewan Butler and Gordon Young, *Marshal Without Glory* (Hodder and Stoughton, 1951), pp. 259-260. The author quotes the French translation, *Goering tel qu'il fut* (Flammarion, 1965), p. 348.
40. Interview with R.L., 21 March, 1973.
41. Letter from R.L. to his family, Rosenheim, 9 Bay, 1945.
42. Interview with R.L., 21 March, 1973.
43. Ibid.

3

The Broadcasting Years

"The voice of Canada, Montreal, Canada" : this introduction identified the programs of the CBC's International Service, * broadcasting on short wave to its overseas audience. When the Service first began in 1943, French-language programming had to be recorded and sent by plane to London and New York where the recordings could be broadcast over occupied France. But once a powerful shortwave transmitter was installed in Sackville, New Brunswick, early in 1945, direct broadcasting began on a daily basis and seventy per cent of all programming was aimed at informing and entertaining Canadians directly or indirectly involved with military operations in Europe.

The end of the war brought important changes : the peacetime function of the International Service was "to reflect faithfully the diverse aspects of Canadian life" and "to lend support to the efforts of international agencies by promoting the principle that peace and prosperity are interdependent goals."

René Lévesque joined the staff of the CBC's International Service on his return from Europe in January 1946. His colleagues included two pioneers of radio, Gérard Arthur and René Garneau, director of the French-language division. Lévesque's experiences in Europe

---

* The English name of the Service was recently changed to Radio-Canada International.

enabled him to speak to his overseas audience in a language they could understand. He briefly describes how he started :

> I went into the short-wave service with that raspy voice I picked up in Alsace and I was stuck with it for the next fifteen years. Since I wasn't a commercial announcer and I really liked reporting, they made me a reporter. The guys who were interested in making money didn't bother with reporting because it wasn't a paying proposition. Quite soon afterwards I had the chance to go back to regular radio as a political reporter. [1]

Lévesque outlined his day-to-day work in a newspaper article :

> This is what we produce in the French division under the direction of René Garneau : two thirty-minute programs every day, which provide news, articles from the papers (we often quote editorials criticizing government policy !), in-depth reports, regular features on mining, agriculture, science, books, Canadian poetry, etc. There are also special features, some drama, and a few bilingual items. [. . .] In other words, our broadcasts have a kind of newsreel format. The purpose of the Voice of Canada is to transmit information, not spread propaganda.

Lévesque closed his article by quoting the remarks of a foreign listener, remarks he found impressive and illuminating : "Radio reminds me a little of the gossip grapevine our grandmothers relied on for their news. In the old days a few rash words could set a small town on its ear. Today, with the coming of the atomic age, those same words broadcast over the radio could easily destroy the whole world." [2] Here again is a theme which has always fascinated Lévesque — the shrinking of our planet by modern communications. He had already mentioned it in his article *"Propos en ondes"* in 1942 * and, thirty years later, commenting on the Christmas mass at the Vatican transmitted by satellite, he described Pope Paul VI as a kind of "village priest."

Lévesque was in his element working for the Voice of Canada, since almost half the programming was devoted to news reporting. Priority was naturally given to Canadian news, but an attempt was always made to place domestic events in an international context. Because the French-language team was small, everyone took turns

---

* See pp. 38-42.

doing different jobs. Lévesque himself was primarily a reporter, but he also worked as a news editor and announcer.

In April 1948, he delivered a broadcast on the signing of the NATO pact in Washington. A year later he covered the election of the new Quebec Liberal Party leader, Georges-Emile Lapalme. Then, on November 7, 1950, he told his European and South American listeners that the first contingent of Canadian troops had just landed in Korea.

Lévesque's assignments became more frequent and increasingly important. On April 8, 1951, French President Vincent Auriol received a warm welcome from 300,000 Montrealers during a four-day visit to Canada. Journalist Jean-Paul Nolet covered the tour for the CBC's domestic service, while over four hours of René Lévesque's report were broadcast by the French section of the International Service. A full three of these four hours were re-broadcast by the French state radio.

Aside from his work in the CBC's International Service, Lévesque published occasional articles in the Liberal daily *Le Canada* : "I wrote a little for *Le Canada* because René Garneau was on the staff. They were a pretty interesting group of people. Even though the paper was Liberal, it was still lively and entertaining for that day and age." [3]

In 1946, he also undertook to write an arts review column for the weekly *Le Clairon de Saint-Hyacinthe*. His format was flexible, to say the least, and covered such diverse figures as Paul Claudel, Jean-Paul Sartre, Orson Welles, Jean Marais, Jean Gascon, Ray Ventura, and Jean Racine. Comparing Claudel's *Le Pain dur* to Sartre's *Huis clos,* Lévesque concluded that while "poetry is compassionate,... philosophy is nothing but mathematics." On other occasions, he had harsh words for the relentless radio soap-operas, "which, like *L'amour tel qu'on n'oserait nulle part le parler* [The love that dares not show its face], threaten to run into their 2500th or 3500th episode. This is the kind of series that alternates endlessly between scenes in which nothing is done and scenes in which nothing is said."

Another of Lévesque's achievements in the post-war period was his program *Les Journalistes au micro* [Journalists at the microphone], which he broadcast every Thursday evening from the Press Club at the Laurentian Hotel in Montreal. "It was an interesting variation on the usual press conference," remarked Lévesque, "because it allowed the journalists to interview each other and

75

discuss matters of common interest. I hosted the program in my capacity as journalist. We had some lively confrontations, and it was a lot of fun. All in all, I think the format was quite workable." [4]

The Korean War : Lévesque is discovered

June 1951 signalled a turning point in Lévesque's life : the International Service offered to send him to Korea as correspondent with the Canadian brigade attached to the United Nations combat forces. Full of confidence after his experiences in Europe, Lévesque accepted the assignment without hesitation. The North Koreans had invaded the South in June 1950, and three months later the United Nations dispatched troops to South Korea. By the following summer, the Korean crisis was sharing headlines in Quebec with the public inquiry into the collapse of the Duplessis Bridge at Three Rivers.

Lévesque therefore left for the scene of the hostilities at the beginning of July as the CBC's French-language war correspondent. He stopped over in Tokyo to pick up his equipment and a soldier's uniform, since no civilians were allowed into Korea at the time. He then rejoined the Canadian contingent and found that he was working with a former CBC colleague, Norman McBain of Montreal, and Norman W. Eaves, a technician from Halifax.

Lévesque sent back report after report and his work was of such high quality that the CBC decided to broadcast his programs on the domestic network as well as on the shortwave service. Starting August 12, he also contributed regular articles about his experience to *Le Petit Journal*. Life in Korea, he wrote, was not heaven on earth :

> It's the day after a gruelling patrol and the 22nd Regiment is now camped in a non-combat zone. If this were Europe during World War II, we'd be several miles behind the front in a town or village that was still relatively intact and had a couple of restaurants, etc. But here . . . the non-combat zone is just a huge waterlogged field. We've come down from the bare mountains which continually loom in the background and in a few days we'll be heading back there. There isn't a house as far as the eye can see, apart from some uninhabitable Korean shanties with their thatched roofs, their tumble-down walls, their filth. When it rains the narrow roads turn to mud, dirty streams cover the camp grounds, and water seeps into the tents, rotting clothes and blankets. We eat wet, we sleep wet. Everyone has a cough. The rain stops, the scorching Ko-

76

rean sun pours down for a few hours and the thick, suffocating dust billows up again in heavy, brown clouds. Everyone's cough gets worse. You can't go near the civilians. It's a country racked with pain and it's hostile as well : the man you see wearing a white peasant costume could just as easily be an enemy soldier. [5]

Lévesque described Lieutenant Roger Halley's frustration at being so far from Montreal's theatres and restaurants, the Forum and the baseball park. He mimicked the voice of radio operator Medland — "Allo, Love-One-Five, pass your message, over . . . ." *
He reported a remark made by Colonel "Jimmy" Dextrase to the effect that the Québécois in the 22nd Regiment were using their French as a kind of secret weapon. He rummaged through the private diary of Maurice Juteau, the sergeant whose generous moustache made him look like a Sicilian bandit. In it he found this passage :

A moment ago I spotted a young Korean girl of about 7 or 8. She stands barefoot in the pouring rain wearing an ankle-length dress, but her head is uncovered. The rain has made her jet-black hair all shiny. She is looking for something to eat and she smiles nervously as she wanders among the soldiers and the trucks . . . . Looking at her I felt ashamed. I was just finishing two chocolate bars. I was hungry, so I ate them, without giving it a further thought. Now I feel terrible. I should have asked her to come and sit beside me in the truck, covered her with my three of four blankets and tried to warm her up . . . . I'm completely amazed at how self-centred I can be . . . .

Lévesque had established himself. His outstanding reports on the Korean conflict placed him in the front rank of Quebec journalists. When he returned to Canada at the end of September, he put together a number of programs on Korea for the CBC and lectured widely on his several months' stay in Asia. The critics were unanimous. Journalist Gérard Pelletier, for example, praised Lévesque's achievements unequivocally :

I believe these broadcasts constitute the best work heard on radio for a very long time. Mr. Lévesque is, in my opinion, the radio discovery of the year and the best French-language (and perhaps also English-language) commentator Canadian radio has ever offered us. Those who have not heard Mr. Lévesque will perhaps find my praise for him too generous. But

---

* In English in the original.

77

having compared him in my mind with all the great figures of his profession, starting with Louis Francoeur,* I make no apologies. My only problem is how to describe fully the reasons for such praise. Not that the evidence is lacking : Mr. Lévesque's programs give one plenty to talk about, plenty of details, plenty of angles from which to make a case. The difficulties arise in trying to reconcile two opposing approaches to the problem : dealing with his work at length but at the risk of getting lost in the details, or dealing with it in the way I always want to deal with something perfectly executed and to the point, namely, by praising it to the skies and leaving it at that. But I feel obliged to explain myself, however briefly, so let's give it a try.

Mr. Lévesque's assignment was quite explicit : to tell the Canadian audience about the Korean War with particular reference to the daily life of the troops Canada had committed there, and to offer his observations on conditions in the Asian countries he had visited. Since Mr. Lévesque was not the first person to talk about these subjects, he was faced with the difficulty of having to avoid repeating past efforts, while still going over the same ground his predecessors had attempted to cover. I say "attempted," because, on hearing Mr. Lévesque's programs, I began to realize, with a growing feeling of admiration (admiration in the Latin sense of "awe"), that until now nobody had managed to bring alive the terrible circumstances behind the war, which descended like a plague on that poor country. The second pitfall he had to avoid was propaganda. These broadcasts might well have become an occasion for sanctimonious clichés in the hands of another reporter. Nothing is easier than climbing on the bandwagon and joining the chorus . . . . But Mr. Lévesque overcame these obstacles with the greatest of ease, as though he had never been aware of their existence. The man we have been listening to is not just any CBC reporter, back from his assignment. René Lévesque is one of our own, a man of independent mind who took overseas with him our sensibility, our hopes, our fears, and our curiosity. What he has been saying to us is precisely what we wanted to know, though we may not have realized it. And he has said it with a candor that does justice to both himself and the CBC.

Having established that much, I could quote page after page of Mr. Lévesque's own words. I could also explain how

---

* Louis Francoeur (1895-1941), a journalist and radio commentator from Montreal. He achieved great popularity and in his day was considered the best radio journalist in the province.

he admirably combines the talents of both the radio journalist whose technique is never labored and the man of culture whose learning is never flaunted. And yet any passage chosen at random from his broadcasts, for example, the stunning recording of the soldiers chatting in the dark, reveals a high degree of technical polish and the careful judgment of a man who does not confuse the farcical ideals of the politicians with the genuine concerns of real human beings. The only criticism I have heard directed at Mr. Lévesque (and this was just an off-hand remark) concerns his voice. I admit that the sound of his voice is husky compared to the dulcet tones of your run-of-the-mill announcer. But I must confess that it is a voice I like, because I like the artful way Mr. Lévesque uses it. His is a voice you feel at home with, one that gives his talks a feeling of intimacy, well suited to the medium of radio. Radio talent of this kind, in other words, is something extremely rare. There is never a shortage of would-be talent, and broadcasting even has its share of the gifted ; but excellence like this only comes along once a year at best. Mr. Lévesque's work as a reporter and broadcaster is nothing less than outstanding. We can only hope that the CBC will withdraw him from the International Service, despite the importance of his contribution there, and give us the chance to hear more often his comments on what is going on in the world around us. [6]

Another listener, student Yvon Côté, described his "discovery" of René Lévesque during the reports on Korea.

One evening not long ago, a report by René Lévesque about Korea came on the air. I had never heard of this man before. But what a revelation to listen to him for the first time ! Within a few moments I felt a friend was in my living room talking to me, invisible behind a cloud of cigarette smoke. René Lévesque was nothing to me at first but a voice ; however, his voice is distinctive, and its slightly husky quality quickly becomes familiar. It has such physical presence that you can almost feel the muscles contracting, inhaling, rounding, and relaxing again, in their natural cycle. [. . .] René Lévesque's subject that evening was Japan, and his program took the form of an interview. The listener was effortlessly transported to a Tokyo street, where he became a fascinated tourist listening to his guide's wonderful description of their surroundings. People's voices, the hum of innumerable background sounds, the small gestures peculiar to this race of people, the continual jostling, even the mannerisms and home life of a person I will never see in the flesh : all this washed over me as I sat in my armchair, half beside myself, captivated by this narrator, experiencing the astonishingly hypnotic effect of real radio. No book — perhaps not even a film — has ever told me more about a country. This was truly radio at its best. René Lévesque is a master of the spoken word, yet his treatment does not simply please the ear ; it also does perfect justice to the ideas which he wishes to put across. His is not the dry talent of the competent announcer, for the purview of his imagination takes in all that is human. René Lévesque's program was indeed a masterpiece.

Similar testimonies in praise of René Lévesque's work on the Korean War abound. At this point, however, we should pause and look at the man more objectively. In 1951, Lévesque was twenty-nine years old. He was quite short and was beginning to lose his hair. He was not a television personality, because the medium was still unknown; neither was he a cabinet minister, nor the leader of a political party. Nevertheless, he had already built up a considerable reputation for his ideas and his mastery of the spoken word, and many people in French Canada were quite simply infatuated with him.

The same student attended a lecture given by Lévesque in February 1952 :

René Lévesque is in a class by himself. His entire outlook on life is both candid and humane. Nervous and incisive, he fills his speeches with images which make his ideas spring to life. His speaking style is almost impressionistic ; he painted a picture of life in present-day Japan and Korea with small deft touches which created a harmonious whole, far more truthful and polished than the labored frescoes of government officials or professional speakers. Mr. Lévesque has no visible axes to grind, no apparent method, and certainly no election to prepare for. He lives by what he does and says, and nothing could be more convincing than this sense of personal commitment. His highly developed powers of observation allow him to discern and recreate things as they really are. A certain movement of the shoulder, a slight arching of the eyebrow, a word emphasized by an intentional slip — all allow him to paint a vivid picture of a soldier sprawling on a ridge of ground somewhere in Korea. He is no less adept at describing the nuances of psychological attitudes, and can give us shrewd glimpses of a mental landscape. [. . .] René Lévesque's words lend a lyrical quality to the simplest acts of everyday life. He knows how to couch the truth in terms that are right for the times ; he is able to accommodate himself to the needs of his listeners and to shape his words in response to their very outlook on life. To many, in a world where truth is at such a premium, his honesty is disconcerting. The strong, clear light René Lévesque sheds on all he discusses is a challenge to those who turn a blind eye and presume to understand better by seeing less. [7]

Gérard Pelletier had suggested that the CBC withdraw Lévesque from their International Service in order to give him wider exposure at home. On his return from Korea, he was in fact instructed to cover the visit to Canada of Princess Elizabeth and the Duke of Edinburgh for both the domestic and international networks. On October 8, Lévesque was at Montreal's Dorval Airport to cover their arrival. The next day, the Montreal daily *Le Devoir* published a parody of his coverage written by Candide, the paper's resident satirist. "I can see her now, ladies and gentlemen, though she's still some distance away. She's wearing a mink coat.... I'm sorry, ladies and gentlemen, it's not really a coat. It seems to be more like ... a ... stole. Her stole, I would say, is made of ... ladies and gentlemen, the princess is too ... far away, and I would hesitate to say what kind of stole her fur is made of, or, to be more precise, what kind of fur her stole is made of." He concluded : "Our radio announcers do their best ; but whose idea is it to give them assignments which amount to nothing more than killing time for thirty minutes, let alone two hours?" A few days later, Gérard Pelletier repied to Candide :

> Who is to blame ? Certainly not our French-language announcers. I have already expressed my admiration for René Lévesque, and this tedious report on the royal visit has in no way diminished it. Mr. Lévesque's talent is not at issue here, but rather the very presence of Her Royal Highness, heir apparent to the throne. How many of our French-Canadian poets have ever written a poem in honor of a British king, let alone an English queen or princess ? There are, it is true, those among us who are royalists in spite of themselves, who believe in the Commonwealth, and stand up for the Crown as a legal fiction which helps balance Ottawa's relations with Washington. But there have never been any French Canadians, apart from a few senile dotards, who have ever felt any genuine sentimental attachment to the royal family. [8]

After following Princess Elizabeth's 23-day tour of Canada, Lévesque finally left the International Service along with his

1953
After returning from Korea, Lévesque became director of the CBC French network's first News Service. One of his major assignments as a commentator was the coronation of Queen Elizabeth.

colleagues Judith Jasmin and Gérard Arthur. Together they founded the CBC French network's first News Service. Lévesque explained its purpose : "We had begun to realize that there was a need for well-trained reporters. Not just people who dabbled in journalism, but real professionals." Jacques Languirand and Jean Ducharme soon joined them. Their proving ground was the program *Carrefour* [Crossroads], which was broadcast every weekday evening and featured interviews and brief reports on many different subjects. Judith Jasmin said of *Carrefour :* "It was a stroke of genius. René Lévesque was the first person to appreciate that people here really wanted to find out about one another. I first met him when he was twenty-three and he was then already much wiser than his years. He's a born professor, as well as a marvellous teacher." [9] *Carrefour* was on the air from 1952 to 1955, in conjunction with *Reportages,* a weekly half-hour program which discussed some of the same subjects in greater depth.

On September 6, 1952, the CBC began transmitting television ✓ programs on a regular basis. What the News Service had done for radio, it could do equally well for television, but some adjustments were in order. Lévesque explained : "At first, the television people were content to use us just for various news items, then, as we got used to the new medium, more and more for reporting. Everybody was trying to get used to it as best they could. Eventually *Carrefour* was moved over to television and for quite a while we did half an hour five days a week." Lévesque was also the moderator of another new television program, *Conférence de presse,* but in 1955 he told a journalist that he was not entirely pleased with it : "What I'd like to do with *Conférence de presse* is to give it the feel of a real debate, the kind of outspokenness which makes similar American programs so effective. But that's not so easy up here." [10] Even though he was head of the News Service, Lévesque had not abandoned his radio work. He appeared regularly on the program *Lettre à une Canadienne,* to discuss various items in the news of interest to women with Marcelle Barthe, and he continued to review films for the *Revue des Arts et des Lettres.*

The notable accomplishments of the CBC News Service naturally coincided with international events of unusual interest, such as the crowning of Queen Elizabeth in 1953. On June 2, Gérard Arthur, Judith Jasmin, and René Lévesque were in London for the coronation.

> Their report created quite a stir. A few weeks before the coronation, a CBC crew went to London and set up for filming the whole ceremony from the BBC telecast. Three RAF jets left London at intervals on the day of the coronation, each carrying part of the precious film to the studios of CBFT in Montreal. At 4:15 on the same day, the three Canadian stations began broadcasting the opening ceremonies while at the same time providing a feed to the national networks in the United States. It all happened in record time : the Canadian viewers actually saw the first part of the ceremony before it was all over in London. [11]

The News Service also covered the Canadian visits of Haile Selassie in June 1954, and of Pierre Mendès-France in November of the same year, as well as the Empire and Commonwealth Games in Vancouver. René Lévesque was on the air for all these events.

A day at Khrushchev's "Summer Cottage"

Over the summer of 1955, Lester B. Pearson, Minister of External Affairs in Louis Saint-Laurent's Liberal cabinet, was preparing to visit the leading capitals of the world. Pearson's tour of the capitals at the height of the Cold War was timed to coincide with a Colombo Plan conference in Singapore, where he was due to arrive on October 12. A number of Canadian journalists accompanied Pearson on the trip, including René Lévesque for the CBC.

The stopovers in London, Paris, and Berlin were uneventful, and on October 5 Pearson landed in Moscow. Because he was the first minister of foreign affairs to come to Moscow since the Geneva Conference in 1954, a large number of western journalists were present. Only Molotov, the Minister of Foreign Affairs, and his assistant Valery Zorin were there to greet Pearson when he arrived. Khrushchev and Bulganin had in fact stayed away deliberately to demonstrate their superiority over the third member of the troika : "The Soviet hierarchy abounds in this kind of fine distinction," explained Lévesque. "It goes on all the time. Depending on where someone is situated in a photograph, for example, the Kremlinologists claim they can tell, up to a certain point, what's happening to that person. The two of them were playing the same game with us." [12] Nevertheless, Pearson expressed the hope that he could exchange ideas on world problems with the Soviet leaders in order to "achieve a better understanding of their respective points of view."

But days passed and still Pearson had no word from Khrushchev and Bulganin. It was felt in diplomatic circles that talks among the three men might give the West some idea of the Soviet position prior to the summit conference in Geneva, where the foreign ministers of the Great Powers were to meet on October 27. Meanwhile, senior Canadian civil servants, including Mitchell Sharp, assistant deputy minister for Commerce, and George Ignatieff, a Russian by birth and head of the liaison division at External Affairs, were attempting to negotiate a trade agreement with Russia concerning wheat and newsprint. Pearson for his part diplomatically underlined how important it was for Canada and Russia — "neighbors across the North Pole" — to work together in peace and mutual understanding.

Finally, after visits to the Bolshoi Theatre, Leningrad, and Lenin's Tomb, and a cold which kept him confined to bed for several hours,

Pearson was told on the morning of October 11 that he would be received that evening by Khrushchev in his Crimean "dacha." Lévesque, who accompanied him on the trip, described what took place :

> They woke us up suddenly that morning and said, "We've got room for two journalists." So somebody said : "Okay, one English and one French." As it turned out, I was lucky enough to go as the French-speaking journalist, because I could do both written and spoken reports. My partner was Richard Needham, who's with the *Globe and Mail* now. So we set off with Pearson, Crépault, one of his assistants, and George Ignatieff. If my information is correct — and this explains part of the story — Ignatieff was apparently the son or the grandson of an old upper middle-class or perhaps even aristocratic family in the time of the Czars. The Russians evidently had him spotted. First we went up to Moscow then down to a town near Yalta, where we caught a taxi which had been waiting for us. Our driver was a strange guy, all the more so because we now found ourselves in a completely foreign environment. He was a real maniac — whenever we were going uphill he floored the gas pedal, and as soon as we were able to coast he turned the engine off. We asked our guide : "For the love of God, can you tell us why he's doing that ?" He replied : "Ah !" The primitive side was still there under the veneer of technical sophistication : he was under the illusion that they were saving fuel. Of course, every time he turned the engine on again, he used up more fuel than he'd saved. We drove with the engine constantly being turned on and off like that all the way to Yalta.

Lévesque talked more about the taxi driver.

> He was interesting in other ways as well. His wife was a doctor, but he was just a driver by profession and not all that bright. This kind of situation gave you an inkling of how far the old social order had been broken down. The great majority of Russian doctors are in fact women. Most of them end up getting married ; there's no social snobbery to prevent them from marrying beneath their station, as the saying goes. It's all right in our society for a man to marry beneath his station, but for a woman, that's another story. It seems to work quite differently over there.

The rest of Lévesque's story takes place behind the scenes of this diplomatic encounter :

85

We finally arrived at Khrushchev's dacha. "Dacha" in this case meant "on the Black Sea." It was right in the middle of a promontory thrusting into the Black Sea, a stone's throw from Yalta. It had originally been a summer resort for the rich, before becoming a retreat for VIP's of the new régime, and it was Khushchev's turn at that point. It was like the big houses you see in Laval-des-Rapides, * cheap and flashy, three stories, lots of rooms, but not exactly a medieval or renaissance chateau. We went inside, where three or four of Khushchev's body guards were waiting for us. The rest of the place was quite unassuming. [13]

Then Khrushchev and Bulganin came forward to shake hands with the Canadian delegation. Lévesque stood off to one side and scrutinized the two men :

Khrushchev was particularly striking. He was the living, breathing antithesis of the rigid and oppressive Stalinism which had become so stifling in its final years. Short and stocky, with pink skin and beady eyes, he was as solid and unkempt as a backwoods peasant, but with the chatty, familiar style of a travelling salesman. When he became excited, that is to say, every time he opened his mouth, his baritone voice quickly got shriller and shriller, he would gesticulate and laugh very loudly. He seemed tireless, naive, curious, insatiable .... You could detect in the demeanor of Khrushchev and his taciturn companion, the very proper and distinguished Bulganin, a certain feeling of newly-won liberation, a liberation so untried that it demanded vigorous assertion. There was a vague smell of confinement about them ; they were like overexcited ex-prisoners flexing their muscles, breathing fresh air once again, and frantically making up for lost time. [14]

Lévesque and Needham were called forward.

Khrushchev was just like his photographs : a kind of peasant with a pink face and beady little eyes, very energetic and full of life. He began to chat, and about half of what he said in Russian was translated. I had a Nagra with me, a portable tape recorder that was very good in its day, but still a lot bulkier than the ones we have now. It was about two or three feet long and at least a foot and a half deep, and I had it slung over my shoulder. In other words, it wasn't very difficult to spot. At one point Khrushchev was jabbering away when he pointed at the Nagra and said, "What's that ?" "Radio ! Radio !" I

---

* A middle class, largely English-speaking Montreal suburb.

told him. He said, "Ah ! Radio ! Radio !" He asked me to put it on the table. I did. He opened it up and made a show of not knowing how to work the machine. I showed him. It was quite simple. Then I handed him the microphone. This kept his interpreter Troyanovsky pretty busy.

At this point Lévesque digressed on the subject of the interpreter, as if to heighten the suspense :

Troyanovsky was another example of how things really worked in Soviet society. He was living proof that patronage and nepotism will always be with us as long as human nature remains the same. Troyanovsky was a man of about thirty, obviously very bright, and he was the official interpreter for Khrushchev and the other government leaders. How had he reached this privileged position ? Because his worthy father, an old Bolshevik, had been the first Soviet ambassador to Washington after Roosevelt recognized Russia in 1933, if I remember correctly. Which meant that the son had obviously learned his English there, American slang and all. Since he was perfectly bilingual, he became an interpreter. Privileged classes always manage to perpetuate themselves no matter what the form of government.

Lévesque resumed his story :

Troyanovsky was busy translating when suddenly Khrushchev tore into Pearson. Keep in mind that this was 1955, the era when there was all that friction over NATO encircling Russia with military bases. So Khrushchev, speaking into the microphone, tore into Pearson, who was completely taken aback. Pearson always objected to this kind of rough-and-tumble — he was a good diplomat, but not exactly aggressive — and didn't put up any defence at all. It was fascinating to watch. This was the first time Khrushchev had ever been so aggressive in public, but that's what he was capable of. Pearson had to stand there and take it.

Now I was the French representative and Needham was the English representative, but at the same time we were both part of the press pool ; in other words, everything we recorded in Yalta had to be sent back to Moscow. We had first priority on the material and the others had the right to use it afterwards. I sent my work to Moscow as was expected. This was the first interview with Khrushchev since he had taken over ; no one else in the West had ever interviewed him before, and here he'd come out with one of his historic tirades. So it really annoyed me when the other journalists in Pearson's party —

the French, the Germans, the British — all jumped on my report, with no thought for Pearson, who by then was looking a bit shaky. Two weeks later, as I passed through various European cities on my way home, I was shown newspapers with eight-column front-page headlines reading, "Interview with Khrushchev : He assails Western policies in shouting match with Lester B. Pearson, etc." It was on front pages everywhere, but not of course under my by-line, because when you *pool,* * anyone else can use your material and its the press agencies that get the credit. But it was still my material, and when I got back to Montreal three weeks later, they hadn't used a word of it, not one line. The CBC had got all upset and wouldn't use it because Ottawa had seen it first and said : "This does not show the Minister in a good light. We think it should not be used." I did get it released here a month later, but it was old hat by then. We did a series of programs about the trip on *Carrefour,* complete with photographs, even though they had been shown on the news in other countries three weeks before. But here, the Minister's image might have suffered — it's a risk you take in External Affairs — so they said, "We can't use it." [15]

Two days after Khrushchev's outburst, *Le Devoir* printed this bulletin from Reuters News Service : "Two Canadian journalists, who accompanied the Minister to the Crimea, reported that the Chairman of the Council of Ministers of the USSR and the Secretary of the Soviet Communist Party received Mr. Pearson in a summer residence about ten miles from Yalta. The journalists were allowed to remain present during the first thirteen minutes of the conversation, which apparently touched mainly on the Atlantic alliance." According to Reuters, Khrushchev advised Pearson to withdraw from NATO, because "the West was obviously bent once more on Russia's destruction." Pearson apparently replied that the purpose of the alliance was purely defensive. [16]

After the exclusive interview, the two journalists were led into a quite sumptuous suite of rooms on the ground floor of the dacha. Lévesque decided to go for a dip in the Black Sea before sitting down to dinner. A good swimmer, he wanted to tease his friends back home in Quebec by telling them that he had gone swimming at "Khrushchev's summer cottage." But the swim was very nearly a disaster :

I went for my swim and almost drowned because I didn't know

* In English in the original.

about the currents in the Black Sea. I scraped myself badly as the current swept me out along the foot of the cape. The water seemed ideal for swimming, just like the Mediterranean, and I thought I was okay, but at one point it looked like I wasn't going to make it back. I ended up swimming all the way around the cape, because I couldn't make it directly to shore. I just wanted a swim in the Black Sea at Khrushchev's, but I got more than I bargained for. When I finally finished this exhausting marathon all by myself, I started in on the vodka and champagne with Needham and we spent a very relaxing evening together. But around midnight or one o'clock we began to hear toilets flushed repeatedly on the floor upstairs — Russian plumbing isn't the most advanced in the world and it makes a lot of noise — where Pearson, Crépault, and Ignatieff had been dining with Khrushchev and his group and supposedly discussing politics. That, after all, is what they were there for. But the toilets just kept on flushing and making a terrible racket for an hour or an hour and a half. The two of us, who had just been sitting there enjoying a good meal, heard all this and asked each other, "What's going on up there, for Christ's sake ?" The next morning, as we were getting ready to leave, our distinguished party came downstairs with Pearson in the lead, all of them looking like ghosts, haggard and completely wiped out by the previous evening's festivities. Eventually the story came out : they had obviously been less than scintillating at dinner and weren't exactly proud of themselves. Khrushchev, you see, wasn't all that eager to talk any more. He'd done his interview and he'd shouted at them. They all chatted a bit, but mostly they just got drunk. The Russians had taken one look at Ignatieff, pigeon-holed him, and said to themselves : "Let's see if we can drink this decadent Russian under the table." And of course Khrushchev had this frightening peasant way about him. What had happened apparently was that about three quarters of the meal was devoted to toasts, a common enough custom in Russia. The Russians must have proposed every toast imaginable, including probably a series of toasts to Queen Elizabeth's health. A toast to this, a toast to that, and with each toast, of course, you have to empty your glass, so that by and by all the Canadians were good and sick. They looked like corpses the next morning. Pearson never did have much to say about that evening. [17]

The Reuters account of the event takes on comic overtones when read against the background of Lévesque's story : "Tuesday evening Mr. Pearson attended a banquet given by Premier Bulganin and Communist Party chief Nikita Khrushchev in the Crimea. A spokesman from the Canadian embassy reported that they held *general discussions.*" [18] Pearson himself said in Karachi on October 13 that "the opinions expressed on both sides had been very frank and quite useful" and that "Mr. Khrushchev had really spoken his mind." Bulganin, for his part, "was present during the talks but did not participate actively, although he did raise his glass to Mr. Saint-Laurent's health." [19]

On his return from Russia, Lévesque was asked to speak to many social clubs, student groups, and women's organizations. Everyone wanted to hear his impressions of a country that had received so much bad press in Quebec and throughout Canada. To many people, the trial of Hungarian Cardinal Mindszenty, who was condemned to life imprisonment in February 1949, had been final confirmation of the evil nature of the Soviet régime. Lévesque accepted many of these invitations and tried to disprove the misconceptions people had about Russia. He was asked : "Is Russia in fact like the Russia we hear about on the radio and read about in books?" Lévesque replied : "Not at all, at least as far as surveillance, ill treatment, and food are concerned. Everything was accessible to us in the cities we visited. No one followed us. You could take pictures, speak Russian if you spoke Russian or English if you met any Russians who could speak English. People seemed no more unhappy than they are anywhere else." [20]

Reactions to his statement were not long forthcoming. The guardians of public morality were on the alert : "Think of it !" wrote Louis Mercure. "To come back from Russia and not say a word about the misery of the people, the concentration camps, or the religious persecution. Mr. Lévesque claims that the Russians seem to be well fed and well clothed. He even claims to have been to mass in a Moscow church, even though everyone is perfectly aware . . . ." [21] Father Ouellette, from the parish of Saint-Jean-de-la-Croix in Montreal, went even further, and had the requests for prayers of some of his parishioners printed up in a "family" bulletin. In addition to pleas for help from an atheist, an alcoholic, a communist couple, and " a stubborn individual who had forsaken religion for twenty-five years," hope was expressed for "the conversion of Gérard Pelletier, René Lévesque, and Jacques Hébert." [22]

But Lévesque went on with his job. He was still doing his evening stint on *Carrefour* with Jasmin, Ducharme, and Languirand ; they were soon joined by Andréanne Lafond and Wilfrid Lemoyne. In

1956, French Premier Guy Mollet visited Quebec and was interviewed by Lévesque, who made a strong impression on the French statesman. Mollet later called him "the most intelligent journalist" he had ever met. [23] Lévesque's work was being broadcast over both radio and television and the critical reception was very favorable. Roland Lorrain wrote :

> René Lévesque's radio journalism is remarkable for its tact, its sense of proportion, and its unfailing human perspective. His skilfully constructed report on Friday the 27th concerning the visit of Father Pierre alternated in a very effective and moving fashion between Father Pierre's voice and René Lévesque's personal observations, which were wise and restrained but quite courageous. This was a remarkable feat in a province where to cast doubt on piety is to commit libel. [24]

Jean Leduc wrote that Lévesque introduced the art of reporting into the CBC :

> Finally René Lévesque stepped into the picture, without any previous experience as an announcer and, furthermore, in my opinion, without any obvious natural talent for this kind of work. But the experience he gained in the CBC's International Service, where his job was to pass on information about Canada to other countries, allowed him to learn the reporter's craft and to develop his own particular style of radio journalism. First we had the special features, the occasional programs, then the regular series, the radio version of *Carrefour,* the television version, the reports on Russia, and so on. The public latched on to this style from the very beginning and remained faithful to it during its evolution. As he went along, Lévesque created the need for programs which did not just present the day-to-day news, but really covered current events and explored them in depth. [25]

Renald Savoie had equally high praise for Lévesque's work :

> He is an indispensable person in an organization which hopes to educate its audience. René Lévesque operates on ideas with the skill of a surgeon : he starts by X-raying his subject in order to get the clearest possible picture of what he is dealing with, takes it apart with his analytic scalpel, and finally sews it all up again into a coherent and vital whole. Abrupt, clever, and plain-spoken, he has a unique way of setting out a problem and finding the right solution to it. I can think of very few matters on which he would be unqualified to express an illuminating

opinion. He has been known to speak with verve, wit, and elegance on subjects as diverse as sports, philosophy, food, and social issues. Nothing seems beyond the grasp of this man. No reporter is more skilful ; no broadcaster is more fascinating to watch. In spite of a voice that is badly suited to his work, he is nevertheless adept at winning over audiences of all ages and backgrounds. *Carrefour* and *Conférence de presse* gave us a taste of this subtle mind at work, and *Les aventures de Max Fuch* is giving us a look at his learning. [26]

Point de Mire

During the winter of 1956, rumor had it that René Lévesque was going to resign his position at the CBC. The rumor was confirmed on February 18 in the pages of *Vrai*, a Quebec weekly.

> Today a much talked-about event has finally become a reality. Almost everyone now knows that René Lévesque, the outstanding CBC broadcaster, has turned in his resignation to the head of the national corporation. Does this mean that we will not see Mr. Lévesque on television any more ? Not necessarily. His resignation is in no way a self-imposed exile. Until last week, René Lévesque was an employee of the CBC, which meant, among other things (!), that he had a regular weekly salary. He has now resigned, however, in order to become a freelancer and he is therefore entitled to work for any employer he chooses. It is quite possible that the CBC will avail itself of Lévesque's freelance services for a particular program, such as *Carrefour* or *Conférence de presse*. This will give Lévesque a lot more freedom and will probably work to his advantage, particularly in regard to salary. It is a well-known fact that more illustrious but incompetent figures earn twice as much as a staff reporter. Although some may find such considerations distasteful, the business of a fair wage cannot be overlooked.

What made René Lévesque decide to go freelance ? The desire for greater freedom of expression ? Higher wages ?

> I was very involved with my work. I really loved it, and it gave me opportunities I'd never had before. From 1952 on, we'd been experimenting with television, putting together news features, then *Carrefour,* then special series. But after a while, I got the feeling that something was missing. At the end of the '54-'55 season, before the following year's schedule

92

had been prepared, I began to talk over the possibility of a program devoted exclusively to current affairs. I mentioned this to Roger Rolland, for example, who I believe was one of the key people in network programming at the time. When we finally got down to details, what we came up with was *Point de Mire* [On Target]. I spent weeks trying to perfect the format with Claude Sylvestre, our producer, and finally the format was accepted. The idea of working as a freelancer was gaining acceptance and it occurred to me that since I had conceived the program myself, I now had the freedom not only to do whatever I wanted but to give myself completely to this one project. At that point I was still head of the News Service. Going freelance allowed me to leave that job, and especially the administrative duties that went with it. My new status allowed me to administer my own program and left me free the rest of the time. But I soon learned that I would have very little evtra time on my hands, because we had to work about eighty hours a week perfecting each program. In other words, I think the choice had to do with being able to concentrate exclusively on this one particular piece of work. On top a that, of course, it was more profitable. It was as well paid as politics, if not more so. [27]

Point de Mire was given the go-ahead and work started in earnest. In the opinion of many people it became the French network's most polished program; it was certainly the most famous series on public affairs. Lévesque described it as "an informative program focussed on one particular item in the week's news." [28] The show's première took place at 11 pm, Sunday, November 4, 1956. In their publicity, the CBC and the *Point de Mire* team carefully explained that "René Lévesque will offer an in-depth look at a major event on the international scene from the previous week which merited world attention."

The first show made the producer of the news program *Téléjournal,* immediately preceding it at 10:30, sick with envy. It was a success from the start, despite the late hour. One critic wrote :

> For his first program René Lévesque chose to give us an account of the Suez crisis, an account which was a kind of masterpiece. It was a particular kind of masterpiece because René Lévesque's masterpieces are like no others. His mind crackles with ideas ; his manner of expressing them, though at first glance deceptively disorganized, is consummately skilful. He has a way of penetrating to the heart of the matter, illuminating details as he goes. This was the René Lévesque we saw

in action Sunday night ; he is a man, as someone once put it, who is always at his best. [29]

The series progressed from week to week, never falling short of the high standards it had set for itself. Lévesque himself made a colorful figure for the critics — "a harsh voice, a piercing look that seems to read your mind, a sharp gesture that expresses a whole mass of ideas, the dishevelled hair, a cigarette, twenty cigarettes." But very few of them remarked on the enormous amount of work the program demanded of everyone. An exception was Fernand Benoit, who wrote about these eighty-hour weeks in a lengthy article.

First of all, once the subject was chosen, Lévesque did a geographical run-down on the area concerned : physical features, climatic conditions, frontiers. Usually some social and economic history was included. On Mondays and Tuesdays, Lévesque read the newspapers and magazines with particular care in order to keep an eye on any important news items which threatened to change the course of events significantly later in the week. "This particular week, an important election was coming up in Nigeria and twenty ships were about to inaugurate the new St. Lawrence Seaway. Which one to choose ? The CBC film library prepared two reels containing all the film footage available on black Africa and the Seaway project respectively." On Wednesday afternoon, René Lévesque was still hesitating between the two subjects. The Seaway was of great economic significance, but people had been talking about it for five years, whereas Nigeria . . . "But time was running out. Claude Sylvestre, the producer, waited in his office for the decisive telephone call . . . . It was to be the Seaway after all. René Paré, a designer in the graphics department, was immediately notified. He pored over the atlases while, over his shoulder, René Lévesque memorized the layout of the different lock systems." Then Lévesque went back to the CBC library where he began the task of going over the history of the Seaway, establishing dates, comparing official statements, and tracing logical connections between events.

Lévesque's approach on *Point de Mire* was typical. His technique was always to reconstruct the puzzle in its entirety and let the individual pieces speak for themselves. Since Lévesque refrained as much as possible from making judgments, in effect he allowed the viewer to make his own analysis of the situation. His skill lay in deciding which pieces of the puzzle to choose and how to present

Hard at work researching material for Point de Mire. *Many viewers had the mistaken impression that Lévesque simply improvised his programs, whereas in fact they demanded an enormous amount of preparatory work each week.*

them so that they would all fit together.

On Saturday they screened all the available footage. Lévesque and Claude Sylvestre selected the material that best illustrated what he had to say on the subject. The producer then shut himself in an editing room for the rest of the day, while Lévesque went back to check the maps for the last time. He felt that the maps had to be clear and accurate, and that he had to use them in the most striking manner possible. "For example, Lévesque himself would write names and figures right on the map during the show. The reason for this was simply that a television audience is easily distracted. In the time it took a viewer to light a cigarette he might miss a figure or date crucial to the understanding of some event. If the viewer was not paying attention, a movement on the screen might catch his eye, so Lévesque wrote the key names and figures on the map himself because he knew the viewer would tend to follow the movement of his hand."

At eleven o'clock in the evening, Sylvestre left the editing room with the film ready to go, and Lévesque left the library feeling slightly pessimistic. He had enough notes for a three-hour lecture. The next morning, half a day before air time, the real thinking began — pruning, compressing, simplifying, shaping. Six hours later, they were finished :

> Now for a rehearsal. The producer fed Lévesque his cues, the points at which he had to stop speaking and let the film roll ; the script assistant, Rita Martel, timed the show, stopwatch in hand. The rehearsal ended and it had taken 42 minutes. The material and to be cut down some more. More crucial facts and more important analogies had to go. Lévesque admitted defeat ; he could not cut any more. There were too many important things to say. The producer gave in and out went a film sequence. But in the end, the broadcast came off without a hitch. Drawing on his more than sufficient fund of information, Lévesque improvised a talk which was clear, simple, and graphic ; he managed to point out the salient features, evaluate the situation, and provide an overview. [30]

In 1957, Lévesque won the prize awarded by the Saint-Jean-Baptiste Society for excellence in journalism. *Point de Mire* was largely responsible for the award. He had gone to Paris to sound out French public opinion on the eve of the Fifth Republic, commented on the conflict over Formosa, interpreted federal statistics on unemployment, and analyzed the results of the American presi-

December 1956. Planning a Point de Mire *broadcast with producer Claude Sylvestre and an assistant.*

dential elections — all this in the hopes of informing and educating his television audience. In December 1956, he was asked if there was a way to channel Canadian public opinion in order to make it a factor in governmental decision-making, and whether he could think of any new approaches to the problem of giving more weight to the popular will in the context of Canadian political life. He replied :

I might as well tell you right away that I hate the word "channel." It makes me think of myself as a docile lamb in a huge herd of sheep, all looking exactly the same, about to be led off and fleeced without so much as a bleat. The way I see it, a vigilant and well-informed public is clearly a collective notion, but it cannot be used effectively except in a nation of aggressive individualists — you have to have both. Even then all these aware and reasonable individuals would by some mysterious process have to agree on certain fundamental principles. Isn't the most important thing to promote high-quality education and honest information and strive to put them into practice? Surely the first step is to know what you're talking about; then you can make intelligent choices on the basis of what you know. We're not cattle, we're free men — or so we're always told. It would be interesting to see what would happen if we acted as though we really believed that. [31]

The critics were unanimous in finding Lévesque's attempts at informing and educating a success. André Laurendeau called him "undisputably the best 'soloist' on television." Roger Brien thought he was "one of the most brilliant and personable broadcasters on television." [32] Gilles Hénault wrote : "This little man with the raucous voice and the trenchant style has something of the teacher, the auctioneer, and the magician about him. In the space of half an hour, he depicts his subject so graphically and makes a wealth of information so accessible that any viewer, no matter how ill-informed to begin with, can come away from the program with opinions of his own." [33] Jean-Marc Rigaud felt that Lévesque's goal was "to make the viewer feel at home with the subject, whether it be a strike, troop movements, or clashes at a strategic border. And thanks to his matchless skill, he nearly always succeeds." [34] Roger Brien was so impressed that he felt the need to write about Lévesque again : "This program has fired the imagination of its audience. René Lévesque's intelligence and enthusiasm have helped to win him a crowd of faithful admirers and he certainly deserves his reputation as the number one commentator on radio and television. His approach to national and international questions is always open-minded and yet completely original." [35] A week later, Brien continued : "It would be laboring the obvious to heap any more praise on this program and its creator .... Each program is as good as the last, and Lévesque continually manages to maintain an interest with a variety of approaches and a vitality that would be

December 1956. A last-minute check before Point de Mire *goes on the air.*

the envy of most performers and broadcasters." [36] Brien could not resist returning to *Point de Mire* for a third time in less than two months : "Every program has been like a highly polished gem, but the last one on France was really magnificent. We have rarely seen the French described like this, with all the pros and cons included. Lévesque's obvious fondness for France did not prevent him from being perfectly objective in revealing the country's present

The Point de Mire *"professor" and his equipment : a microphone, a pencil, a blackboard brush, dozens of cigarettes, and a husky but captivating voice.*

weaknesses." [37] Martine Lefebvre, Brien's successor, added : *"Point de Mire* continues to be in a class by itself. Although it is possible to take issue with some of René Lévesque's opinions, you can't help admiring his talent and the skill with which he explains the issues behind the most complex events, not only in record time, but also in the most stimulating fashion." [38]

The least one can say of *Point de Mire* is that the critics were pretty well unanimous in their feelings about it. Gérard Bergeron summarized this period in René Lévesque's life :

March 1957. The Saint-Jean-Baptiste Society awards its 1957 prize for excellence in journalism to Lévesque. From left to right: Raymond Dupuis, president of the Canadian Chamber of Commerce; Paul Guertin, incoming SJBS president; and F.-Eugène Therrien, outgoing president of the Society.

The television program *Point de Mire* made Lévesque a star. He had been biding his time for three years, but when his turn finally came, he had the good fortune to be launched virtually overnight. The show's première took place on the last Sunday in October 1956, after the week of bloodshed caused by the crises in Hungary and the Suez. Lévesque scored 100 per cent with this program. An excellent reporter (he has a gift for conveying atmosphere), but a poor interviewer (his questions are too long and often leading), Lévesque has proven that he can popularize a subject brilliantly. Week after week, he makes intelligible to all the world what a handful of specialists can only comprehend with difficuly. He knows how to explain a subject before analyzing it, but then he is forced to analyze without drawing conclusions because, at the CBC, "objectivity" is sacrosanct. But the proper conclusions can be drawn simply from the presentation of the problem, as is always the case when the problem is well presented . . . . There is something in his program for everyone — the well-informed intellectual and the specialist, the uninformed and even the uninterested, regardless of age or background. Lévesque is an unheard-of phenomenon : without any appropriate university training and with no other resources than the McGill University Library, he manages to select and digest, from a mass of completely disconnected material, the essential elements, the parameters, and the variables of every kind of crisis — without, of course, ever using "scientific" jargon ! He is a craftsman with the fierce independence of a lone wolf, which he is by instinct and no doubt always will be. Lévesque is, moreover, the living contradiction of the ideal broadcaster : he has no voice and no charm, but nervous tics by the dozen ; he smokes like an impatient locomotive, talks in incredibly long sentences full of the most unlikely combinations of ideas and, to top it all off, he has revived that good old educational standby, the blackboard, as his main prop ! But the message is crystal clear . . . . There has never been anything like Lévesque before, and there will probably never again be anyone like him on television anywhere. There is a tribal quality in his success that suggests a parallel with Louis Francoeur, * whom Lévesque admired so much, except that his instrument is a hundred times more powerful and resourceful than the medium Francoeur had at his disposal twenty years earlier. What Lévesque accomplished in these three years was nothing less than miraculous. [39]

The Korean War made René Lévesque known to the public ; *Point de Mire* made him a star. Perhaps one day we will regard this program's success as the first political awakening of a people soon to undergo their "quiet revolution." Some fourteen years later the broadcaster had this to say about the whole experience :

Personally I found it one of the most satisfying jobs I ever did. I was far from fed up with it when the strike brought us to an abrupt halt, but after that it was simply time for a change. One thing that still strikes me about it today — and from time to time I meet people who confirm this observation — was that we really reached the public . . . . It was extremely hard

* See note on p. 78.

work each week to simplify, summarize, and illustrate what was often an enormous subject without doing the material an injustice. And half an hour, even an hour, isn't much time to do it in. I think we must have had the right *touch,* * because we did manage to reach people. Common everyday viewers told us and sometimes still do : "Thanks to your program we were able to follow what was going on in the outside world." This was particularly important because here in Quebec we were a little isolated and needed to take a look around. Television has an important role to play here. We seemed to have succeeded, because we had a damned good *rating.* † That's what struck me most about the show, and, as I say, people tell me the same thing when they look back on what we did. [40]

But on December 29, 1958, production of *Point de Mire* and all other regular programs on the CBC's French network was brought to a halt.

The Producer's Strike

On that day at a quarter to five in the afternoon, in the old Ford Hotel on Dorchester Boulevard, Fernand Quirion, the tall, thoughtful fellow who produces *Les belles histoires des pays d'En-Haut,* told us in an expressionless voice — "That's it, we're on strike." There had been more than three weeks of meetings between his colleagues (74 producers of the CBC's French television network in Montreal) and their bosses, in particular Gérard Lamarche and André Ouimet, head of the main station of the French network. The meetings did nothing but confirm and harden from day to day the heavy paternalism which is one of the most striking features of the CBC bureaucracy and well known to all who have ever been exposed to it. [41]

This was René Lévesque talking, and he had few kind words for the CBC. "It is a structure at once rigid and flabby, one which allows those incapable of making decisions to tread water and pass the buck, while those who are ambitious or authoritarian enlarge and consolidate, at the expense of others, their little empires where their slightest whims are divine law." [42]

So on December 29, 1958, the Montreal producers left their posts. Why ? Essentially because CBC management would not recognize their salaried employees' union, on the grounds that producers had always been considered managerial staff. At the

* In English in the original.
† In English in the original.

beginning, the positions of the two sides were firm. On the evening of the first day of the strike, the producers won the support of 2000 other unionized workers — machinists, make-up artists, costume designers, office workers, performers, musicians, and writers. Management held to the position that the producers were managerial staff and therefore could not form a united front against "themselves," but they were confident that the strike would only last a few days.

The next day, December 30, negotiations were resumed, but the producers would not budge : they demanded recognition of their right to organize and recognition of their association as the producers' bargaining agent with the CBC. They also demanded written guarantees from management that there would be no reprisals against producers who participated in the strike or in the organization of the union. Meanwhile, the president of the *Union des Artistes,* * Jean Duceppe, assured them that his membership would respect the picket lines.

Television programming was hit hard by the strike. All live programs, for example, had to be cancelled, and feature films and documentaries were broadcast instead. CBC radio offered only music and the occasional news bulletin.

The Montreal daily *Le Devoir* quickly came out in support of the strikers. In an article printed on December 31, André Laurendeau was highly critical of the producers' working conditions: "Unless the nature of the work changes or the rhythm of production slows down, it is hard to see how these employees can be expected to grow old happily working for the CBC." *Le Devoir*'s support of the strike turned out to be very important to the producers, since the paper not only lent moral support but also made space available for statements by the strikers. Picketing continued in front of the Dorchester Boulevard studios in Montreal. The striking producers included Fernand Quirion, Claude Sylvestre, Gilles Sénécal, Guy Beaulne, Guy Leduc, Jacques Blouin, and Louis-Georges Carrier.

On January 5, 1959, in a special bulletin broadcast on television, management ordered all union employees who were out in support of the producers back to work, but they refused. Jean Hamelin, radio and TV columnist for *Le Devoir,* wrote on January 6 : "In their tenacious struggle for the right to organize, the CBC producers have earned the respect of all those who might have harbored

---

* The Quebec performers' union.

any doubts about the merits of their case. And by giving them full support, the performers and technicians have also acted in a spirit of admirable professional solidarity." The next day, in an open letter to the CBC printed in the newspapers, 66 radio and television celebrities, including actors, authors, and broadcasters, blamed management for the strike and gave their unconditional support to the producers. Among those who signed was René Lévesque.

This was the first time since the beginning of the strike that Lévesque's name had appeared in the newspapers. The star of *Point de Mire* was not one of the prime movers behind this strike, which was the expression of a newly found solidarity on the part of his professional comrades. As the strike progressed, the names of producers like Quirion, Fugère, and Sylvestre, and of Jean Duceppe and Jean-Louis Roux (president of the *Société des Auteurs* *), figured just as prominently in the headlines as Lévesque's. His role in these events must be examined with these reservations in mind.

On January 8, the producers made their first direct appeal to Prime Minister John Diefenbaker and his Minister of Labor, Michael Starr. They were called upon to intervene in the dispute because negotiations had reached a standstill. The two politicians turned a deaf ear, and *Le Devoir* wrote : "The Ministry of Labor has made it quite clear that, since the *Association des réalisateurs* † is not a legal entity, there is nothing the Minister and his office can do." [43] For the moment, scarcely anyone interpreted this refusal to intervene as a deliberately hostile act.

After the strike had gone on for eleven days, the CBC's 1600 unionized employees held a special meeting. They reaffirmed their support for the producers and stated that they would continue to respect the picket lines. But some were not entirely content. *Le Devoir* reported :

> Although the meeting took place behind closed doors, we have reason to believe that a lively debate preceded the voting on this resolution and that it was opposed by a number of prominent personalities. But it appears that the intervention of Jean Duceppe, president of the *Union des Artistes,* René Lévesque, Jean-Louis Roux, and Madame Denise Pelletier made a strong impression on those members who were hesitant about sup-

* The Quebec writers' union.
† The disputed producers' association.

porting the strikers. However, they constituted only a small proportion of those present. [44]

The union members did not stop at moral support ; they also decided to organize a huge benefit for those hit hardest by the strike. A show called *Difficultés temporaires* * was presented at the *Comédie canadienne* on January 12 and ran for three months. Lévesque was among the fifty performers who helped put the show together. After opening night, Jean Hamelin wrote in *Le Devoir :*

> The hero of the evening was certainly René Lévesque. He received a warm ovation as he took the stage and for nearly half an hour he delivered a lively and forthright talk in the style of *Point de Mire* which elicited a thunderous round of cheering and applause. Having made his mark in an area of television where no attempts are made to win over the audience, René Lévesque could finally see for himself, if he did not already know it, that his following among television viewers is of vast proportions. Only a tiny fraction of his viewing public was there last night, but he managed to inform them about the discussions and made them aware of problems with which the public in general was not familiar, while they for their part expressed unequivocal admiration for the man and his achievements. [45]

On January 16, negotiations were broken off completely. John Diefenbaker's government was still deaf to all entreaties and would not intervene. Was this attitude perhaps founded on the belief that the dispute involved only French Canadians and was therefore of no concern to English Canadians ? André Laurendeau commented :

> What we are witnessing here is the unfolding of a crisis in French Canada which will have to be resolved from outside this province either by authorities who draw their power from the federal government, or else by the federal government itself — in other words, by men from a milieu untouched by this conflict and who are virtually impervious to any kind of outside influence. [. . .] The facts are that this country is divided into two communities, each going its own way ; that a crisis in one community hardly ever affects the other, not even in areas where there are close ties nor when union solidarity should be playing a part ; and that it is in this other, indifferent, perhaps hostile community that the crisis will have to be resolved, simply because it constitutes the majority. [. . .]

* "Trouble is temporary" – an allusion to the "please do not adjust your set" formula.

It has become clear that in their struggle to save their own institutions, the producers and their supporters throughout Quebec cannot make their case heard effectively outside the province, even though that is where their case will be tried. So we come face to face once more with the tragedy of the French-Canadian situation : French Canada is not master of its own institutions, and, in times of crisis, the outside support on which the very idea of Canadian unity should depend is not forthcoming. It would be unwise to keep Quebec for very long in such a condition. [46]

On the morning of Wednesday, January 21, a general meeting of performers and CBC unionized employees was held in the Orpheum Theatre. All the speakers pledged continued support for the producers. Jean Duceppe and Jean-Louis Roux said they were certain that their members would not cross the picket lines. René Lévesque argued that a *family compact* * operating within the CBC was responsible for the present situation.

According to René Lévesque, André Ouimet owes his job as head of television for Quebec to the influence of his brother, Alphonse Ouimet, president of the Corporation. He added that Alphonse Ouimet and Clive McKee, who also holds an important position in the CBC, had already shown their anti-unionist sympathies by organizing ARTEC † on the model of a shop union. [47] He said that it had become necessary to take the dispute to Parliament, because the directors of the CBC are playing havoc with the Corporation. "As far as I'm concerned," concluded Lévesque, "I will not set foot inside the CBC until this conflict has been settled in an equitable fashion." [48]

In his description of Lévesque's evolution, Gérard Bergeron alludes to the Bergsonian concepts of impatience and indignation, two qualities whose absence in our society he regards as particularly serious. Bergeron then goes on to say that, during his career as a journalist, Lévesque had held his own sense of impatience and indignation in check up until the time of he CBC producers' strike. Since December 29, 1958, according to Bergeron, a new man was evolving, or rather, emerging from the old, a man more true to himself. The new Lévesque did not hesitate to speak forcefully ; he now showed his capacity for impatience and indignation. [49]

---

* In English in the original.
† Association of Radio and Television Employees of Canada.

107

On the evening of January 21, 1959, Lévesque introduced André Laurendeau to the audience at the *Comédie canadienne*. The editor-in-chief of *Le Devoir* proceeded to read out an editorial entitled "Will Ottawa let the CBC scuttle its French network ?" in which he demanded action on the part of the federal government :

> Anything — mediation, arbitration, a special law — is better than having Ottawa wash its hands of this affair. We believe that a conflict which has paralyzed the whole French network of the CBC — and thereby affected nearly one third of Canada, in fact all those Canadians who speak French and pay taxes — we believe that such a conflict deserves a little attention from Ottawa and some meaningful gesture of reconciliation on the part of those in power. [50]

Not only did this appeal go unanswered, but the next day CBC management released a bombshell statement to the press, which made it clear that they did not recognize the *Association des réalisateurs* and refused to deal with them any longer. They told their 1600 unionized employees to go back to work or risk losing their jobs. CBC management was planning to resume regular television programming and would do so by "hiring the necessary personnel" and starting the work begun six years before "from scratch." There was now little doubt that they were determined to intimidate the unions.

Late that afternoon, CBC management called a press conference to answer journalists' questions. Michel Roy described the prevailing atmosphere :

> The battle lines were drawn. A veteran producer could not have put together a more controversial, action-packed scenario. There were about forty journalists present, clouds of smoke, flash-bulbs popping, questions and interruptions from all over the place in both languages. Two spokesmen appeared on behalf of the Corporation, both affable in the extreme : Marcel Carter, administrative chief, and Ron Fraser, a typical PRO, the national director of publicity and information services, who had come straight from Ottawa. Standing behind them was the placid Jean-Jules Trudeau, head of public relations for the Montreal office. They handed out their press release and, sitting up straight at the front of the narrow room, smilingly awaited questions. Our English-speaking colleagues opened fire.
>
> "Gentlemen, the Corporation has been accused of being anti-unionist. What have you got to say about this ?"

108

The Corporation is not anti-unionist. This is an absurd accusation. Our relations with the unions are excellent . . . ."

"But who are you counting on to resume your regular service ?"

"We would be happy to have our producers back, and of course our performers too. We would obviously prefer to keep our old employees."

From this point on, the situation deteriorated. One after another — Ernest Pallascio-Morin (CKAC), Gérald Dany (*Le Petit Journal*), André Roche (*Vedettes*), Marc Thibeault (*La Presse*), several English journalists who for once objected to the cold aloofness of these tedious *briefings* * — and right at the back that familiar silhouette, immobile, apparently calm and collected, René Lévesque . . .

There was a stir in the room. Carter and Fraser threw questioning glances at the imperturbable Jean-Jules Trudeau, who shrewdly took the offensive : "Is Mr. Lévesque here as the representative of a newspaper ? Which one, might I ask . . . . *Le Monde* perhaps ?" "I represent the *Association des réalisateurs* and perhaps some of the taxpayers whose contributions finance the Corporation as well . . . . May I ask the question no one wants to answer, the question everyone here wants to ask, the question the public is asking at this very moment : how does the CBC intend — if indeed it intends anything at all — to resume what it absurdly refers to as regular television service ?" There was a mumbled reply. But Lévesque repeated his question. "Come to the point and tell us which producers, which performers, which technicians, which journalists you're going to use to resume your regular service ?"

"This question is presently under study, and CBC management will announce its decision in due course." [51]

In the end the press conference cleared up very few questions, but the producers and their supporters would not allow themselves to be intimidated. On the same day as the corporation's declaration, the strikers staged a boisterous demonstration in front of the CBC offices on Dorchester Boulevard. Morale was high.

The next day Lévesque published an article in *Le Devoir* entitled : "We will not go back on our hands and knees !" He summarized the attitude of the corporation's directors "who," he wrote, "are waiting cold-bloodedly for this exercise of ill will to be forgotten after the strikers are routed and forced to return to work

---

* In English in the original.

on their hands and knees, so that their own heavy-handed stupidity and unshakeable arrogance will be miraculously transformed into fair-mindedness and good sense. Where this kind of thing is concerned, human nature has not progressed much beyond the ancient ethic — Survival of the fittest ! ... The losers have nobody to blame except themselves. ...." Alluding to Murdochville, * Lévesque appealed to the reading public :

> This strike must not be allowed to come to such a dishonorable conclusion that after three weeks we will see the strikers, still convinced of their rights, forced to go crawling back to their jobs, humiliated and broken by worry, hunger, and panic on the part of their wives and children. This is the fate I saw inflicted on the miners in the Gaspé not so long ago. Because they were isolated, they were beaten before the real extent of their misery became known. So they went back, those who still could, terrible caricatures of the men they used to be, their rights trampled on and ridiculed, their spirit broken by callous indifference. They did not believe in anybody any more : neither the moralists, who sermonized on Sunday and passed the buck on Monday ; nor the sociologists, who warmed to their cause and were about to write fine articles on their courage — in six months ; and certainly not the politicians, who wallow every four years in talk of social justice and inviolable rights but are never around when it comes to putting a clear, intelligent working definition on what they pretend to value. Here in Montreal, French Canada's largest city, [. . .] we have no excuse for not perceiving the situation clearly, for not trying to understand what is going on — before it's too late. In the meantime, we urge you to see the show presented by the *Union des Artistes,* and to bring your friends too, so that while we await some action on the part of our unhurried do-gooders and prudent politicians, our friends are not defeated by hunger, worry, and humiliation, and will be able to go back to their jobs — which they love and are very committed to — with their heads held high. [52]

Faced with the federal government's refusal to intervene, the strikers organized a protest march in Ottawa. On January 27, 1500 union members descended on Ottawa for a demonstration in front of the parliament buildings where they were addressed by Jean

---

* A mining town in the Gaspé where a strike was ended by means of collusion between the employers and the Duplessis government, at the expense of the striking miners.

Marchand, secretary general of the CTCC, * Jean Duceppe, and René Lévesque. Lévesque announced that in the preceding four days, 25,000 people had signed the strikers' petitions in Montreal alone. He stressed that the CBC's ultimatum was "the height of complacency and stupidity." He also pointed to the "deep-seated dishonesty" of the men running the CBC in Montreal, once again denounced the pace at which the negotiations were proceeding, and added finally that management was motivated solely by the need to "save face and protect the house of cards which makes up their empire." [53]

But for Lévesque, the demonstration in Ottawa became more than just an occasion for airing grievances : it was later recognized as the turning point of his life. This is how he described the demonstrators' reception in Ottawa by the federal government to journalist Pierre de Bellefeuille :

> We went up to Ottawa and came back empty-handed after seeing Michael Starr, who at that time was the responsible Conservative minister. The poor devil didn't have the faintest idea what we were talking about. I guess you really couldn't blame him because nobody in Ottawa cared much about what was happening. So the French network of the CBC had been shut down for three weeks or a month — why all the fuss ? We came back without even having made them understand what the problem was and said to ourselves : "If the English network had shut down in Toronto, it wouldn't have taken the government and Parliament more than 24 hours to set things straight, even if they'd had to call in the army." But the fact that the French network had folded, or at least was temporarily defunct, didn't bother them at all. Basically they didn't give a damn. On top of that, some of the professional nitwits who represent Quebec ridings in Ottawa came up to us and said, off the record of course, that we had their support but that unfortunately they couldn't do anything — not even put in a good word for us — because of the party line and all that. So by the time we got back we were really fed up. [54]

Lévesque added : "I remember Laurendeau telling me a few days later : 'You may not realize it yet, but you're about to launch a political career which might really take you places'." And Lévesque replied : "I don't know. Maybe. I have no idea what will happen." [55]

In any event, Lévesque was not about to give up the struggle.

---

* *Confédération des Travailleurs catholiques du Canada.* See note on p. 10.

He and Gérard Pelletier were responsible for co-ordinating union activities during the strike, and worked hand-in-hand with Fernand Quirion, Jean Duceppe, Jean-Louis Roux, and Jean Marchand. The creator of *Point de Mire* took advantage of every forum offered him to publicize the dispute and explain the producers' position. On January 30, he spoke on television for a quarter of an hour in Sherbrooke. Nine days later, he made another appearance on a commercial television station in Quebec City, where a group of sympathizers helped defray the costs of the program. On February 9, all the union members held another general meeting. Lévesque asked the strikers to be patient and to "stick it out to the end," then announced that the show taken on tour around the province by the *Union des Artistes* had been well received. [56]

Two days later, a French-speaking Conservative finally spoke up in the House :

> The Conservative member for Berthier-Maskinongé, Mr. Rémi Paul, said in the Commons yesterday that the CBC producers' strike will at least be useful insofar as it will give French Canadians a rest from the "belly-aching of Jean Marchand, René Lévesque, André Laurendeau, and Gérard Filion." Once good sense prevails, he added, and the CBC has rid itself of André Laurendeau, René Lévesque, Michel Chartrand, Jean Marchand, and the others, the CBC strike will be settled to everyone's satisfaction. [57]

Almost every day there was fresh hope of a settlement, but each time hopes were dashed. Jean-Louis Roux, one of the principals in the strike, wrote :

> The strike began on a Monday afternoon and by the following Friday morning there was already talk of an imminent settlement. Things went on that way for sixty-eight days, with new hope of a settlement springing up several times a week, if not every day. Every time the problem seemed on the point of being resolved, some unforeseen development would set it back. The suspense could not have been more gripping if it had been plotted in advance : no novel can match the exciting and almost unbelievable ups and downs of daily life. [58]

On March 2, there was another dramatic turn of events. After a general meeting of the strikers that morning, more than 1000 demonstrators gathered in front of the offices of the CBC at exactly twelve noon. Hundreds of Montreal policemen, some on horseback, charged into the crowd on the pretext that they had been "provoked" and arrested twenty-eight people. Among those detained were René Lévesque, Jean Marchand, Louis Morisset (vice-president of the *Société des Auteurs dramatiques* *), Mia Riddez, Madeleine Langlois, Raymond Couture (the principal strike organizer), André Roche, Pierre Duceppe, Roland Chenail, Jean-Guy Benjamin, Monique Bosco, Thérèse Arbic, François Lavigne, Monique Nadeau, Jean Lebel, Jean Poirier, and Michel van Schendel.

Chief of police Albert Langlois had placed Inspector W. Minogue in charge of maintaining order and it appears that Minogue's men were somewhat over-anxious to do their job well. *Le Devoir* wrote :

> This demonstration, which the strikers intended to keep as orderly as previous demonstrations, did not get out of hand until the Montreal police, in an attempt to enforce the letter of the law with regard to a parade permit, adopted a hostile attitude towards the crowd and committed acts of brutality worthy of the Gestapo. [59]

Those arrested were released four hours later. The next day, Chief Langlois was called before the executive committee of Montreal City Council to explain the behavior of his men.

> When asked to explain the conduct of the mounted policemen and those on foot who had used such violent methods to break up the CBC strikers' demonstration, Chief Albert Langlois maintained — in all seriousness — that his undercover agents had got wind of a *conspiracy* : he told the executive committee that the demonstrators were planning to "invade CBC headquarters" and had to be stopped. [60]

Gérard Filion, the publisher of *Le Devoir,* rejected this explanation out of hand. In a typical editorial (Filion was well known for his hatchet jobs), he levelled a scathing attack on Chief Langlois :

> When the man who heads such a large police force adds the insult of *post facto* rationalization to the injury of police brutality, he has certainly shown his true colors. This kind of birdbrain does not have enough grey matter to direct traffic in the suburbs. He had no business appearing before the Executive Council of the City of Montreal — he should have been shipped off to an asylum instead. [61]

Once again, John Diefenbaker made it clear that he and his

---

* The Quebec playwrights' union.

Minister of Labor, Michael Starr, would not under any circumstances intervene in the conflict. On March 4, another demonstration, led by Roger Mathieu, president of the CTCC, was held in front of the CBC offices. This time the rumors of a supposed plot seemed to have gone unheeded, since the police did not interfere with the demonstrators.

Hope for an early settlement grew dim. At the same time, both sides had begun to grow weary of the struggle. Lévesque, angry with the federal government's disdainful attitude throughout the crisis and anxious to dispel certain misconceptions, decided to publish a statement in English for the benefit of those who could not, or would not, see the strikers' point of view. This statement was printed on page 2 of *Le Devoir,* March 7, 1959, and was entitled *"Radio-Canada ** is a lie ! The truth is called the 'CBC'." Several lengthy extracts have been reprinted on the following pages because this article marks an important stage in Lévesque's political evolution.

Here is the introduction : †

> This affair has lasted 68 days. It is now one month to the day since the CBC initialed an agreement and undertook to respect it. A week ago tomorrow the CBC violated this undertaking by openly changing an already difficult strike situation into a lock-out which has transformed this crown corporation into a scandalous public monster. Throughout these 68 days, behind a silence broken only by outrageous ultimatums and acts of bad faith, this intangible presence supported by taxpayers' money has encouraged bureaucrats great and small to indulge their brutal irresponsibility. There is something else as well . . . . Something almost as intangible and at the same time grotesque, which obstinately refuses to show its face. If by chance we should ever succeed in unmasking it, this face will desperately try to twist itself ino a grotesque smile. The statement which follows has been written in the only language this intangible entity understands. It is, I believe, as dispassionate as two wearying months of frustration and disillusionment will allow.

The first aspect of this face Lévesque dealt with was an editorial which appeared on March 3 in the *Montreal Star,* entitled "CBC Deadlock and Rowdyism."

> One example is enough to put the *Star,* as far as we are concerned, among dishonest newspapers forever. "Frustration, it

---

* French name of the Corporation.
† The title and introduction originally appeared in French, and the main text in English.

wrote, led to unruly conduct on the picket line. The police moved in." What had happened the day before was in fact that the strikers' frustration led to nothing more than a peaceful march and the singing of "O Canada" in front of the CBC. The facts are that the police moved in first, under orders, and that whatever unruly conduct broke out afterwards was the result of this stupid provocation. Such facts the *Star*'s editorial writers had, or should have had, from their reporters. They chose to fabricate their own.

That, unfortunately, is also nothing but the latest in a long series of slanted and biased presentations of facts by that paper. As for the *Star*'s opinions, they naturally are those of its owners, whose basic attitude — well reflected throughout this strike — is fundamentally hostile to any attempt by French Canadians at anything but proverbial "pittoresque" and quaintness.

Lévesque was not well disposed towards the English-language Montreal daily. His feelings towards the *Gazette* were no less critical : "This worthy sheet has tenets on this matter which are exactly the same as the *Star*'s, only more so."

Lévesque saw CBC management as another aspect of this "intangible and grotesque something."

The CBC itself, quite predominantly in its higher echelons, is English. During most of the conflict, its acting president has been Mr. Bushnell, whose knowledge of the French language is a very doubtful quantity indeed. On return-to-work — which after three weeks of an incredible game of cat & mouse came to look exactly what it was : a spiteful starving out of French employees and artists — its chief negotiators were gentlemen named Bruce Raymond and Clive McKee. Its PRO is a Mr. Ron Fraser, who, a certain day in January, became a slightly legendary figure in French Canada when he talked about "rebuilding the French network from scratch," but was obviously and smilingly unable not only to say it in French, but even to appreciate the meaning of his own words.

The federal government constituted yet another aspect of the face.

In Ottawa, there is also a House of Commons controlled by a political party in which the overwhelming majority of MPs are English. Honi soit qui mal y pense. But they are the final authority over public radio and television. And three ministers,

115

almost exclusively, have had to answer recent questions about the CBC.

All three are English. One is the hon. Michael Starr of Labour, another smiling man. Consistently he has refused to intervene in this strike — thereby maintaining, with perseverance worthy of a better cause, the natural confusion in the public's mind between political intervention, and intervention under the Labour Law which is an implied duty of his.

Another is the hon. George Nowlan of National Revenue. He is the man who answers for the CBC in the Commons. One of his first offerings was that the producers' strike was illegal. That, by modest estimation, was enough by itself to delay any real negotiations and embitter the conflict for at least an additional, useless and painful week. The hon. gentleman later admitted that such an opinion, which in the first place was none of his business to give, might have been slightly erroneous . . .

The third honorable English spokesman is the Prime Minister himself. Three times in a row, on March 2, Mr. Diefenbaker gave negative answers to Mr. Lionel Chevrier's repeated requests for some kind of government action. Thereby equalling saint Peter's score on one of the least glorious days in his life. Obvious to a French mind, there was a quality of quiet desperation to Mr. Chevrier's appeals. But that, it is evident, is something that couldn't register on Mr. Diefenbaker's solidly unilingual grey matter.

Then Lévesque explained to the English-speaking audience what the French network of the CBC means to French Canadians.

It's about one of French Canada's most potent and rapidly-growing cultural outlets. The French network's Public Affairs programs are one of our main platforms of opinion. Its regular "tele-theatre" is a TV stage the equivalent of which is nowhere to be found in English. Its Concert Hour is a trans-Canada feature. Its popular serials, unique while far from perfect, are both a part of folklore and bread-and-butter for such topflight writers as Roger Lemelin, Robert Choquette, Germaine Guèvremont, C.-H. Grignon, Marcel Dubé, etc. . .

The creator of *Point de Mire* was fed up. He had reached the point of no return. Any illusions he might have had concerning a Canada united by mutual understanding and sympathy were gone :

Many, many weeks back, some people said that a racial cry

116

was being raised, when it was advanced that a prolonged strike could mean ruin or at least serious damage to a valuable public property of French Canada. So a lot of us stopped saying that truth as we saw it.

Now most of the damage has been done. CBC's higher-ups have run the gamut from corporate irresponsibility to anonymous viciousness. Cabinet ministers have stood up in the House like knights in incredible armors of denseness, small-town vanity and brutal indifference.

Some of us, maybe a lot of us, will come out of this permanently disgusted with a certain ideal called National Unity. Never before have we felt that apart from pleas every four years in painful "political French" National Unity is something designed almost exclusively to keep negligible minorities nice and quiet.

Never before we have felt that our affairs are bound to be either tragically or comically mismanaged, as long as they remain in the hands of men who have no understanding of them and make it quite clear that they don't consider such lack as any kind of a personal flaw.

Some of us, and maybe many, come out of this with a tired and unworthy feeling that if such a strike had happened on English CBC, it would — as the hon. George Nowlan said, and on this occasion not erroneously — have lasted no more than half an hour. To this day, ours has lasted 66 days. Of such signal advantages is the privilege of being French made up in this country!

The very day this statement appeared in *Le Devoir* — March 7, 1959 — a spokesman for the CBC announced to the parliamentary press gallery in Ottawa that the national corporation had just signed an agreement with the *Association des réalisateurs*. The strike was over and work resumed on the following Monday, March 9.

That same Saturday evening, the 1500 striking CBC employees gathered in the *Comédie canadienne* to celebrate the end of the strike. A number of speakers took the stage : first of all, the producers Quirion, Fugère, and Sylvestre ; then Jean Philip, François Péladeau, Father Ambroise Lafortune, Jean Marchand, Jean Duceppe, and Jean-Louis Roux. René Lévesque, exhausted like the rest, had this to say :

We've all lost something in this struggle — a little money, a lot of sleep, peace of mind. But we can take great encouragement from the fact that on Monday morning, we will go back to the CBC in full command of the French network. Let's not forget the serious responsibilities that implies. When our programs bring the screen to life again, people will see our collective influence behind every name in the credits and we as a group will have to share both the praise and the criticism. We will go back to work with our heads held high, strengthened by our devotion to the common cause. We must strive to maintain this precious unity forged out of great hardship and self-sacrifice. We must also be careful not to let our high spirits get the better of us, and see to it that those most vulnerable among us are the most carefully protected. [62]

André Laurendeau and René Lévesque had worked side by side throughout the strike, and had exchanged many ideas about the political significance of the crisis. After presenting some personal opinions on the conflict, the editor-in-chief of *Le Devoir* came to the conclusion that Lévesque was right. His editorial of March 16 was entitled, "Yes, two solitudes !"

We did not see racist overtones in this conflict overnight. Little by little we got the feeling that our interests were being pushed aside by the tide of Anglo-Saxon opinion, that is, by the majority, and we finally said so. [...] But from that point on, the nationalist sentiments involved were no longer founded on chauvinism or racism, but simply on injured pride. This is how nationalist movements usually begin. A man may find that his situation defines him as a second-class citizen, as a colonial powerless before the distant but almighty mother country, or as a black whose suffering prompts no sympathy from those who dominate his life. This man must choose between an utterly self-effacing moral enslavement and the struggle to rebuild his shattered dignity. No matter what he does, his life has become affected by this realization. Many of us here in Quebec know what it feels like. [...] Our situation is clearly such that we have two communities living side by side scarcely aware of each other's existence, which, in times of crisis, become estranged and solitary partners, the stronger one leading and the weaker left with no option but to revolt. [63]

Gérard Bergeron observed : "After the strike it was apparent that everyone had lost out, as is usually the case in any costly war with such uncertain objectives. *Point de Mire* came back on the air for a few months just for appearances' sake. But like other programs, it had lost its spark, because it was difficult to rejuvenate people's sagging spirits." [64]

Lévesque commented on this analysis :

That's what Bergeron thinks — he may be right, he may be wrong. It's all a matter of opinion. As far as I can remember, our spirits weren't sagging, although we did come out of the strike in pretty bad shape. There was no getting around that. It's difficult to pick up where you left off after two and a half or three months. But one thing I knew all along was that because of the role I had played in the strike and the quasi-political positions I had adopted, they intended to cancel the series at the end of the season. Any fool could have seen that. They didn't want to be too obvious about it, however, so they were prepared just to let the contract expire. But there was no doubt about the fact that they weren't going to renew it, and that does curb your enthusiasm. [65]

In any event, the *Point de Mire* team did not waste any time getting down to work after the strike. Newfoundland was the trouble spot that week, and it was chosen as the subject of the first post-strike program. Journalist Michel Roy described the crisis in the following terms :

The lumberjacks' strike continues ; a special law declares their union illegal and the premier substitutes his own in its place ; there are outbreaks of violence ; a policeman dies ; Ottawa refuses to send the reinforcements demanded by St. John's ; the RCMP commissioner resigns ; there is a violent reaction in the Commons ; the Liberals are divided ; doubts are cast on the whole grants system under the "Act of Union" ; "It's treason !" exclaim the Newfoundlanders, literally going into mourning and cursing the mainlanders. And to top it all off, Joseph Roberts Smallwood, the uncontested boss of the province, has said he would resign if he could be sure that his departure would facilitate a settlement.[66]

The *Point de Mire* crew, headed by Lévesque and the producer, flew out to Newfoundland to take stock of the situation. The program they brought back did not seem to reveal any lack of enthusiasm, at least according to reviewer Jean Hamelin :

Point de Mire dealt with the situation in Newfoundland, where a conflict between Mr. Smallwood and the International Wood-workers of America has resulted from the strike that has plagued the province for nearly three months. René Lévesque's treatment of the crisis was in keeping with the gravity of the situation. He

119

and his producer, Claude Sylvestre, made their investigations on the spot. Lévesque interviewed IWA union leaders, lumberjacks, and several of those in charge of the union set up by the premier. He even went to the extent of showing us Mr. Smallwood in action denouncing outside interference in Newfoundland's affairs. [. . .]

This is not the place to discuss the opinions expressed in the course of the program. Such editorializing has been done elsewhere by people far more competent than myself. I would, however, like to venture the following remark. Last Monday's *Point de Mire* was of exceptional dramatic interest, because René Lévesque succeeded in getting us involved in this idea of "solidarity" which I mentioned earlier. Nevertheless, the program was not perfect. For example, the attempt to provide simultaneous translations of interviews conducted in English resulted in a few moments of confusion. But this was almost inevitable, considering that the program was hastily put together and involved a number of virtually insurmountable difficulties. [67]

The *Point de Mire* team continued to turn out programs of great interest from March 23, the date of the Newfoundland show, until the end of May, when winter programming made way for the summer season. As expected, *Point de Mire* was not renewed for the following year.

However, Lévesque did not sever all connections with the CBC. After a few weeks of summer vacation, he returned in the fall to take part in a number of public affairs programs :

I worked, still as a freelancer, on programs for *Premier Plan* and *Conférence de presse* as well, I believe. These series were just stop-gap affairs, because the CBC had dropped *Point de Mire* from their schedule and needed some eye-catching public affairs programs to make up for it. The style they developed for *Premier Plan* in a way foreshadowed today's *Format 60,* a kind of weekly news magazine featuring three or four items either produced by us or brought in from outside. That kept me fairly busy. Gérard Pelletier was also around at that time, I think, and Judith Jasmin too. [68]

In September 1959, Maurice Duplessis died in Schefferville and was succeeded by Paul Sauvé as the leader of the Union Nationale party. Sauvé's takeover was a blow to rival political forces in Quebec, according to Georges-Emile Lapalme, house leader of the provincial Liberal Party at the time :

120

June 1959. Lévesque had a large audience for his daily news commentary on CKAC.

Sauvé was extremely intelligent and knew how to get the most out of those around him. When he took over, I was worried that he would be much harder to deal with than Duplessis. At that point I was saying : "It's all over for us." This feeling was confirmed by a poll taken during November and December which showed that if there had been an election the Liberal Party would have been virtually wiped out. [69]

September 1959. Lévesque and Claude Sylvestre at work on a broadcast for the CBC program Premier Plan.

But for the majority of Quebec intellectuals Duplessis' death was far from discouraging. Opponents of his régime, some of whom Duplessis used to refer to as *joueurs de piano,* * looked forward to significant changes in the Quebec political climate. A sign of the times was a conference on freedom organized by the Canadian

---

* Literally, "piano players," one of Duplessis' favorite epithets for "intellectuals," who were not to his liking.

Institute of Public Affairs in September 1959. There is no doubt that Sauvé, who was much younger than Duplessis and came from a quite different background, changed the course of Quebec's history. In fact many observers associate the beginnings of the Quiet Revolution with Sauve's slogan, *Désormais* [From now on], which quickly became synonymous with the idea of change.

As a freelancer, Lévesque was able to work on programs for the CBC as well as write for the newspapers, including *Le Devoir*. He also accepted speaking engagements and continued to express his views on political affairs. In November 1959, he gave a talk to the North Montreal Businessmen's Association, in which he emphasized that Sauvé's plan to offer grants to universities and classical colleges represented a complete break with the spirit of the previous administration. Lévesque also suggested that if one had to find a label to distinguish Sauvé from his predecessor, he might aptly be called a "leftist."

This speech drew an angry reply from the Union Nationale newspaper *Le Temps*. "What happened at the recent meeting of the North Montreal Businessmen's Association should serve as a lesson to other organizations who are on the lookout for a speaker, namely, that most audiences will not be pleased by what René Lévesque has to say. Other speakers are available with greater experience and a better sense of perspective." [70]

When Lévesque referred to Paul Sauvé as a "leftist," he was hurling a challenge at those who denounced the so-called left-wing elements in French-Canadian life. Among them was Robert Rumilly, an historian who published a book in 1956 entitled *Quinze années de réalisations* [Fifteen years of accomplishments], in which he heaped praise on the government then in power. He concluded by saying:

> The province of Quebec has taken the lead and is setting the pace in many fields. In their desire to injure the government, certain members of the opposition have chosen to run down their province, or rather, to be completely honest, commit libel. The province of Quebec is bursting with life. We are witnessing and experiencing a veritable ferment of new ideas, experiments, and undertakings in every field — intellectual, artistic, economic. [...] The province of Quebec today is one of the most exciting places in the world to live. [71]

Furthermore, Rumilly had harsh words for those who, at one time or another, had spoken out against certain policies of the

Duplessis régime. He expressed these views in several publications whose contents are echoed in their titles : *L'infiltration gauchiste au Canada français* [Left-wing infiltration in French Canada], *La tactique des gauchistes démasquée* [Left-wing tactics revealed], and *Les socialistes dominent le réseau gauchiste* [The socialists dominate the left-wing element]. He was quite convinced that there existed in Quebec

> a left-wing conspiracy in which Jean-Louis Gagnon * figures as one of the leading lights. [. . .] Let's make no mistake about it : the situation has become quite serious. In the first place, a handful of individuals has taken advantage of widespread publicity to assume a certain importance in the public eye. The *Revue de l'institut Pie XI* pointed out on April 25, 1959, that the CBC has provided a forum for René Lévesque and his reporting — with its "pre-determined interpretations" — which has made him one of the country's most influential broadcasters in the field of public affairs. I have already made a similar observation regarding Pierre Elliott Trudeau. The CBC extends invitations to Jean-Louis Gagnon, René Lévesque, and Pierre Elliott Trudeau ; students extend invitations to Jean-Louis Gagnon, René Lévesque, and Pierre Elliott Trudeau ; the labor unions extend invitations to Jean-Louis Gagnon, René Lévesque, and Pierre Elliott Trudeau. Everywhere you look, French Canadians are listening to the gospel preached by these three wise men. [72]

Taking his cue from the Union Nationale's official paper, Rumilly also attacked Lévesque's speech to the businessmen of North Montreal. According to him, the journalist "defined right and left in his own peculiar way, naturally attributing all folly to the right and all virtue to the left." "The left," Rumilly continued, "owes its origins and inspiration to the French Revolution. It rejects authority." On November 24, Lévesque replied to Rumilly in a speech delivered to the Maisonneuve Richelieu Club. † He completely denied having made any such division between "left" and "right." He reminded his audience that the term "left" implies a certain openness to change. But he added, "a person may not be favorably disposed towards all kinds of change. The attitude of an extremist, whether of the left or the right, in regard to a particular problem

---

* A prominent journalist, formerly head of Information Canada and co-chairman of the Royal Commission on Bilingualism and Biculturalism.
† The Richelieu clubs of Quebec are the counterpart of English Canada's Rotary and Lions clubs.

November 1959. Lévesque on Premier Plan *with the celebrated French journalist Pierre Lazareff.*

will be determined by his political commitment. But the person who is willing to submit his position to constant revision and who has not decided beforehand, is quite likely to take a left-wing stand on one matter and a right-wing stand on another." [73]

Lévesque then took issue with Rumilly's association of "left-wing" with the French Revolution. He denounced "the tendency to identify a man of the left with the revolutionary of 1789, as if, for example, the leftist had no choice but to be anti-clerical. Though the term 'left' may have been introduced during the French Revolution, what it stands for has no such historical limitations." [74] Finally, Lévesque labelled as "idiotic" Rumilly's statement that the left rejects authority. "The left simply believes," said Lévesque, echoing the teaching of Father Georges-Henri Lévesque, * "that freedom must come before authority. Free will was our first gift; freedom has priority, and we need to remember that here perhaps more than elsewhere." [75]

Having explained his point, Lévesque did not allow himself to become trapped in a quarrel over semantics. Afterwards he tried to avoid it as much as possible and became annoyed when journalists later persisted in questioning him on the subject. Despite his protests, Lévesque quickly acquired a reputation as a "leftist," a reputation he would not soon shake off.

On December 18, Lévesque addressed a public meeting in the auditorium of the University of Montreal on the political problems, both national and international, connected with the dangers of radio-active fall-out.

> It is incredible that matters of life and death involving our society are left in the hands of private enterprise. Defence and arms production should be the responsibility of government alone. We allow large private interests, who by their very nature are only interested in increasing their profits, to make their money from the power over life and death, a power that should belong to society as a whole. This point of view may be "leftist," but only because the left-wing stand on this question is founded on common sense and an instinct for self-preservation. [76]

René Lévesque had his views concerning the ideal society and never hesitated to diagnose society's problems. His contribution to public affairs, however, might have been limited to social criticism had he not shortly changed the course of his life and taken the plunge into politics.

---

* See note on p. 132.

Chapter 3 — References

1. Interview with R.L., 21 March, 1973.
2. René Lévesque, "La Voix du Canada, Montréal, Canada," *Le Clairon de Saint-Hyacinthe.*
3. Interview with R.L., 21 March, 1973.
4. Ibid.
5. René Lévesque, *Le Petit Journal,* 16 September, 1951.
6. Gérard Pelletier, "M. René Lévesque, reporter et commentateur émérite," *Le Devoir,* 6 October, 1951.
7. Yvon Côté, "René Lévesque," *Le Quartier Latin,* 7 February, 1952.
8. Gérard Pelletier, "Parlons, en retard, de la Princesse," *Le Devoir,* 24 November, 1951.
9. Hélène Pilotte, *Châtelaine,* April 1966, pp. 96-97.
10. Rémy Le Poittevin, "René Lévesque ne vit que pour tout voir et tout comprendre," *Le Journal des Vedettes,* 9 October, 1955.
11. Florent Forget, "L'actualité à la télévision," *Le livre de l'année 1954* (Société Grolier, 1954).
12. Interview with R.L., 9 May, 1973.
13. Ibid.
14. René Lévesque, "Staline parmi nous," *Vrai,* 10 March, 1956.
15. Interview with R.L., 9 May, 1973.
16. *Le Devoir,* 13 October, 1955.
17. Interview with R.L., 9 May, 1973.
18. *Le Devoir,* 12 October, 1955.
19. Ibid., 14 October, 1955.
20. Renald Savoie, "Un espion du Canada en Russie," *Vrai,* 12 November, 1955.
21. "Les grenouilles de bénitier contre René Lévesque," *Vrai,* 26 November, 1955.
22. *Vrai,* 28 April, 1956.
23. "René Lévesque, un dynamo humain! *Nouvelles et Potins,* 1 June, 1956.
24. Roland Lorrain, *Vrai,* 11 June, 1956.
25. Jean Leduc, *Vrai,* 25 February, 1956.
26. Renald Savoie, *Vrai,* 3 March, 1956.
27. Interview with R.L., 9 May, 1973.
28. *Le Droit,* 10 July, 1957.
29. Jean-Marc Rigaud, *Vrai,* 10 November, 1956.
30. Fernand Benoit, "Point de Mire ou l'art de cerner l'actualité," *La semaine à Radio-Canada,* 23 May, 1959.
31. *Vrai,* 15 December, 1956.
32. Roger Brien, *Revue de l'Institut Pie XI,* 17 November, 1959.
33. Gilles Hénault, *Le Journal des Vedettes,* 9 June, 1957.
34. Jean-Marc Rigaud, *Vrai,* 8 June, 1957.
35. Roger Brien, *Revue de l'Institut Pie XI,* 5 October, 1957.
36. Ibid., 12 October, 1957.
37. Ibid., 30 November, 1957.
38. Martine Lefebvre, *Revue de l'Institut Pie XI,* 10 May, 1958.
39. Gérard Bergeron, *Ne bougez plus! Portraits de 40 de nos politiciens* (Editions du Jour, 1968), pp. 149-150.
40. Interview with R.L., 9 May, 1973.
41. *Le Devoir,* 22 January, 1959.
42. Ibid.
43. *Le Devoir,* 10 January, 1959.

44. *Ibid.*
45. Jean Hamelin, *Le Devoir,* 14 January, 1959.
46. André Laurendeau, *Le Devoir,* 19 January, 1959.
47. The reader seeking more information about the various unions involved should consult a study by Jean-Louis Roux entitled *Radio-Canada, 1959,* which appears in *En Grève! L'histoire de la C.S.N. et des luttes menées par ses militants de 1937 à 1963.* (Editions du Jour, 1963).
48. *Le Devoir,* 22 January, 1959.
49. Bergeron, p. 148.
50. André Laurendeau, *Le Devoir,* 22 January, 1959.
51. Michel Roy, *Le Devoir,* 23 January, 1959.
52. René Lévesque, *Le Devoir,* 23 January, 1959.
53. *Le Devoir,* 28 January, 1959.
54. Extract from a series of 13 one-hour documentaries on *La Révolution Tranquille,* produced by Pierre de Bellefeuille and Jean-Pierre Bergeron for CBC radio. Second program, 17 June, 1972.
55. Ibid.
56. *Le Devoir,* 10 February, 1959.
57. *Le Devoir,* 12 February, 1959.
58. *En Grève! L'histoire de la C.S.N.,* p. 181.
59. *Le Devoir,* 3 March, 1959.
60. *Le Devoir,* 4 March, 1959.
61. Ibid.
62. *Le Devoir,* 9 March, 1959.
63. André Laurendeau, *Le Devoir,* 16 March, 1959.
64. Bergeron, pp. 150-151.
65. Interview with R.L., 9 May, 1973.
66. Michel Roy, "Terre-Neuve . . . 10e province," *Le Devoir,* 30 March, 1959.
67. Jean Hamelin, *Le Devoir,* 28 March, 1959.
68. Interview with R.L., 9 May, 1973.
69. De Bellefeuille and Bergeron.
70. *Le Temps,* 12 November, 1959.
71. Robert Rumilly, *Quinze années de réalisations* (Montréal, 1956) p. 227.
72. Robert Rumilly, *Les socialistes dominent le réseau gauchiste* (Published by the author, 1959), pp. 132-133.
73. *La Presse,* 25 November, 1959.
74. Ibid.
75. Ibid.
76. *La Presse,* 19 December, 1959.

4

Political commitment and the quiet revolution

For many years the political power of Maurice Duplessis played havoc with the fortunes of Quebec's Liberal Party as it struggled to find a coherent philosophy, a platform, and a winning slogan. There were good men like Georges-Emile Lapalme and Jean-Marie Nadeau in the party, but they were far too few. Lapalme, among others, described the situation this way :

> Apart from the Official Opposition — or official oppositions — virtually no one was willing to stick his neck out. I know, because in 1952 and again in 1956 I tried to involve a number of people in the fight against Duplessis who all refused for various reasons — everyone had some excuse. But then when the régime was finally toppled, they went around taking the credit for it, which was completely untrue. The Liberal Party was alone in its opposition to Duplessis and we paid the price for standing up to him. The point I'm making is that being a member of the Liberal Party during those years meant that you'd burned all your bridges. [1]

In 1958, Lapalme was replaced as leader of the party by Jean Lesage, who had just moved from federal to provincial politics and therefore had no seat. Lapalme himself had already formulated the guiding principle of the revitalized Liberals' new program : "The

Liberal Party stands for social justice." Full of enthusiasm, Lesage hoped to succeed where Lapalme had failed by attempting to win the support of outstanding public figures. In January 1959, he stated : "Unless we plan to let our society go rotten at the core and collapse, then it is high time some of our more talented people stopped repeating that politics is dirty and that getting involved in public affairs is not worth the trouble." He launched an appeal "to all men of good will and liberal inclinations, whatever their political beliefs, inviting them to work with the Liberal Party in order to save democracy in Quebec." The Liberal leader warned that "the Union Nationale is doing its best to undermine democracy and install a régime based on the rule of wealth and privilege." On the same occasion he defined his concept of democracy for the McGill University student audience : "In the economic sphere, this liberalism falls between two extremes — complete absence of intervention on the part of the state and the dogmatic control proposed by socialism. The Liberal Party is therefore prepared to apply government controls when it would be in the public interest to do so, especially with regard to public utilities." [2]

Lesage's appeal to "men of good will" was not without a certain interest. It showed quite clearly his conception of the Liberal Party : a group of democrats "prepared to apply government controls when it would be in the public interest to do so." But in January 1959, it did not appear that Lesage's appeal would be any more successful than those made by Georges-Emile Lapalme.

The following month, Jean Drapeau, honorary president of *L'Action civique,* which had made a name for itself with an inquiry into public morality, took Lesage's pronouncement one step further. Drapeau was still politically uncommitted, but this did not prevent him from thinking out loud. He asserted that it was futile to attack the régime in power without also attempting to destroy the system that created it. He continued :

> The problem lies in the system itself, which is founded on favoritism, patronage, and the domination of vested interests. It is typical of this system that the very man who committed himself to a program of economic liberation and social reform in 1933 has in the meantime had striking workers clubbed, while just recently he has sold off one of our most valuable resources, natural gas, to American interests. [...] As for myself, in any event, I am leading a fight not only to overthrow a régime and its leader but also to create a program

for Quebec which will ensure spiritual growth and material well-being for its people in a climate of confidence and dignity. [3]

Jean Drapeau's words inspired new hope; but it was questionable whether he could avoid similar pitfalls in his own career.

Sauvé's takeover after Duplessis' death plunged the Liberal members in Quebec City into deep despair, whereas in the province as a whole it was treated more optimistically. "Only a few weeks had gone by with Sauvé at the helm," explained Georges-Emile Lapalme,

> but already the whole climate was different — often all a revolution needs to get started is a simple change in climate. Some of the revolutionary goings-on in France would never have taken place if people had awakened to find that it was 25° below zero. They just wouldn't have turned up for the demonstration. The physical climate and the other kind of climate can both be influential. Back then, a certain climate pervaded the whole province and everybody was expecting something to happen, but nobody knew exactly what. [4]

Suddenly, on the morning of January 2, 1960, Paul Sauvé died after being in office only one hundred days. This was cause for political celebration as far as the Liberals were concerned. "It was the opportunity the Liberal Party had been waiting for. We were convinced when Barrette took over as the third premier in a row that the Union Nationale wouldn't hold out." [5] Lapalme later wrote in his memoirs :

> Paul Sauvé, premier of Quebec for one hundred days, disappeared from the scene and left the way open for Jean Lesage ; there was nothing to stop the Liberal leader now. We used to have friendly arguments about our luck : when it came to politics I always had to blast my way through, but everything fell into place for Lesage, who never had to lift a finger. [6]

By the fall of 1959, René Lévesque seemed more and more interested in playing an active part in political life. A number of observers had felt it coming. From time to time he talked politics with Gérard Pelletier, Jean Marchand, and Pierre Elliott Trudeau.

> I had been a sort of stop-gap contributor on a very infrequent basis to Cité Libre, * which was still at the height of its

---

* A left-wing Quebec periodical whose founders included Trudeau and Pelletier. The various contributors shared one main preoccupation – the struggle against Duplessis.

success, I think, and still pretty influential. That's how I got to be professionally associated with Pelletier, as well as Marchand, whom I'd known for a long time since our days at university, and Trudeau, whom I only ran into occasionally. We met now and then to talk over what was going on and we had connections with various university people, particularly in Quebec City. These included Marchand himself, René Tremblay, Maurice Lamontagne, and others who had worked on the Liberal Party program — the Father Lévesque team, so to speak. * The Liberal program for 1960 taken as a whole represented a big improvement on what Quebec had been familiar with before — catch-phrases, hollow promises, and so on. For once, there was an attempt to come to grips with a series of problems in a very concrete way, and it was all written down. We took an interest in the program and tossed it around in group discussions. At the same time, there was a kind of ongoing discussion about whether or not it was worthwhile going into politics. Marchand and some of the others kept coming back to this point. [7]

These discussions concerning the Liberal Party program lasted from January to March, 1960. But it was time to make a decision. The last provincial election had been held in 1956 and, since the Barrette government did not have the stamina of Paul Sauvé's administration, general elections were almost certain to be held soon. The question was : when ? The Liberals could only guess, but it was probably just a matter of weeks. The Liberal Party accepted in essence the recommendations presented to them by this coterie of Quebec intellectuals, and it was anxious to recruit a few candidates from among those who had taken part in the discussions, since they had clearly demonstrated the keenest interest in the party's future. "Lesage finally got in touch with us," explains Lévesque,

> through whom I don't remember — it may have been Marchand or perhaps Lamontagne. He wanted to know if any of us in this indecisive group connected with *Cité Libre* and the unions were interested in being candidates, because the elections were just around the corner. That was in early spring. We got together and talked it over a number of times. [8]

Most of the men concerned, however, were not in a position to take any risks. They all had steady work which they did not

---

* Georges-Henri Lévesque was a Dominican who founded the Faculty of Social Sciences at Laval University in the forties and gathered around him a number of young left-wing intellectuals committed to social change in Quebec.

want to jeopardize by going into politics. Moreover, they felt that they could be just as useful in their present positions, at least for the time being.

Time was running short. When the election campaign reached its second week, Lesage could not wait any longer ; he had to complete his list of candidates. Lévesque describes what happened :

> On the final evening, Lesage waited for us at the Windsor Hotel, while we were practically next door in Marchand's room at the Mount Royal. If I remember correctly, Trudeau, Pelletier, and Marchand were there and probably two or three others. We had to make up our minds because Lesage had said, "I'd like to know by this evening. There aren't that many ridings left." That's what it is like in any election — once the campaign is under way, you can't wait for the latecomers. So Lesage told us, "There aren't many ridings left, especially in the Montreal area, and I'd like to know how many of you have decided to join us. Two ? three ? four ?" In the end, I was the only one who went. At midnight or one o'clock, I phoned Lesage and went to the Windsor. "Here I am," I said, "the others just aren't ready." [9]

René Lévesque had taken the plunge into politics. Why ? One reason, of course, was that he liked the Liberal Party's new program. But there were other factors too, as he explained to journalist Jacques Guay :

> I did it for all kinds of reasons. Following political affairs can be very frustrating. I was already in it up to the neck, what with Canadian conventions and American conventions and Quebec conventions. In 1956, I covered the last stages of Pierre Laporte's campaign when he was beaten as a Liberal candidate. [. . .] A few months later, Fathers Dion and O'Neil published their book *Le chrétien et les élections* [Elections and the Christian], which attacked electioneering abuses. Then there was the *Rassemblement des forces démocratiques* [Rally of democratic forces], that kind of alternative political group that Trudeau tried to get off the ground in 1958. It was all very well to keep complaining about Duplessis, but that wasn't really enough. In 1960, I was impressed by the Liberal program and especially by Lapalme. He was probably more committed to social justice than many of those who go around jabbering about it these days. In any event, I was the only member of the Pelletier-Marchand-Trudeau group who could afford to weigh anchor, so I jumped on board. [10]

Lévesque's description of himself as "up to the neck" in politics is quite accurate, since time and time again the CBC assigned him to various elections and political conventions.

> Thus he covered the 1952, '56, and '58 conventions and elections in the United States, the 1953, '57, and '58 Canadian federal elections, and the 1952, '56, and '58 Quebec provincial elections. Parties and programs were an old story to him, and, of them all, he liked the 1960 Quebec Liberal platform best. "It was a good beginning," he said later. [11]

Lévesque discussed the reasons for his decision in greater detail with three Quebec journalists who asked him, "Was your entry into politics prompted by force of circumstances or by your own personal convictions ?"

> I'm not too good at that kind of self-analysis. As a journalist in those last few years before I went into politics, which also happened to be the last few years of the Duplessis régime, I followed political affairs very closely. If you spend your time studying what other people are doing or not doing in a certain field, you end up wanting to get involved in it yourself. In my line of work getting involved in politics was a kind of occupational hazard. On top of that there was the fact that Duplessis died in '59. Who knows, if Sauvé had lived ... but he died and that was that. Then along came Barrette, and we wondered if it was finally all over for them. After sixteen years we were anxious to see someone else in power. The group stuck together at first, but I ended up as the only one who took the big step because the others all had good reasons not to. The group looked at it this way: "There's no point discussing the merits of the Liberal Party itself — we all know it's just one of the old parties. But, God, we have to get rid of the Union Nationale somehow, because if we don't, we might as well pack our bags and leave !" At that point I was thirty-seven years old. [12]

The reasons for René Lévesque's decision were clear. First, through his work he had developed a taste for political life ; second, like many others, he felt the need to pitch in and help bring about the Union Nationale's defeat ; and, finally, he was attracted by the program of the Liberal Party. But there was another factor — the presence of Georges-Emile Lapalme, whose sense of justice Lévesque admired so much. Perhaps he also had in mind the former Liberal leader's "realistic" candor and his stubborn and unyielding opposition to Duplessis, a struggle unselfishly motivated on Lapalme's part since it was virtually without hope of success. Lapalme wrote in this regard :

> Was I really a factor in his decision to join our ranks, as he stated both publicly and privately ? [...] Was it the program ? Was it the fact that I was one of the candidates ? Was it my political record ? I am naturally very flattered that René Lévesque gave me some of the credit for his decision to join the Liberal Party. [13]

Moreover, there is no doubt that Lapalme and Jean Lesage were overjoyed at Lévesque's decision. "By the time the election campaign was in full swing," wrote Lapalme,

> we had been blessed with three strokes of good fortune : a strong slate of candidates, an outstanding public figure, and a made-to-measure scandal. This little man who seemed larger than life in the eyes of his public, was not simply René Lévesque ; no, despite his cracked voice and unimposing physical presence, he was TELEVISION personified. His program *Point de Mire,* which was ten times better than Pierre Lazareff's *Cinq colonnes à la une* in Paris and displayed a command of the medium and a scope which have not been equalled since, made him the star of television. As Jean Lesage flipped through his lists of names looking for good party material, he stopped at Lévesque's name and wondered out loud, "What do you think ?" It was a great idea, but was it possible ? And then everything came together in the end. [14]

Lévesque was to be the Liberal candidate in the Montreal riding of Laurier. The decision was made at the Windsor Hotel the same evening Lévesque told Lesage of his decision to join the party :

> I remember he offered me a choice between two ridings, on condition that the party leaders agreed. One was Laurier and the other was in the west end, Saint-Laurent or something like that. I chose Laurier because in my TV work one of our favorite places for man-in-the-street interviews — which I always enjoyed a lot, getting other people's opinions and reactions and so on — was Saint-Hubert Plaza. And Saint-Hubert Plaza was on Saint-Hubert Street, smack in the middle of Laurier riding. "Hell," I said, "I know that area and I'm sure I'd feel at home there." I didn't really know anything about politics so I said, "Sure, I'll give Laurier a try." And that's how it was all decided. [15]

On May 6, Lévesque announced publicly that he was running as a candidate in Laurier. His Union Nationale opponent, Arsène Gagné, had held the seat since 1955. The new candidate explained to the press and to the public his reasons for "plunging into this campaign with all the strength and resourcefulness at my command." We are already familiar with some of these reasons :

> In my humble opinion, the Liberal Party's program provides solutions to our most substantial and immediate problems, and I believe quite simply that it is worth some personal sacrifice to try and sell the program to the electorate, and then, if the electorate is willing, to work towards its implementation. I am convinced, as are the majority of Québécois, or at least so I hope, that the ranks of the Union Nationale are filled with the leftovers from an old régime. If we are to preserve the well-being and dignity of the province and all its inhabitants, changes are in order. Men like Lesage, Lapalme, Gérin-Lajoie, Hamel, and many others, by sticking tenaciously to their principles, by democratizing the party structure, and by adopting this remarkable party program, have shown that they are the new team we so urgently need if we are not to lapse into a humiliating state of political paralysis. [16]

But what in fact were the contents of this much-praised party program ? It comprised fifty-four articles : some merely adjusted the old system so that it would run more smoothly, while other measures were intended to change fundamentally the face of Quebec. Its overall concern was to make a serious effort to put Quebec's public affairs in order. In the area of education it proposed, among other items, free tuition for all levels of schooling and the creation of a royal commission enquiry into education. It promised the creation of an economic advisory council to act as "the central planning agency for the economic and industrial sector." A ministry of natural resources would also be created to see that all untapped hydro-electric resources were turned over to Hydro-Quebec. Electricity rates would be made uniform throughout the province and, as needs be, lowered in places where they were too high. The most important proposals in the realm of social security were the immediate establishment of government-sponsored hospital insurance, the formulation of a labor code, and the creation of workmen's compensation boards. Finally, the Liberals promised a royal commission enquiry into the administration of the civil service under the Union

Nationale régime, as well as reforms in the provincial bureaucracy and the electoral system. Strict controls would be imposed on the handling of public finances, and these same finances would be strengthened by abolishing favoritism in the awarding of contracts ✓ for public works and replacing it with a system which would call for the submission of public tenders. [17]

On April 27, Premier Antonio Barrette announced the forthcoming general elections. Like an old-fashioned steam locomotive, the campaign got off to a slow start, but its rhythm quickly became more frenzied. On May 6, just as René Lévesque announced his candidacy, Jean Lesage revealed the Liberal Party program to the public at a news conference in the Queen Elizabeth Hotel.

In the following week, Lévesque concentrated on planning his own campaign. Although his opponent Arsène Gagné had defeated Pierre Laporte in 1956, the riding had a certain tradition of political non-conformism and in 1948 had elected André Laurendeau, then provincial leader of the *Bloc Populaire*. * But the fight would not be easy. From the beginning, Lévesque's opponents decided to attack him personally, despite the fact that there had never before been so much talk of cleaning up campaign tactics. On May 13, *Le Devoir* wrote :

> Let's see what has been accomplished by the current insistence on better behavior and higher ethical standards in the election campaign. Laurier riding, of course, is being contested by Arsène Gagné (UN) and René Lévesque (L). "A clean fight is predicted for ... Laurier," we are told on page 2 of *Le Guide du Nord,* an upstanding local newspaper owned by Jacques Francoeur (son of the late Louis) and one seemingly well endowed as you will notice if you take the trouble to examine pages 8 and 9, which are filled with publicity for the Union Nationale and where we find the following question : "Who is René Lévesque's best friend ?" The answer : a photograph of Khrushchev with an inset picture of René Lévesque and an unsigned article by Gaston Houde, in which the broadcaster is taken to task for a speech he gave on Russia and Nikita Khrushchev. This is all part of a Union Nationale advertisement promoting Mr. Gagné. The elections are slated for June 22. Today is May 13 : the campaign is off to a fine start !

---

* A Quebec-based party founded in 1942, which succeeded in getting candidates elected to both Ottawa and Quebec City. It was opposed to conscription and to the federal government's centralist tendencies.

But Lévesque paid no attention to the slur printed in *Le Guide du Nord* ; he was too busy raising the curtain on the Liberals' new program. He gave one of his first speeches as a politician at the Saint-Marc parish hall in Shawinigan, part of the Saint-Maurice riding represented by Liberal incumbent René Hamel. The press reported that Lévesque's arrival in the hall was greeted with thunderous applause. He told the audience that, once in power, a Liberal government would demand "royalties based on twentieth-century prices" for Quebec's natural resources, and that the mining companies and other large firms concerned would be required to employ "people from the province of Quebec before they handed over key jobs to Americans." He also attacked the Union Nationale for their "mustard-plaster" style of government.

Maurice Duplessis had often campaigned on slogans designed to exploit the autonomist sentiments of the Québécois, fully aware that he was the one who called the shots. In 1960, when Antonio Barrette saw that the entire Liberal platform was based on the notion of cultural and economic development for the Québécois, he too decided to play up the theme of provincial autonomy for all it was worth. The tactic had worked successfully for previous governments, after all : why not for his as well ?

The Liberals had difficulty attacking this position because it had already brought them to grief in 1954, when the provincial income tax system was introduced. * But Lévesque laid his cards on the table in Shawinigan. He declared that the whole issue was just a smoke screen and that the Union Nationale's concept of autonomy was all talk and no action. He added that "the Union Nationale is using the word autonomy like one of those mechanical rabbits that dogs are made to chase at the track. For fifteen years the Union Nationale has used autonomy to keep us on the run." [18]

Lévesque was encouraged by his reception in Shawinigan but in his own riding his troubles had just begun. On May 20, the Union Nationale party organizers managed to force Lévesque out of his campaign headquarters. *Le Devoir* reported :

---

* Duplessis introduced provincial income tax in 1954 and accordingly demanded that Ottawa reduce the federal tax by 10 per cent. The Quebec Liberal Party, assured by Prime Minister Louis Saint-Laurent that he would never yield to such a demand, assailed Duplessis' position. It was not long, however, before the federal Liberals did acquiesce, thus leaving the Quebec Liberals in a position of great political embarrassment.

The election headquarters of Mr. René Lévesque, Liberal candidate for the Montreal riding of Laurier, are no longer to be found at 7060 Saint-Hubert Street. The owner of the building in question, who sometimes rents out his premises for weddings, dances, and other social functions requiring a temporary permit from the Quebec Liquor Board, told Mr. Lévesque yesterday morning that he would have to vacate. He explained that men working for Mr. Arsène Gagné, the Union Nationale candidate for this riding, warned him that if he continued to rent his premises to Mr. Lévesque during the campaign they would see to it that he received no more temporary liquor permits. Mr. Lévesque's headquarters have therefore been moved a few doors north to 7175 Saint-Hubert Street. [19]

The personal attacks against Lévesque were not restricted to his riding alone. One daily newspaper, *Montréal-Matin,* which was then owned by the Union Nationale, also entered the fray. The paper argued the case of Louis-Joseph Pigeon, a Quebec MP :

A member of Parliament has attempted to find out in the House of Commons how much the CBC used to pay broadcaster René Lévesque, who is now the Liberal candidate for Montreal-Laurier. As usual, obtaining this information was impossible ; it is another of the CBC's jealously guarded secrets. The taxpayers have to pay up and then see their money turned over to questionable persons for questionable reasons with questionable results, without even being allowed to find out what is going on. Nevertheless it has been established that from April to November, 1958, in other words a period of eight months, the CBC paid René Lévesque close to $28,000. [. . .] We are not all that curious about Mr. Lévesque's former income. But the public has a right to know how much it's paying and in particular how much it has paid in the past to make a star of René Lévesque, whose only interest was in finding a springboard from which to launch his political career. Mr. Lesage has provided him with just such a springboard and on June 22, they will both find themselves in over their heads, soundly defeated along with most of the other Liberal candidates. [20]

Just as the Union Nationale daily was publishing this article, Gérard Filion, editorial writer for *Le Devoir,* was noting with satisfaction the high quality of the election publicity produced since the beginning of the campaign. "The public has undoubtedly been aware of the dignity which has typified the publicity efforts of both parties since the campaign began. With the exception of a smear directed at René Lévesque, apparently the work of a low-ranking party official, campaign publicity has not resorted to prejudice or, what is worse, slandering members of the opposing party." [21]

On the whole the campaign was indeed remarkably free of smear tactics and Filion had good reason to be satisfied. But it seemed that Lévesque's presence in the front ranks of the Liberal Party irritated the Union Nationale, who redoubled their efforts to identify him with "communism." *Le Devoir* wrote : *"Nouvelles Illustrées,* that outspoken newspaper which sees every issue in terms of 'good guys' and 'bad guys,' [...] has printed the very same election propaganda in its May 28 edition as appeared in the pages of *Le Guide du Nord.* [...] This unseemly piece of electioneering is undoubtedly 'the work of a low-ranking party official' !" the Montreal daily concluded. [22]

But even while the weekly was spreading this propaganda, Jean Lesage was using similar tactics to discredit the American financier Cyrus Eaton. Lesage called on Premier Barrette to take back the iron-ore concessions granted Mr. Eaton in Ungava, "because," as he put it, "this individual has gone and heaped accolades on Khrushchev, a man who has shown the greatest disrespect for the President of the United States and the free world." André Laurendeau registered his exasperation with these tactics : "I can understand that Mr. Lesage may have been tempted to give the Union Nationale a little of their own medicine. But in doing so he has virtually legitimized mud-slinging tactics : the slanders perpetrated by the Union Nationale do not justify those perpetrated by the Liberals." Laurendeau then compared Lesage's accusation to the attacks on Lévesque :

> If the Liberal leader allows himself to make accusations so obviously far removed from the truth, then he is at the same time justifying in a way the ravings directed against Mr. René Lévesque by certain subordinates in the Union Nationale hierarchy. Is Lévesque really a friend of Khrushchev's ? No one at Union Nationale headquarters believes that for a minute. It is simply more election propaganda put out in the hopes of impressing the ignorant or the fanatical and, since the end always seems to justify the means in politics, the attitude seems to be "why not use it ?" But why not announce a moratorium on name-calling so that we can clear the decks and agree to argue the real issues ? [23]

140

Lévesque had no more to say about the propaganda in *Nouvelles Illustrées* than about *Le Guide du Nord* or the slur in *Montréal-Matin*. He was busy with his campaign, and his organization was working on a new formula he later used a great deal — the "kitchen meeting," as *Le Devoir* called it :

> The Liberal candidate for Montreal-Laurier, Mr. René Lévesque, is conducting a relatively unusual door-to-door campaign. Mr. Lévesque visits what averages out to three homes every evening, and a small group gathers at each house to have an informal chat with him. It appears that the "gimmick" has been very successful. [24]

But because he was one of the "stars" of the Liberal Party from the very beginning of the campaign, Lévesque had to keep leaving his own riding in order to speak in other areas. He turned up in Thetford Mines to support the Liberal candidate, Emilien Maheux, where as usual he touched on a number of subjects, including the natural gas scandal, a favorite topic of Liberal speakers. This Lévesque regarded as "the most notorious successful highway robbery in history." "Certain cabinet ministers," he said, "have made enormous profits at public expense. Three Ontario politicians accused of having made money by peddling their influence were immediately relieved of their posts, while in Quebec all the ministers implicated in the gas deal are still in power." There was more. According to Lévesque, the Union Nationale party itself was politically obsolete :

> Let's not forget that the party's two former leaders aren't around any more to look after the province. No, I repeat, the present government is simply not capable of meeting its obligations in the modern world of today. The late Honorable Maurice Duplessis himself pointed out that a government in power for fifteen straight years is a corrupt government. In point of fact, they no longer have a blueprint for the future, nor do they have any new ideas. It is a leaderless party, which is now concerned exclusively with protecting the interests of its members and their friends. [25]

Meanwhile the Union Nationale's attacks on the ex-journalist continued. Lévesque's opponents believed they had finally uncovered a scandal which would ensure his defeat. Writing in the June 4 issue of the Union Nationale newspaper *Notre Temps,* journalist Jean-Paul Poitras violently attacked Lévesque and the CBC. Poitras took great exception to the presence of the Liberal candidate for

Laurier on one of the Corporation's programs :

On Monday, May 23, CBC Television, which had decided for some unknown reason to televise the award ceremonies of the first *Congrès du spectacle,* * arranged a little surprise for René Lévesque. This gesture amounted to an endorsement by the CBC of their favorite broadcaster and a direct contribution to his campaign coffers. The show was carefully put together to give the impression that nothing unusual was going on. Trophies were handed out here and there until we came to René Lévesque, who won the prize for broadcaster-commentator-announcer. The real reason for the award was not revealed, namely, his Liberal candidacy in Laurier. The trick worked. The claque nearly brought down the house and there was prolonged applause (in the words of some Russian news report describing Khrushchev's grunts). It was enough to make you believe that for once the whole artistic community was of one mind. [. . .] But the viewers were not so easily fooled. They saw through the charade and realized that regular programming had been pre-empted that evening to give René Lévesque a little free publicity — at the taxpayers' expense, of course.

This was not the only revelation in Poitras' article. Why had the federal government refused to divulge René Lévesque's CBC salary when asked to do so by MP Louis-Joseph Pigeon ? Poitras believed he had the answer :

The Corporation did not wish to reveal the amounts paid out to their favorite broadcaster, René Lévesque, because they knew he had received fabulous sums from the public treasury over a period of three years and that this fact might be used against their hero. After such a revelation it would have been difficult for Mr. Lévesque to sound off over the so-called natural gas scandal and to criticize those on the provincial payroll. How greedy can a man get ? It is rumored that for 1956, 1957, and 1958 alone he was paid more than a federal MP makes in fifteen years and more than a provincial MPP makes in twenty-five years. [26]

But Lévesque paid no heed to these attacks until late in the campaign. At the beginning of June, he stepped up the pace. Each week, Monday through Saturday, from 6:00 to 6:10 pm, he came on the air at radio station CKAC to deliver a kind of political

---

* Poitras is in fact referring erroneously to the *Gala des artistes,* an annual event honoring the outstanding performers of the year.

Point de Mire, during which he discussed the election campaign. A commercial for the Liberal Party introduced his talks. Lévesque's schedule was becoming increasingly hectic. On Sunday, June 5, for example, he left Montreal around noon to speak in Mont-Laurier at 2 o'clock. That evening he addressed the citizens of La Tuque, and the next morning he was back in his Montreal riding to clear up some business before giving a talk in Saint-Hyacinthe at noon.

He then made his way to Quebec City where he was the guest speaker that evening at a Liberal rally held in the *Palais Montcalm* on behalf of Henri Beaupré, the candidate for Quebec-Centre. After outlining the main features of the Liberal program, Lévesque tried to explain to his audience just how much things had changed in the province of Quebec :

> The Union Nationale is actually proud of not having changed its program since 1931 and is surprised that the Liberals have an entirely new one. Anybody with an ounce of common sense can see to what extent things have changed since 1931. The population of Quebec alone has more than doubled. We've had industrialization, we've had the war, new communications media, and rapidly accelerating progress in all areas of endeavor. Yet the Union Nationale can come to the people of this province and say that it sees no need for a new program and no reason why the Liberals should put forward a new program. Statements like that show what nonsense these people are capable of.

Lévesque then attacked the basic principles of the old Duplessis machine :

> No one in the Union Nationale ranks is capable of holding the party together any more. It used to be that only one man counted in this party. Until recently, you never heard of any real discussions among its members. The Union Nationale caucus was like a collection of robots incapable of expressing personal opinions. All the decisions were made at the top. Even Mr. Barrette's appointment seems to have been the work of a small group who met secretly behind closed doors and ignored the wishes of the elected members. The Union Nationale can boast of unanimity simply because it has no ideas to offer : ideas would threaten their complacency. Personal gain is all that has ever mattered to that party, and as long as there was a strong man to pay off the membership with one hand and impose

143

order with the other, no dissenting voices were raised. But now that war has been declared on the vested interests . . . [27]

Before official nominations for the Quebec election closed on June 8, someone named René Lévesque — but not the "real" René Lévesque — was entered as a candidate in Montreal-Laurier. Was this another move on the part of the Union Nationale to confuse the voters and help bring about Lévesque's defeat? No one knew for sure. In any event René Lévesque, the journalist, had no choice but to compete against his unknown namesake, who gave his occupation as "performer," because this manoeuvre was not strictly speaking illegal.

The publicity put out by the Laurier Liberal organization attempted to create a definite image for their candidate. One advertisement read : "René Lévesque, the Liberal of the year, offers the people of Montreal-Laurier a voice which is hoarse but can nevertheless be heard throughout the province ; a voice familiar to everyone in Quebec, a voice which addresses itself above all to OUR problems, a voice which insists on speaking the truth and presenting the facts as they affect us all." A sharp contrast was drawn with his opponent Arsène Gagné, "a typical Union Nationale voice, which speaks up for a few days around election time . . . and then falls silent again for the next four years." It would be in the interests of the voters of Laurier to elect René Lévesque, the advertisement continued, because "he represents a new breed of politician who will not stoop to slander, is not interested in damaging reputations, and yet says exactly what he thinks." The voters were then urged to support the "Liberal reconstruction" which promised "work for all able-bodied citizens, a guaranteed education for all, security for widows, the elderly, the disabled, and the blind, and new hope and support instead of fear and abuse." [28]

Montréal-Matin, which felt the need to talk about Lévesque every day, was undaunted by the Liberals' propaganda :

> We write about Mr. Lévesque quite frequently for the good reason that he is the most blatant leftist the Liberal Party has ever included in its ranks, and for the good reason that he started off as a perfect stranger to the Liberal Party and yet suddenly became the candidate Mr. Lesage has paraded around most. Mr. Lévesque is sure to be defeated and will forfeit his deposit. What interests us, however, is how far he and the Liberals will go in order to deceive public opinion. [29]

144

Lévesque's campaign continued. At Saint-Hyacinthe, he developed a new theme : equal educational opportunities for all. He accused the Union Nationale of systematically short-changing Quebec's most important resource, its young people, by allowing "half of them to waste their lives through sheer lack of opportunity to develop their talents fully or pursue their studies, simply because they were too poor to do so." Lévesque continued :

> Free education at all levels, as proposed by the Liberals, is the only measure that will put a quick stop to the systematic dehumanization perpetrated by the Union Nationale's outmoded administration. I chose to enter politics only because I felt that the province was in serious trouble. If we don't act promptly we'll all end up like them and democracy will be rendered meaningless by the old system of patronage for the few and deprivation for the many, which has ensured the helplessness of the individual while the disintegration of the province continues unchecked. This incompetent government is beneath the intellectual and moral level of the French-Canadian race. We deserve better. As guardians and trustees of French culture in America, we must make every effort to preserve what we have retained of this heritage. [30]

The following evening, June 9, a rally was held in Mercier riding for Liberal candidate Jean-Baptiste Crépeau. The speakers included Antonio Lamer, André Nadeau, Georges Lachance, Jacques Vadeboncoeur, and René Lévesque, who gave a particularly lively talk. After warning the audience about "election confectioners," "patronage fall-out," and "statistical half truths," he pointed to a province-wide shift in public opinion indicating that "the people have had enough of the Union Nationale, which has been doing a rotten job for sixteen years and isn't even aware that there's a bad smell around." "All we've had in these sixteen years," he added, "is a lot of patching, paving, and bridge-building." [31]

At Roxton Falls on June 10, Lévesque attacked the Union Nationale even more severely :

> There are three kinds of cabinet minister in Quebec — those who can, or rather, those who could say, "Yes, Mr. Premier," those who said, "Yes, Maurice," and, finally, Paul Sauvé. Paul Sauvé's death left the Union Nationale without anyone strong enough to guide the party or run an efficient government, so that today the party finds itself with a leader who was simply imposed on it from above. [. . .] The unseemly methods used

by the Union Nationale hide behind the interests they wish to protect, namely, their own. They will not hesitate to resort to intimidation and blackmail in order to obtain votes and remain in power. An incompetent administration camouflages the absence of any program or ideas with a policy of papering over the cracks and handing out contracts on the basis of favoritism. If the people of Quebec continue with such men as their leaders they will end up resembling them, and this would be a great shame. The most neglected problems are those most crucial to French Canadians. Education and hospital insurance have been good examples of this for years. I could go on and on about the blunders these men have committed, their incompetence, the lack of patriotic spirit shown by this bunch of politicians. The degradation of the individual by this administration has reached such a point that in order to merit their attention, which in a democracy should be the natural right of every free citizen, we have to go crawling to them on our knees and kiss their feet. Our leaders are selling our province to outside interests, while we are left without any legitimate profits to call our own. [32]

It appeared that Lévesque would never allude to the Union Nationale propaganda which made him out to be "best friends" with Nikita Khrushchev. After the meeting in Roxton Falls, he made an appearance at the Magog town hall to speak on behalf of the Liberal candidate, Georges Vaillancourt. Lévesque explained that the Union Nationale organizers had chosen not to use the word they really had in mind because, as he put it, "they're cowards." He added : "I'll tell you what it is however — the word is *communist*. It's funny because it's not a dirty word, but it can really shock people just the same. And all this happened simply because I wanted to be well informed and satisfy my curiosity! The day people really start getting curious and start wanting to find out how this province is run, there won't be any more Union Nationale in Quebec." Lévesque went on to attack the politics of Antonio Barrette.

As Minister of Labor, Mr. Barrette expressed his dissatisfaction with Mr. Duplessis' policies by going home to sulk like a little child, but he didn't forget to take his portfolio along with his bag of candies. Now the little boy who went home to sulk for a while has become the third leader of the party, and here he is harking back to his days as a worker. I remember the strike at Louiseville when the Honorable Mr. Barrette, in his capacity

146

as Minister of Labor, was acting as mediator. He promised that the strike would be settled and indeed it was — with pistol butts and billy-clubs. The Honorable Mr. Barrette has told the electorate, "I have not changed." He certainly hasn't — he's been stuck in the same groove for the last thirty-five years. [33]

On June 13, the Shawinigan Water and Power Company placed a full-page advertisement in the Quebec newspapers under the headline "Quebec supplies the world with asbestos." The advertisement concluded : "One more area in which hydro-electric power plays a leading role in our province." [34] Had this hydro-electric company seen the writing on the wall despite the fact that Lévesque had never once mentioned the possibility of nationalization ?

On the evening of June 14, the first big public rally for Lévesque was held in Montreal. The response was tremendous : more than 1500 people crowded into the basement beneath the church of Saint-Jean-de-la-Croix and listened until nearly midnight as he attacked the Union Nationale for over two hours. The audience was not disappointed ; Lévesque pulled out all the stops. This is how a journalist described it : "He was biting, sarcastic, cruel ; he belabored his opponents with sharp tirades and closely reasoned arguments, explaining in his own way the most complex social and political problems so that everyone could understand them." He reviewed the arguments he had developed elsewhere in Quebec, then summed up his position with the following words : "I am a Liberal candidate for three main reasons : first of all because the Union Nationale government is a bad government ; secondly, because the Liberal platform answers the needs of the people of Quebec ; and, finally, because I want to make sure the Liberal election promises are carried out." [35]

In a Quebec still haunted by the strikes in Asbestos, Louiseville, and Murdochville, it was a relief to hear a candidate declare himself a staunch defender of union interests. "Mr. Lévesque," continued the same journalist,

> dealt with the union question as no other politician has done before. He explained the meaning of the right of association, spoke of the need for both workers and employers to accept trade unions, and pointed out that, in Quebec, this right to organize is not respected. He described how he had gone to Schefferville five years ago and discovered that in order to get

in touch with local workers, a union organizer was forced to gain access to the restricted area by jumping from a plane. He remained in hiding during the day and only came out after nightfall to meet the workers in dark secluded corners of their camps so that they could build a union organization. [36]

The campaign Lévesque was conducting seemed to be bearing fruit for the Liberal Party, as *Le Devoir* concluded in an assessment which appeared less than a week before the election :

> Those who have followed Mr. Barrette around the province and those who, if only out of idle curiosity, have examined the Union Nationale propaganda, have been amazed at the determination with which speakers, publicity agents, and party plotters have tried to belittle, if not destroy, René Lévesque, the Liberal candidate in Laurier. For those who are amazed to hear the Premier attack René Lévesque in every one of his speeches, who read in the newspapers supported by the Union Nationale the insults and attacks hurled daily at René Lévesque, and who wonder why Lévesque has become the Union Nationale's *"point de mire"* [target], the answer is simple: they should go some evening and listen to Lévesque talk about provincial politics, the Union Nationale, and the Liberal platform, and they will see why the Union Nationale has to shoot down René Lévesque as soon as possible, because he is single-handedly going to bury them. René Lévesque is well known. He is influential. He is intelligent. He is a speaker who is convinced and convincing. On June 22, he will earn the Liberal Party tens of thousands of votes, not counting those he will win in his own riding of Laurier. Right now he is the most sought-after speaker in the party. Hordes of people crowd in together to hear him, sometimes listening religiously, sometimes according him thunderous applause. As one party worker put it, no one leaves the rally unconverted to the Liberal cause. These are the reasons behind Lévesque's magnetic appeal and the cause of the Union Nationale's despair. [37]

Georges-Emile Lapalme gives a similar account :

> In the 1960 campaign, he tore the Union Nationale apart from top to bottom. Jean Lesage acquitted himself well in the fight and I threw myself into it with as much enthusiasm as if I had been the leader of the party, but it was René Lévesque who really drew the crowds. The refreshing style of his speeches — vivid, anecdotal, full of literary gems — held his listeners

148

captive for hours. They came to see a celebrity and discovered a politician. Has a political party ever had such a star as a last-minute recruit ? He was one of the major contributors to our victory. [38]

On the eve of the big rally held for Lévesque in Montreal on June 14, an astonishing event took place in the riding of Montmorency. After fifteen years, René Lévesque's voice lost its huskiness and returned to normal. The newspapers reported the incident :

> Whether by a miracle or through natural causes, René Lévesque has recovered his voice, a pleasant and agreeable one at that. This is how Lévesque described the transformation : "On Monday evening I found myself in the riding of Montmorency, near Sainte-Anne-de-Beaupré, travelling in a convertible with my head uncovered. The next morning (did the good Saint Anne perform a miracle so that I could continue my campaign of purification ?), my voice had returned to normal." Mr. Barrette will now have to stop making remarks about Mr. Lévesque's thin, squeaky voice. It's a voice worth thousands of votes to the Liberal Party. [39]

The weekend of June 18-19 was the last weekend before election day and, true to form, the Union Nationale and the newspapers under its control launched an all-out personal attack on the Liberal candidate for Laurier. *Nouvelles Illustrées* wrote : "René Lévesque lacks dignity and behaves like the frog who takes himself for a bull." *Notre Temps* went further, referring to Lévesque as "a militant radical left-winger, an unbridled socialist who cannot disguise his tremendous admiration for Khrushchev and all that goes on in Soviet Russia." Alluding to a statement by Cardinal Alfredo Ottaviani to the effect that "the fellow-travellers will open the door for Anti-Christ," the paper continued :

> No, René Lévesque, the people of Quebec have no admiration for communist Russia nor the terrible dictatorships of the other Iron Curtain countries. We are not interested under any circumstances in having our people, from workers to scientists, trampled under the cruel boot of a merciless bureaucracy backed up by some frightful Gestapo. No, the Soviet "paradise" holds no attraction for us, and we are not impressed by their calculating actions and vile propaganda. Our healthy Christian upbringing has taught us to despise all forms of left-wing thought and radical socialism. We may only possess average

149

intelligence, but we find it ridiculous that some pretentious little nobody could come along and make the stupid, blasphemous claim that *Jesus Christ* was a *leftist,* the greatest *revolutionary,* indeed the *greatest leftist of all time.* * We're sorry, René, but there was nothing revolutionary about Christ. All he brought to this world were words of truth, goodness, peace, and charity. [40]

This method of attacking reformist opponents was part of a long Union Nationale tradition. As early as the 1930's, Duplessis pushed through the famous "padlock law," which forbade anyone from using his home for the propagation of bolshevism or communism. By defining "communist" in fairly wide-ranging terms, the Union Nationale was in a good position to identify any opponent who, backed by the international conspiracy, might attempt to lay his threatening hands on Quebec. Duplessis liked to be regarded as a defender of liberty and a guardian against this "insidious menace."

During this last weekend of the campaign, Antonio Barrette hit back at Lévesque. At a meeting in Saint-Jean d'Iberville for Paul Beaulieu he announced that "if Mr. René Lévesque goes back to the CBC after losing his deposit as the Liberal candidate in Laurier, the province of Quebec will take steps to set up its own broadcasting network. [...] We will not allow a self-styled intellectual to spend his time denigrating and slandering the leaders of this province." With specific regard to journalists, Mr. Barrette promised that, after June 22, "every time a journalist makes an accusation against one of our public leaders he will have to prove his accusations. He will have to prove them and explain where he obtained his information. If he does not prove his accusations, he will have to make an apology." [41]

Meanwhile Lesage was winding up his campaign with visits to Chicoutimi, Saint-Hyacinthe, and Shawinigan. He spoke at half a dozen rallies and gave numerous radio talks. At Saint-Hyacinthe he sharply criticized the Union Nationale's publicity campaign and also attacked Robert Rumilly :

Then we have the campaign against "creeping socialism." They've brought in this outsider Rumilly, † a viper we've nurtur-

---

* This refers to the speech given by Lévesque to the North Montreal Businessmen's Association on November 3, 1959. [Author's note.] See p. 123.

† Rumilly was born in France where he was active in right-wing political movements during the thirties.

ed at our breast a little too long, who now turns on French Canadians and poisons their opinions. So he wants people to believe that we Liberals despise the Catholic religion does he ? Mr. Rumilly, go back where you came from — you've got nothing to say to us. If you claim that the Church has condemned free education, you're a bald-faced liar. I was a member of the Saint-Laurent cabinet and I was Minister of Northern Affairs and in that capacity I had schools built in the North — Catholic federal schools. I was in charge of an area where Catholics were in a minority and I was a cabinet minister in the government of a country which is predominantly non-Catholic. And yet they would have people believe that a government under my leadership would pose a threat to religion ? What a bunch of hypocrites ! *Operation Mud-slinging* is the name for their campaign. They have tried to destroy the reputation of one of the most respected men in the province, Mr. René Lévesque. They parade Claude-Henri Grignon before your eyes because he claims to have broken away from the Liberal Party. He couldn't have broken away from the Liberal Party because he never belonged to it. In 1930, he turned Conservative and voted for Bennett's Tory régime. The Liberal Party favors neither the left nor the right. Like the prow of a ship, it is the centre which points the way for both sides and its goal is progress for the province of Quebec. Fear is what's behind all these last-minute Union Nationale machinations. Fear has changed sides in this campaign : they're the ones who are scared to death now. [42]

With the election imminent, René Lévesque gave this advice to the voters of Montreal-Laurier : "Every citizen must make an effort to insure that tampering with the votes next Wednesday is minimized." He urged all citizens to vote and warned them to refuse any money they might be offered in an attempt to buy their votes or otherwise influence their choice. He also advised them how to handle manoeuvres such as the nomination of another Lévesque on the Laurier ballot :

> To counter these dishonest tactics, the voters must find out just who their candidates are. The residents of Montreal-Laurier, for example, should remember that if they want to avoid playing into the hands of those who have engineered this dirty trick and cast their vote for the Liberal candidate, they must vote for René Lévesque the journalist and not the Lévesque who calls himself a "performer." [43]

151

These words of advice to the voters about keeping a watchful eye on the Union Nationale were delivered at a rally held on June 19 in the Notre-Dame-du-Rosaire parish hall in Montreal.

Lévesque · had good reason to be concerned, since the Union Nationale was turning to physical intimidation as a last resort. *Le Devoir* wrote :

> The Union Nationale's determination to beat René Lévesque knows no bounds. As if their pronouncements, their publicity handouts, and all their other gimmicks were not enough, they have now decided to bring in the goon squad. Over the week-end, a car belonging to Mr. Laurent Kochenburger, one of the Liberal organizers in Laurier, was damaged while parked opposite 7319 Boyer Street. In addition, a mail box at the corner of Jean-Talon and Saint-Hubert, a few steps from Mr. Lévesque's headquarters, was set on fire in what seems to have been an attempt to destroy election publicity being sent through the mail to the local voters. But that's not all. Also on the weekend, several unidentified persons telephoned Mr. Eugène Tanguay, chief returning officer for Montreal-Laurier, and demanded that he *sell* them ballot forms. When he replied that he was a man of principle and had no intentions whatsoever of being a party to such dealings, the callers warned him that they were going to carry out a raid on his home. "That way your conscience will be clear," they added. And in fact there was a break-in Sunday at Mr. Tanguay's residence, but the thieves were thwarted by swift intervention on the part of the police. Mr. Tanguay had taken the precaution of alerting them following the telephone call he had received earlier. [44]

But the Liberals were carrying the fight to the Union Nationale, who had been on the defensive ever since Lesage opened the campaign at Louiseville on May 8. The change of climate described by Lapalme was working in the Liberals' favor and they had managed to keep the Duplessis machine constantly on the run. On June 20, Lesage, Lapalme, and Lévesque — or the three "L's" as they were known in the Liberal publicity in opposition to the Union Nationale's three "B's" (Barrette, Bellemare, and Bégin) — all took the stage together in Montreal. *Le Devoir* described the scene :

> The *Palais du Commerce* was full to bursting. There was a sea of people stretching from the rostrum to the very back of the hall where the crowd disappeared behind clouds of smoke.

Even more people stood outside. The police estimated the crowd at roughly 25,000. Berri Street was completely closed to traffic between Montigny and Ontario streets. The three main speakers all received long ovations, and a good ten minutes elapsed after the Liberal leader was introduced to the crowd before he was able to begin speaking. [45]

Lesage's associates had been afraid that he might be too exhausted to finish off the campaign, but he was in top form that evening. Rounds of applause punctuated his inspired oratory.

> Never before has a people been so determined to achieve liberation. Tonight's demonstration foreshadows the great cry of relief which will be heard everywhere next Wednesday evening. We are not only ready for this liberation but also for the new order which will begin on the morning of June 23. With this goal in mind we have a comprehensive program of government prepared by a group of men who have studied all the problems within this province's jurisdiction and who have made dynamic proposals which will put Quebec back in front where she belongs. Look at the wonderful team seated around me here ready to carry out this program. Consider their experience, their qualifications, their enthusiasm. With your help, all of us together can start this province on the road to justice, prosperity, and progress.

Then Lévesque stepped forward to praise the Liberal Party and its leaders :

> If I could be sure I'd always have an audience like this one, I wouldn't have to go on television any more and Mr. Barrette would be happy again ! I am particularly proud to be associated with the two most accomplished and magnanimous politicians I have ever known, Mr. Lesage and Mr. Lapalme. To Mr. Godbout we owe the two greatest achievements of the last quarter century — female suffrage and Hydro-Quebec. Now Mr. Lesage and Mr. Lapalme are going to bring us another generation of progress. The Liberal Party offers us the means to build a Quebec whose destiny we can control. The Liberal Federation offers us the means each year to put the government's accomplishments on trial. The Liberal Party treats us like responsible men and women. The worn-out, corrupt government that we have now treats the people of Quebec with contempt and lies to their faces. It claims to be the party of the working man and talks about its blue-collar sympathies, but

the truth of the matter is that 25 years ago it abandoned the workers to the clubs of the provincial police. [46]

The pundits were impressed by the success of this huge rally and many placed their money on the Liberals to win. Meanwhile, the Union Nationale, which a week earlier had counted on 75 of the 95 seats, was now talking about winning 56.

On June 21, the day before the election, Gérard Filion, the publisher of *Le Devoir,* faithfully carried out a long-standing election tradition. At the end of every campaign this Montreal daily tries to separate the wheat from the chaff by outlining and endorsing the particular virtues of certain candidates and the policies they represent. In his editorial entitled "Do we need a change ?" Filion did not severely criticize the Union Nationale ; nevertheless he concluded :

> Should our support of the Opposition go so far as to replace the Government ? We cannot see why not. After all, sixteen years in power is enough and in the case of the Union Nationale it is perhaps too much. When the Liberals held power in Ottawa for twenty-one years they became arrogant and autocratic. Man for man, the government of John Diefenbaker cannot hold a candle to that of Louis Saint-Laurent. Yet the change of leadership had its good effects, particularly in showing the Liberals that they did not hold a permanent mortgage on the government of this country. It's now time for the voters of Quebec to drive the same message home to the Union Nationale. Parliamentary democracy draws its strength from the delicate balance between government and opposition and each party must have its turn in power. In Quebec, after sixteen years of uninterrupted government by one party, it's time for a change. [47]

Filion's support was unequivocal : his final words echoed the Liberal campaign slogan, "It's Time for a Change."

Robert Rumilly did not share Filion's opinion. Just hours before the polls opened, a leaflet signed by Rumilly was distributed among Quebec's churchmen. *Le Devoir* reported the incident :

> On the very eve of the election, the Union Nationale's propaganda campaign has once again focussed on the clergy of the province, who were all sent a leaflet penned by Robert Rumilly entitled *A Hotbed of Leftists.* In this leaflet, printed in a blue type-face, the celebrated (!) historian of the late Mr. Duplessis vigorously attacks the "instigator," the "publicist," and the

154

"prime candidate" of the provincial Liberal Party, namely Jacques Hébert, Jean-Louis Gagnon, and René Lévesque. He denounces what he calls their sympathies for — not to say connections with — communism and Soviet Russia. The leaflet is accompanied by a 30-page pamphlet discussing left-wing tendencies within the Liberal Party. Needless to say, the author of the pamphlet is also Mr. Rumilly. [48]

The Union Nationale were obviously determined to employ desperate measures until the bitter end.

But it was June 22 : the bets had been made and the politicians were silent after fifty-five days of delivering their messages to the people. It was up to the 2,500,000 voters throughout Quebec's 95 ridings to make their will known. The Union Nationale's campaign had been waged in the traditional style — would they try some of their old tricks on election day too ? Would they again engage in "a vast conspiracy designed to suppress freedom and buy the silence of the people" ? These are the terms in which Jean and Marcel Hamelin have described the age-old electoral tactics employed to maintain a party in power when used on a large scale. "The usual methods — strong-arm persuasion, tampering with the voters' lists, substituting certain people to vote for others, false ballots — were used in urban ridings, and any riding where a defeat would have had province-wide repercussions." [49] On June 22, 1960, most of Quebec was spared these traditional practices.

But it was a long day in the riding of Montreal-Laurier because this was an urban riding where a Liberal defeat would have far-reaching implications. Early in the day, some twenty polling stations received a visit from five thugs who pushed around the voting officials, then locked them all into rooms beside the polling booths so that they could stuff the ballot boxes without interference. All day long goon squads patrolled the riding to intimidate anyone they suspected of having Liberal sympathies. Around 5:30, representatives of the "other" René Lévesque visited a large number of polling stations with credentials allegedly authorizing them to replace the representatives of the official Liberal candidate. Finally, a large number of counterfeit ballots already marked in favor of the Union Nationale candidate were seized in the riding. These counterfeit ballots, as it turned out, were also used in a number of other Montreal ridings. Le Devoir concluded that it was 1956 all over again and that criminal activity was rampant in Laurier.

155

Historians Jean and Marcel Hamelin classed the election incidents in that riding with the worst excesses of the 1850's.

It looked as if Laurier could go either way. When the polling stations closed at 6:30 pm, early projections showed that the election overall was being hotly contested. In Laurier, the lead changed hands each time a new result came in. Paul Earl, the Liberal for Montreal-Notre-Dame-de-Grâce, was the first member to be elected. William Cottingham, Minister of Mines, re-elected. Paul Beaulieu, Minister of Industry and Commerce, defeated in Saint-Jean. Antonio Barrette, re-elected. Wilfrid Labbé, UN, defeated. Georges-Emile Lapalme, re-elected. Jean Lesage, elected. Johnny Bourque, Minister of Finance, defeated. Paul Dozois, re-elected. Antoine Rivard and Joseph-Damase Bégin, in difficulty. Yves Prévost, Provincial Secretary, re-elected. Armand Maltais, re-elected.

At 9:30 p m, René Lévesque — the "real" René Lévesque — was declared the winner in Laurier, but only by the skin of his teeth, as he later pointed out. Officially he received 14,015 votes to 13,878 for his Union Nationale opponent. But if it had not been for the "false" René Lévesque, who received 910 votes, Lévesque's 137-vote majority probably would have been greater. His real majority was also reduced by the fraudulent voting procedures used against him. The day after the election it was estimated that 5000 illegal ballots marked in favor of the Union Nationale candidate had been cast.

At the moment Lévesque's election was announced, the battle between the two parties was at its height. The Union Nationale had elected 25 members, the Liberals 24, and one independent had managed to slip in between them. The 45 seats left undecided would make all the difference. Gérard Filion wrote that, whatever the outcome of the election, it was the end of the political era dominated by Duplessis :

> Politics in this province will never be the same in the years to come. The new era that began with Mr. Sauvé will continue to unfold. The methods of the Duplessis régime, which for a generation paid handsome dividends, have been completely discredited. The people of Quebec will no longer allow themselves to be pushed around as they have been since 1944. Mr. Lesage knew how to take full advantage of the situation and during the campaign displayed remarkable energy and keen political insight. He made no errors of judgment, no regrettable pronouncements. Whether it happens next week or next year,

obviously he will be next Premier of the province of Quebec. [50]

Lesage did not have to wait that long : he became Premier of Quebec on the evening of June 22. At 11:00 p m, it was announced that the Liberal Party had won the election with 51 seats to 43 for the Union Nationale.

> This was perhaps one of the closest elections in the history of Quebec politics : 61 of the candidates elected had majorities of less than 10 per cent, and 34 had less than 5 per cent. One unexpected and significant aspect of the vote was that the winning party had an urban power base. Although the Liberals took only 28 of the 58 rural seats, they captured 23 of the 37 urban seats. This was the first time that a party drawing most of its support from urban centres had taken power in Quebec, with the possible exception of the 1939 election when the Liberals had also relied on urban majorities. [51]

The television coverage that evening showed the Liberal Party in its glory. Lesage cried out to his supporters in Quebec City, "Ladies and gentlemen, we have unmasked and destroyed the devil's hideous machinery." René Lévesque, long awaited by many viewers that evening, made a very brief appearance. He said in his newly-found voice :

> It appears that in spite of all the threats and the intimidating power wielded by this régime, there were a lot of people in the province who were just fed up. First of all we must eliminate the kind of dirty voting tactics that we saw today. I watched officers of the Provincial Police actually leading thugs in groups of six into the polling stations. I would like to thank all those who voted for me and I hope I will live up to their expectations. Finally, let me add that I am very happy to be here this evening doing a program for the CBC. [52]

Lévesque's election to office completed the major change that had taken place in his life since the CBC producers' strike. According to commentator Gérard Bergeron, Lévesque was unique in two ways : "(1) As a result of his career in journalism, he is one of the few people whose cosmopolitanism has actually been acquired outside Quebec ; (2) he was the first and only person of that particular ideological bent to make the big leap and join an old party. This fact is all the more remarkable considering that his ideological beliefs were as deeply rooted as those of the men who entered politics later on or even held back until the present day." [53]

157

It is worth noting as well that his decision to join a provincial rather than a federal party was a clear indication of the relative importance he attached to the two levels of government.

The day after the election, a rumor began to circulate that Lévesque would be named Secretary of the province and head a new ministry of cultural affairs. On July 5, Lesage announced his cabinet appointments. His right-hand man, Georges-Emile Lapalme, became Attorney General. The rumor about Lévesque turned out to be false : he was given the portfolio of Hydraulic Resources and Public Works. Paul Gérin-Lajoie was named to the Ministry of Youth, Bona Arsenault to Lands and Forests, Gérard-D. Lévesque to Fishing and Hunting, Lionel Bertrand to the provincial Secretariat, Bernard Pinard to Highways, Paul Earl to Mines, René Hamel to Labor and Municipal Affairs, Alcide Courcy to Agriculture and Colonization, Gérard Cournoyer to Transport and Communications, Emilien Lafrance to Welfare, J.-Alphonse Couturier to Health, and André Rousseau to Industry and Commerce. C.-A. Kirkland was named Secretary of State.

Journalist Jean O'Neil described the swearing-in ceremony :

> The lovely ladies suddenly stopped their whispering and rustling. Jean Lesage appeared and lined up his colleagues. A short man could be seen in fifth place behind Lesage, Lapalme, Hamel, and Gérin-Lajoie. All the others were in formal attire, but he was satisfied to appear in a very plain, dark blue suit with trousers short enough to reveal a pair of baby-blue socks. To tell the truth, René Lévesque looked a little out of place. He waited, hands fidgeting, nervously shifting his weight from one foot to the other. His colleagues held their heads high, throwing smiles of greeting right and left to the assembled wives. When all the ministers had been sworn in and all the speakers had said their piece, there was a flurry of handshaking and congratulations. Lévesque disappeared in the confusion, and was probably greatly relieved to have escaped so easily. You knew then that Lévesque's position in the Cabinet would be the same as that of our province in Confederation — different from the rest. [54]

There was never in fact any possibility that Lévesque might be Secretary of the province and Minister of Cultural Affairs. Everything was decided on June 24 in Saint-Jovite, north of Montreal. The day before, he had received a call from Lapalme. "When I became a candidate," Lévesque explained,

I had told Lesage that I was particularly interested in one thing — natural resources. But there was no question then of a cabinet post. I had also told him that there were certain things in the program concerning natural resources I didn't like. I had some disturbing memories of the Gaspé which made me feel that the program was too vague on the subject of electricity. I let Lesage know I would soon come back to that part of the program. Lesage was still pretty flexible at that point, as you would expect before an election, so he told me : "OK, we'll talk about it." On June 22, I was elected by the skin of my teeth and soon afterwards I got a phone call from Lapalme. Lesage had put him in charge of the Montreal area while he went off to Saint-Jovite to do some thinking. Lapalme called me and said : "Lesage is expecting you tomorrow morning at Saint-Jovite. It's a nice spot, etc." I asked him, "What does he want ?" Lapalme replied, "He's in the middle of putting together the cabinet and apparently he wants you in it." That was the first time I had heard about such a possibility — there had been no previous discussion whatsoever, either specifically or in general terms. I said to Lapalme, "Fine, in that case I guess I'd better go." He said to me, "Yes, you'd better ; there have been lots of phone calls from others who want to go, but Lesage specifically asked that you go up to see him. Maybe it's because you didn't ask. Hurry on up there." So I went, and it turned out that Lesage had latched on to the idea that I should look after Hydraulic Resources. He also asked me to take over Public Works but only for a transitional period long enough to allow him to get the government functioning. [55]

By placing Lévesque in charge of Public Works, the new premier was acknowledging the confidence he had in his colleague. The main source of patronage under the old government, Public Works was in need of a good housecleaning. Lesage himself, as Premier and Minister of Finance, was overburdened with work. Lévesque therefore had to act as caretaker for Public Works while the Salvas inquiry, named after the presiding judge, examined the dealings of the previous administration. As far as Hydraulic Resources was concerned, Lévesque considered Hydro-Quebec the most important and interesting part of the portfolio. As he said, "It is the only thing that really belongs to us." [56]

The Liberal team set to work immediately in a flurry of activity. On August 6, *Le Devoir* wrote : "Though it may not be a matter of much concern to most people, this has been an exhausting month

159

for journalists. Not only the Premier but also most of his cabinet have had a lot of news to tell us. Press conferences have been so frequent that occasionally two have been called at the same time." Lapalme wrote : "The change-over was quick and decisive. Few protests were raised in that atmosphere of joyful discovery, except by those who were afraid that the new light shed on their affairs would cast them into political obscurity." [57] Under the old administration only builders who were friends of the régime obtained government contracts and the Union Nationale treasurer went so far as to hand out millions in public funds on all sides. But in July 1960, for the first time in sixteen years, the Liberal government called for public tenders on provincial works projects. Paul Gérin-Lajoie asked for tenders on the construction of the Teachers' College in Three Rivers, as did Lévesque on the bridge at Shawinigan.

The Liberals had to close out the fiscal year according to the budget inherited from the Union Nationale, but they tried to save funds where they could. Projects begun on contracts signed before the elections were stopped whenever possible and tenders called for. Lévesque stressed that the government stood to save a vast amount of money by proceeding on the basis of tenders : "He said that under the old régime contracts were granted before plans were even finished and that most of these contracts were based on the 'cost plus' formula. For those unfamiliar with the phrase, it simply means that the more a project costs, the more profitable it is for the contractor because he is given a percentage of the total cost. This method certainly does not encourage economy." [58]

Although Lévesque's mind was concentrating on Public Works, his heart was more concerned with Hydraulic Resources. But this was far from the most important ministry in the Quebec government. "Hydraulic Resources," explained Lévesque,

> was a tiny ministry of little importance at that point because there was nothing much to be looked after except a few problems relating to drainage, waterways, grants, and that kind of thing. But there was one other big task and that was to assume political responsibility for Hydro-Quebec, where I soon found myself up to my neck in work. Then our key man, Michel Bélanger, arrived. He was an economist : up to that point the ministry had never had one.

The arrival of men like Bélanger was vital to the Quebec government. As Lévesque said, it was necessary to find some "prime movers" who held important positions in private enterprise and attract them to the public service, because you cannot stop the business of government just to go back to school. It's a little like a motorist who learns how to drive at sixty miles an hour knowing that the political machine under him is an old heap. In other words, the mechanics have to do their repairs while the vehicle is in motion. [59]

Later, after he had gained some experience, Lévesque expanded this statement. There is no doubt that without the help of certain senior civil servants in the Quebec government, many of the Lesage administration's projects would never have been completed. In 1960, Lévesque admitted : "We are apprentice ministers." Eleven years later he said :

By 1960, the Union Nationale had been in power for sixteen years. The first thing we realized, of course, was that we were all completely inexperienced in matters of government. After sixteen years, there aren't likely to be very many experienced men left among the opposition. Strangely enough, in fact, out of the whole cabinet the only person who had ever run a ministry was Lesage himself, when he was in Ottawa. But because that had been at the federal level, even he had to make adjustments to a new environment and new methods. As for the rest of us, we had to start completely from scratch ! There wasn't a soul among us with any previous experience. We weren't even sure where to find our offices and hang our hats. But perhaps the most important consideration in my case — everyone has their own way of doing things — was that I was a journalist and therefore a non-specialist. A journalist is by definition a jack-of-all-trades — you know a little bit about a lot of subjects, but you don't know very much about any single one of them. So the first thing that happened — and this saved my life, or at least gave me a chance insofar as it allowed me to function properly — was that I realized — I was in Public Works for a year at that point so my connections to Hydro were actually through another ministry — that I wasn't an economist, an engineer, or an architect, and therefore I wasn't professionally equipped to deal with the problems that would come my way. I got together as quickly as possible the best team I could find, which meant stealing a couple of guys from Ottawa, particularly Michel Bélanger, who, as it happened, was the first professional economist to work for the Quebec government. In other words, we managed to scrape

161

through by building up a team as quickly as the situation at Hydro allowed, a new team of men who were ready to come up with reforms or at least take a fresh look at things. That is what saved me — getting together a team of competent people as fast as possible who would be easy to work with and who knew the problems. [60]

The team running Hydraulic Resources developed a program which was made public by the minister on October 18, 1960. It was based on "making all the citizens of Quebec shareholders in the development of the vast natural resources at their disposal through Hydro-Quebec." The program foresaw the creation of a ministry of natural resources during the next session, the development of these resources, government aid for the establishment of new industries in this sector, the hiring of Québécois at all administrative and technical levels, the creation of a mining institute, the granting of all undeveloped hydro resources to Hydro-Quebec, and the turning over to Hydro of the natural gas network sold by the Union Nationale to private interests. "It's not much ; it's only a beginning," said the minister. "But this beginning will allow us to gather information on which to base a new policy whose aim will be to put Québécois in charge of their province and to ensure them a role in the development of these resources." [61]

In this same speech, delivered at the closing dinner of the seventeenth plenary congress of provincial mining ministers, Lévesque, speaking in his usual picturesque style, compared Quebec to a ten-year-old boy, "who is going to feel very frustrated if he keeps being turned down by the neighborhood football team. Even though he has stepped right onto the field equipped with his oversized helmet, they seem to consider him too delicate. And if they do decide to take him on as a second stringer, he will still not get a chance to play." [62]

Lévesque continued to take advantage of every speaking opportunity offered him. He shared his thoughts with the people of Quebec and kept them informed on what was going on in the province. But some of his colleagues, not only ministers but backbenchers as well, were not too pleased with this, as Lapalme explains in his memoirs :

> There is something about a celebrity that annoys people, even though they may not be exactly jealous. When I was a celebrity (if you could have called me that), my all-too-obvious dis-

162

pleasure with certain glaring abuses and well-known public figures earned me some sharp criticism. René Lévesque's every move, however insignificant, was followed closely on television and radio. Beneath that modest exterior, which could have been either calculated or quite spontaneous, he seemed to glory in the attention heaped on him every day. What made us think so was the fact that he always accepted every invitation to lead a discussion or give a lecture. I remember somebody making us all laugh by remarking, "All it takes is an invitation from forty old tarts in Beauce or Abitibi and he'll drop whatever is going on in parliament !"[63]

While it is easy to understand such an attitude, there are other possible reasons for Lévesque's behavior. First of all, he often had more respect for the "old tarts" than for the party workers. Perhaps it was also his way of sounding out the electorate and legitimizing his mandate between elections. In many ways it was simply a case of his wanting to make a new voice heard. After the long silent years of the Duplessis régime, Lévesque was among the first to create an atmosphere of open discussion in Quebec — naming something is a good way of exorcising it. Finally, his urge to speak on every possible occasion may have been a matter of professional habit since he had spent fifteen years analyzing and commenting on national and international politics.

The author had noted this tendency of Lévesque's before Lapalme's remarks were in print and questioned him about it : "I have the impression that while you were in power you communicated with the public through the press more than anyone else. The journalists claim you also had the highest rate of absenteeism from the Assembly. I realized in the end that it would be possible to write a biography of René Lévesque based on nothing but newspaper reports. I'm not saying you didn't put forward some good proposals in the Assembly, but how would you explain your attitude — your apparent lack of interest in parliamentary procedure and your preference for speaking through the various media ?" Lévesque replied :

I think you're right about the highest rate of absenteeism while I was in the government. But when it came to discharging my responsibilities in the House, whether it was a budget debate or discussion on a bill that concerned me, I had to have my brief ready and be there to present it. And I was. But I believe that parliament itself, which in the British system is built along party lines, is becoming discredited, as some have remarked, or worse, is losing its purpose. The members themselves often feel that the important things are happening elsewhere. The cabinet and its technical advisors make all the important decisions and any government that really wants to, can virtually eliminate serious debate from parliament if it has complete control over its *backbenchers.* * The ministers are only in the House long enough to tell the other members to keep quiet. There is nothing worse than playing *backbencher* to a bunch of ministers — you practically have to get permission to go and pee. This very quickly takes away from parliament its atmosphere of urgent necessity. It's true that I wasn't particularly interested in parliamentary free-for-alls except when I had to be. On the other hand, partly because of ingrained professional habit and partly because I never feel comfortable in a closed environment, I went out to sort of renew myself by talking to people. Sometimes there were journalists present, who reported what happened. Since I was a journalist myself, maybe I knew more than other people just how far I could go with them. You'll find reports here and there about these lectures and meetings because I liked doing that kind of thing, that's all. I found you could keep in better touch with the things that affected your ministry by going out to see people and getting their reactions than by spending all your time with the élite gang that hangs around parliament. But that's just my personal opinion. [64]

In any event, soon after the election Lévesque was seeking the active support of people entirely unconnected with the government because certain Liberal businessmen who had been "doing penance for sixteen years" were now eager to ingratiate themselves with the new administration. On November 2, he asked the Liberals of Quebec-East to support the government in its fight against patronage. Though few of the other ministers or deputies were expressing any concern, Lévesque observed that since June 22 there had been a veritable flood of demands on the government from certain Liberal supporters: "If our leaders do not exercise some restraint, then this will become a government of privilege and favoritism fed on by parasites, and our party will be in danger of becoming another Union Nationale." He then broached a subject which was as touchy for the Liberals as it was for the Union Nationale — the question of

---

* In English in the original.

campaign contributions. Under the traditional system, Lévesque explained, the government is indebted to any dubious financial interests which happen to have filled its campaign coffers. "Then it is not the government that rules but those who have bankrolled it." He accordingly proposed that campaign expenses be paid for from public funds.

Despite the fact that the Liberal Party was now in power, conservative forces were still very strong in Quebec, as the Minister of Public Works, who continued to seek broad support for the government, could testify. He discussed this conservatism more openly before an audience of three hundred young people in Drummondville : "Pressures intended to serve private interests which run against the grain of our policies are regularly brought to bear on various ministers. We want to see the balance righted and you can help us do that." [65] Lévesque was no doubt alluding to a problem which Lapalme later made more explicit :

> Being in power was a very disappointing experience for me in every way. First of all the Liberals had been in opposition for such a long time. You wouldn't believe what a can of worms we had to contend with — it would take a book to describe it. There were people who told you while you were in opposition that they'd fight beside you on your behalf for the sake of certain principles and as soon as you got into power asked for half the province of Quebec. It really made me sick. [66]

During the first session Lévesque spoke frequently in support of the government's policies — hospital insurance, income tax reform, measures to be taken by his own ministry, etc. Daniel Johnson, the Union Nationale member for Bagot, was his most vocal adversary. He harassed Lévesque constantly, and their exchanges were lively. For example, Johnson expressed his dislike for the royal commission investigating the Union Nationale's administration, which began work on October 5, 1960. Lévesque responded by enumerating blatant cases of favoritism. Johnson accused the Minister of Public Works of being "the gravedigger of the denominational school." Lévesque replied that Johnson was "the most sick-making person" he had ever known in public life. Many of their exchanges were never accurately recorded because transcripts of the Assembly debates were not yet being made.

In January 1961, the Liberal government submitted a bill to parliament proposing the creation of a ministry of natural resources through the amalgamation of two other ministries, Mines and Hydraulic Resources. This was the first proposal put forward after months of thought on the part of the new team brought together in Hydraulic Resources by Lévesque, who was the bill's sponsor in the Assembly. He took this opportunity to promote a line of political thinking which gave priority to Quebec's interests. Though he stopped short of calling the federal structure into question, he nevertheless proposed that Quebec take full advantage of whatever possibilities Confederation offered. He said that the people of Quebec had only one tool they could really call their own — the provincial government. He reproached the Union Nationale for having turned the government into "a kind of bogey man which made people afraid of their own shadows" and added : "As French Canadians we must look upon our government as something precious because we are a minority nation. French Canadians must use their government to help abolish their subservient status." Referring to a remark made by the member from Maisonneuve, Lucien Tremblay, to the effect that the Americans were not about to demolish their steel mills in Pittsburgh in order to come and start all over again in Quebec, Lévesque continued :

> This kind of thinking suggests that we have always got the short end of the stick and, if we're to believe the Union Nationale, that we always will. Why, for a start, don't we think in terms of supplying our own market ? The province of Quebec buys millions of tons of iron each year : why does it always have to come from outside the province ? This is how the opposition sidesteps one of the most agonizing problems facing French Canadians today — by taking the easy way out.

The Liberal minister had some harsh words for Maurice Duplessis. Recalling that Gérard Thibault, Union Nationale member for Mercier, had remarked that two portfolios were too much for one man, Lévesque replied by asking if he had forgotten that there was a time when one man, in the Union Nationale's opinion the greatest man in Quebec history, ruled every aspect of their lives year in and year out on the basis of his personal preferences, while not one of those who praised him so highly today had dared disagree with him or even discuss his orders. Lévesque added :

> While we wait for the definitive judgment of history on this historic genius, we may be permitted a provisional judgment, not of the man but of the way in which he dealt unilaterally

with matters affecting us all, without the possibility of any discussion, not even within the Union Nationale. [...] The province of Quebec was left for much too long in the hands of a little lawyer brought up in the '90s, with whom no one dared discuss anything and whose orders no one dared contravene.

Returning to the arguments of Tremblay and Thibault, he said : "There you have an example of the extent to which all members of the Union Nationale have been affected by what went on when the province was run by the greatest dictator it has ever known." He ended his speech by quoting a statement made by General de Gaulle in April 1960, while he was visiting Montreal : "It is time French Canadians enjoyed full citizenship." [67] On February 22, the law creating Quebec's Ministry of Natural Resources received royal assent.

After restructuring Natural Resources, the Liberal government created on March 24 the Ministry of Federal-Provincial Affairs whose purpose was to promote full development of provincial autonomy as well as intergovernmental co-operation. On the same day, the Ministry of Cultural Affairs came into being. This general reorganization also established the Office of the French Language and the Arts Council. On March 3, Lévesque was called upon to speak in the House in support of the bill creating the Ministry of Cultural Affairs and he took advantage of the occasion to announce that in future all contracts issued by his ministry would be drawn up in French. The first budget proposed for Cultural Affairs was minimal, as Lévesque himself admitted ; he even called it a "symbolic budget." But he added : "Before a budget can be voted on, priorities must be established, those in charge of the ministry must find their feet, and operational procedures must be set in motion." [68] During the debate on the new Ministry of Natural Resources, Lévesque had already stressed the importance of exploiting the possibilities offered by Confederation to their fullest extent. A month later, in the course of the debate on the Cultural Affairs bill, he reiterated this idea : "The best way to guarantee real autonomy is to move right into those areas over which Canada's constitution has given Quebec jurisdiction."

Lévesque's observations were not always partisan. From time to time he would step back into the role of analyst and offer objective political commentary, a new approach for a Quebec politician. On March 5, for example, during a televised press conference in which there were four student participants, he pointed out that our established political parties are not ideological rallying points, as in Europe, but rather conglomerations flexible enough to accommodate many different points of view. He also reiterated one of his favorite ideas, namely, that all citizens deserve to be kept as well informed as possible : "Government has a duty to inform public opinion and explain clearly the reasons for its decisions. A government has no right to use force when applying its policies."

The budget of April 1961, the first the Liberals could really call their own, included a tax increase which Lesage, as Minister of Finance, was called upon to justify. But Lévesque typically wanted to explain the reason for the increase himself : "Asking the taxpayers for more money," he said, "is not the easiest way to win popularity." This was especially true since the Union Nationale had often managed to accumulate budget surpluses. The new Minister of Natural Resources continued :

> However, we were elected to solve the problems facing us today. We have been left with an incredible legacy of old debts that have to be paid off now. To do this we must ask the citizens of Quebec for their help because it is important that we balance the books without creating undue hardship. The simpletons in the Union Nationale reduced the debt by adhering to a backward kind of peasant economics more suited to the Middle Ages. The result of the Union Nationale's lower spending was to cripple the province severely in all respects. It is now a relief to work in the atmosphere of debate introduced by the Liberals. Things change in time, and our new approach to the budget is no exception. As for the money spent on education, we have no choice because Quebec will fall apart at the seams if we keep trailing behind the rest of the country in this field. [69]

Education was a theme Lévesque returned to many times in the next few years.

During 1961, he continued to make his mark as a unique political figure. At a screening and public debate organized by the Citizens League of Saint-Jean, he was asked if it was possible for a politician to remain honest. He believed it was, given that eight conditions were fulfilled. In the first place, a politician must not accept any money other than his salary and expense allowances. He must avoid direct or indirect involvement in any firm that does

168

business with the government. In return, he must insist on adequate remuneration for his work, "to avoid temptation." Lévesque also recommended that a politician keep an eye on his associates and ignore rumors and gossip. If he discovers someone untrustworthy among those close to him, he must sever the connection immediately before trouble starts. A politician must recognize that the public has an absolute right to know how the country is being administered. He must take all criticism, even the most severe, into account and sift out what is valid from what is not. He must encourage the free exchange of ideas, including those he may not like. "Only inert matter is static ; where there's life, there's movement. A public figure who stands in the way of the free flow of ideas and opinions paralyzes the life of the community and betrays his mission." Finally, the politician must not be afraid to exercise leadership : "He must not be a feather to every wind." [70]

Lévesque had much more to say ; he was becoming an iconoclast bent on shaking up the old order. On Saint-Jean-Baptiste Day he said :

> Only a nation of robots or sheep adheres slavishly to the ways of the past. A nation needs its misfits, its rowdies, its grumblers, its visionaries, and, at times, its rebels. Some people are frightened by the very thought of this new road we are all about to take. Some people are just naturally afraid of change, of the vertigo that accompanies innovation, because for a while the ground seems to give out from under their feet and they are no longer certain of their destination. [71]

Since the conquest of space and the stirrings of student protest had just begun, these words were bound to be favorably received by the youth of Quebec, whose only memory of Maurice Duplessis was that of a kind father handing out dimes to his children. From then on, they showed great interest in and sympathy with the evolution of this new Quebec politician.

Lévesque's public statements that year touched on both political and economic questions. Politically speaking, he noted, the people of Quebec were living under the yoke of colonialism. There was a pressing need, therefore, to "realize our destiny through the exercise of intelligence and expertise and not through the revenge of the cradle." Because Quebec was short of competent men, Lévesque felt that opposition to universal education could only come from the rich man concerned about whether there would be anyone left to mow his lawn. [72] Better education would perhaps help eradicate the worst enemy of progress — fear. "We must stop being afraid of thinking, speaking, and saying what we think. We must assert ourselves and realize our potential." [73]

While education can allow the individual to free himself from this yoke, a government can allow an entire nation to do the same. Lévesque believed that there was no turning back for the Liberals, because their program had committed the party to setting this process of liberation in motion : "We must not forget that we are part of the western world, engaged in a vast ideological, political, economic, and social conflict and that the stakes involve global domination and our very survival as a civilization. It is more important than ever that we take care not to lull ourselves into a state of apathy with false ideas." [74] Clearly it was "unthinkable that 95 per cent of the population of Quebec should control only 10 per cent of the economy." [75] In October 1961, Lévesque announced to students of the University of Montreal that in the next session the government would introduce a bill proposing the creation of a general investment corporation, one of whose first projects would be the financing of an iron and steel complex located in Quebec. He also took the position that the hydro-electric industry's future lay in the public sector, particularly since, as far as natural resources were concerned, "Quebec is a millionaire but gets only a beggar's share of the profits." [76] This situation could not continue, said Lévesque, because "economically that means being second-class citizens, something we simply cannot tolerate."

The Minister of Natural Resources explained that, with regard to electricity,

> Hydro-Quebec's distribution network is concentrated in the Montreal area. In other regions of the province, distribution is carried out by private firms who were granted the right to harness certain waterfalls. There are no more unharnessed waterfalls left in the province, and since consumption has been doubling every fifteen years, these private firms have had to be supplied by Hydro-Quebec. The result is that private enterprise buys the electricity it needs from Hydro at practically cost price and sells it again at a profit to its customers who have no choice but to pay the price. The private companies are therefore making profits by re-selling electricity produced with the taxpayers' money. Would it not be better to let the whole province benefit from the low cost price of electricity

170

by turning over all distribution to Hydro-Quebec ? In the present situation we have a form of socialism from which private enterprise is making money. In this case they are not complaining because socialism is allowing them to make a profit. [77]

This situation could not be allowed to continue. But the question was : what steps should be taken ? At the end of November, the minister announced that a decision had not yet been reached in this regard. But he promised a reporter from the newspaper *Le Nouveau Journal* that a statement would soon be made outlining in a general way a large-scale plan for hydro development and distribution. "Just because Hydro-Quebec has been paralyzed for the last fifteen years does not mean it has to stay that way." [78]

If education and state intervention might help free the people of Quebec from the "colonial yoke," they would certainly not tolerate any interference with this process of emancipation on the part of the larger political structure which included Quebec. Lévesque was willing to refrain from calling this larger political structure into question but, from September 1961 on, he let it be known that Quebec would stretch the federal system as far as possible. On October 26, he spoke at an international conference on "Resources and the Future" held in Montreal, which brought together delegates from the eleven Canadian governments as well as several from abroad. He began by saying that he wanted to be as frank in English as he had been in French and then explained that it would be unnatural to give the federal government responsibility for planning and policy-making with regard to resources.

> It would be unnatural because it would be just like trying to build a house by starting with the roof before pouring the foundations and putting up the walls. We in Quebec feel it is essential that the responsibility for those foundations — in this field as well as in many others — must rest with us at the provincial level. The Constitution has delegated these responsibilities to us, and, in terms of our national interest, it is of vital importance to French Canadians that the day-to-day handling of economic affairs such as planning and policy-making, no matter what their nature, be left to us. All the facts must be in before a policy can be laid down and implemented. And we Québécois are the only ones who can do this inside Quebec with regard to employment and economic progress for the Québécois, always keeping in mind that 85 per cent of the people of Quebec are French Canadians. Otherwise

we will never get on our feet. Any scheme failing to take this into account would in our opinion be too insubstantial to be worth even considering. Since, first of all, a sense of duty must inform our actions, our own needs must take priority where development funds are concerned, and we therefore believe that a restructuring of revenue arrangements under Confederation is necessary if we are to keep Confederation in good health. Otherwise we will keep running into problems which will become more difficult as the years go by. Finally, it is of course understood that we would like to see closer co-operation and further opportunities such as this where views can be exchanged. [79]

There was nothing peevish in Lévesque's carefully measured words. He simply intended to exploit fully the opportunities offered by Confederation, to take what he felt Quebec deserved. But he cautioned against getting lost in debates and discussions on the subject of the Canadian constitution, because "too often they are just a flood of words which leave us thirsting for solutions," as he declared to the Congress on Canadian Affairs at Laval University on November 17. Lévesque was impatient ; the province of Quebec could not suffer from "constitutionitis" indefinitely, any more than he could. "All this verbiage does not solve anything. Meanwhile there is an urgent need to rethink what action has to be taken on problems presented by Confederation as it now stands, given the concrete priorities and needs it is up against." For him, Confederation was only "an experiment compromised by a cumulative series of errors repeated unthinkingly for decades. If the necessary adjustments are not made, the experiment will simply fail."

Lévesque then directed an even sterner warning specifically at his English-speaking listeners : "We have no real need of you as a group. The great threat to Confederation lies in the fact that — to take myself as an example — I am only interested in it out of a sense of obligation rather than real concern, and believe me, many French Canadians share this attitude." Lévesque's reaction to the recent announcement by federal cabinet minister Davie Fulton that Canada's constitution would soon be repatriated was "So what ?" * He then accused the federal government of perhaps having used the two world wars and the Depression to its advantage in an attempt to transform the federal structure into a legislative union. [80]

* In English in the original.

The attack had the desired effect. It hit English Canada like a thunderbolt and left people wondering what had overcome Quebec's Minister of Natural Resources. Lévesque's statement seemed even more surprising when viewed in the light of a speech given two days later by Premier Lesage himself at a luncheon sponsored by the Quebec government for the delegates to the Congress on Canadian Affairs. Lesage remarked :

> The Canadian experiment is neither a success nor a failure. In other words, we cannot draw any conclusions from the facts at our disposal based on the use that has or has not been made of one of its basic elements — the federal system. I do not in any way believe it is necessary to change the act of Confederation, because we already have at hand all that we, as citizens of Canada or of one of the ten provinces, need to make a real success of the great experiment begun barely one hundred years ago. [81]

But Lévesque was not about to let this stop him. On December 2, without actually attacking Confederation, he returned to the theme of economic betterment for Quebec and punctuated his message with Errol Bouchette's * slogan — *"Soyons maîtres chez nous !"* [Let's be master of our own house !]. [82]

During the election campaign of 1960, the Liberals had made a firm commitment by publishing their program. November 1961 marked the end of their first full year in office. A start had been on the universal education scheme, the liquor laws had been completely reorganized, hospital and compulsory automobile insurance had been introduced, the handling of public funds was more carefully supervised, government contracts were being issued strictly on the basis of public tenders, and the civil service was undergoing a housecleaning. But there was still a lot to be done. Lévesque outlined these urgent priorities in a talk delivered to the Lévis Liberal Women's Association : the development of human resources through education, the development of natural resources, a complete reform of the electoral system, and a reorganization of the government bureaucracy. "We have the best chance in the world, with our 5 or 6 million people, of becoming a kind of earthly paradise," he said. [83]

---

* Errol Bouchette (1863-1912), a writer and civil servant who promoted the cause of economic autonomy for Quebec. He was the first Québécois to suggest that the province's hydro-electric resources should be nationalized.

Pierre Elliott Trudeau, then a professor at the University of Montreal, echoed his sentiments : "And think how much faster this revolution — for it is a revolution — would have gone if there were more people like Lévesque in power, if *all* the forces of democracy were represented in the government now." [84]

The Electricity Gamble

In November 1961, Lévesque had disclosed to a journalist that the main outline of a vast hydro-electric development and distribution scheme would soon be announced. Lévesque's statement was not meant to imply that nothing had been accomplished in this field since June 1960. On the contrary : as the Minister of Natural Resources put it, "Hydro-Quebec has rapidly become a kind of pioneer in social change as far as Quebec is concerned, because it belongs to the whole population." Unionization of its employees was permitted almost immediately, and the American and Ontario engineers who had been brought in by the previous government to take charge of the Carillon generating station were replaced by Québécois. Meanwhile the new team in Natural Resources led by Michel Bélanger had been at work on the vast development and distribution scheme. In January 1962, their voluminous Blue Book was ready.

The new session opened in Quebec City in mid-January. On January 16, Daniel Johnson, the new leader of the Union Nationale, delivered the reply to the speech from the throne. He criticized the Liberals for seeking greater governmental control over life in Quebec. The Minister of Natural Resources, armed with the documentation in the Blue Book, took advantage of this occasion to reply to the member from Bagot. First of all, he deplored the fact that, under the Union Nationale, Hydro-Quebec had been forced to make large capital investments in order to produce electricity that was in large part sold off to private companies. If the government had carried the nationalization of Montreal Light and Power and the Beauharnois power dam in 1944 to its logical conclusion, Hydro-Quebec would have been able to extend its distribution network through the orderly acquisition of the private companies. "Such intervention on the government's part would have brought about a lowering of electricity costs to the benefit of the consumer, who would have seen a corresponding rise in his real income."

The next day, January 18, *Le Devoir* ran a headline which read, "Mr. Lévesque hints at impending nationalization of hydro-electric resources." The private power companies were alarmed and began to keep a watchful eye on Lévesque.

On February 11, the Minister of Natural Resources, speaking to seven hundred Liberals in the riding of Bagot, returned to this subject: "'The provincial government, which is in fact the people of Quebec, must take bold initiatives in those fields where it can expect to produce positive results, such as the development of our hydro-electric resources and the construction of a steel mill." [85] The next day, he delivered a speech entitled "Electricity in Quebec" to members of the electric power industry from the Montreal area, who were gathered at the Queen Elizabeth Hotel for Electricity Week. Most observers felt that this speech marked the beginning of the campaign to nationalize the power companies and, because of its great importance in this connection, it deserves careful attention.

He first explained to his listeners the functions of Hydro-Quebec, the Electricity and Gas Board, and the Office of Rural Electrification. He pointed out in passing that several rural areas were underdeveloped as far as electricity was concerned because they were unprofitable, and private companies had therefore refused to provide them with electricity. He marshalled a large number of statistics on production capacity, which amounted to slightly more than thirteen million horsepower, and then discussed the revenues collected by the government in the form of rents, royalties, taxes, and duties.

Distribution was the next subject. In 1960, Quebec had 1,420,296 electricity customers who were supplied by four kinds of enterprises: Hydro-Quebec (38.6%), the co-operatives (4.2%), the municipalities (6.2%), and forty-six companies licensed by the Electricity and Gas Board (48.3%). In this last category of 686,000 customers, 98% were supplied by five large distributors: the Shawinigan group (Shawinigan, Southern and Quebec Power), with 492,164 customers (71.7%); Gatineau, with 101,832 customers (14.8%); Northern Quebec with 15,903 customers (2.3%); the Lower Saint Lawrence Power Company, with 33,280 customers (4.8%); and the Saguenay Electric Company (Aluminum Co.), with 36,812 customers (5.3%). The other 41 companies served 5209 customers all together (1.4%). Hydro-Quebec itself furnished electricity directly to consumers only on the island of Montreal and in a few neighboring municipalities.

175

The result in those regions unable to produce enough to meet their own demands has been a duplication of supply lines, which means that distribution costs are far more expensive than they should be. Moreover, because the Board must allow the companies to charge rates high enough to attract investment; flagrant disparities are inevitable. On the whole, Hydro-Quebec's rates are the lowest. In some regions, customers must pay up to twice what a Montreal customer pays for the same amount of power.

Backed by these hard facts, the Minister of Natural Resources came to some inevitable conclusions :

Such a ridiculous and costly mess cannot be allowed to continue if we intend to get on with the rational development of our economy instead of just talking about it. There are five major disadvantages in the present organization of the electric power industry : (1) lack of investment co-ordination and consequently a rise in development costs ; (2) no opportunity, because of the present investment situation, to use the water at maximum efficiency and thereby lower costs ; (3) multiplication of basic costs because every distributor has to maintain separate administrative offices ; [. . .] (5) direct subsidies paid by customers in our province to those in other provinces with government-run systems through the payment of federal taxes.

Reforms are in order. We can start from the axiom that the electric power industry is vital to Quebec and must constitute a well-integrated whole if it is to give the best returns. Only the gradual amalgamation of the whole system will allow a standardization of rates on a basis that is in the best interests of both consumers and industrial development, and only amalgamation will put an end to the massive subsidies being paid out to non-residents of the province. This gradual amalgamation must be undertaken by Hydro-Quebec, in the public sector. [. . .] Electric power is an area where it is particularly important that the Quebec government take the lead, both in the interests of Quebec's economy as a whole and in the interests of the citizens themselves. Based on a knowledge of the facts presented in a study which has lasted a year and a half, I can honestly draw no other conclusion and still consider myself fit to run the ministry with which I have been entrusted. [86]

The conclusion — nationalization. It had been discussed for a year in a roundabout way without being called by name. Even in this speech the Minister of Natural Resources was careful not to

October 1962, at radio station CKAC. Lévesque shakes up Quebec with his proposal to nationalize the electric power companies. "Anyone who can't see the facts for what they are must be either blind or dishonest . . . ."

use the term. Was he afraid to use it or had the policy not yet been approved by the full cabinet ? Lévesque said,

> No, I wasn't much of a strategist, but our studies hadn't been completed. After more than a year the only concrete thing in the whole project was one huge brick, our Blue Book. But if we had talked about it prematurely, before the project was all ready and before we had been around long enough to be sure of ourselves, we would have been crucified on the spot. We just wouldn't have been able to defend ourselves adequately. I finally made it public, appropriately enough, in a speech during Electricity Week. The cabinet was far from being in agreement, but I had dropped hints and had tried to broach the subject in a general way even though we weren't really ready. [87]

The next day, presidents Fuller, Mainguy, Béique, and Rattee of Shawinigan Water and Power, Quebec Power, and Southern Canada Power, held a hastily organized press conference. They declared that they could not see any validity in the minister's claims, nor any proof that public enterprise could be as efficient as private enterprise. They concluded with this warning : "The errors committed by a public monopoly are no one's responsibility and the taxpayer is always left to pay the bill." [88]

Lévesque was happy to see that, even though he had not named any names, the Shawinigan group had been stung to the quick and reacted sharply. The Minister of Natural Resources was also pleased that he had the support of the principal Quebec dailies, including *Le Devoir* and *La Presse*. Journalist Vincent Prince wrote : "I have no intention of becoming too involved in the debate, but in spite of the companies' response I still believe that the minister is basically right. [. . .] Mr. Lévesque is working from a position of strength and the people of this province are hoping he'll stick to his guns." [89] On February 15, the Minister of Natural Resources launched a counter-attack :

> The Shawinigan group executives took it upon themselves to reply to the talk I gave on Monday concerning the electric power situation in this province. Yet I assigned no responsibility for the present state of affairs to any particular group. I was rather surprised, therefore, when these gentlemen from the Shawinigan group reacted as though they had been singled out for attack ! [. . .] They have a perfect right to defend their interests. But as far as I am concerned, though I respect these interests for what they are, I am duty-bound to consider the general interest of the province first, even when that flies in the face of certain other interests, however compelling they may be.

Lévesque then presented facts and figures to refute the private companies' main arguments against his thesis. He finished by saying :

> In any event, this brings us into the realm of political decision-making. Though in the first place it is the prerogative of the Minister of Natural Resources to suggest policy options, it is up to the government as a whole, and the government alone, to decide on policy [. . .] I am making this statement simply to set the record straight and put the facts in their proper perspective. I believe that the people of Quebec have the right to

be given enough information about electric power, one of our most precious resources, to enable them to understand clearly what is going on. [90]

The Minister of Natural Resources had proposed the idea of nationalization and it was now up to the government to make a decision. But the Liberal government was very displeased with Lévesque's attitude. His attacks on patronage and campaign fund abuses had been unassailable, even though there had been no need to implicate certain individuals. But this time he had gone too far. Lapalme wrote :

> One morning stands out in my memory. It was the day after the papers had carried a story about the electric power policy proposed unilaterally by René Lévesque. Jean Lesage was furious, and so were the rest of us. We had good reason to be ! The principle of cabinet solidarity had been blown sky high. After that day the Liberal government was never the same, because Lévesque's dissident attitude generated a great deal of bitter feeling in the cabinet, especially when he was absent, which was often the case. Lesage was urged to bring him into line. The Premier could not conceal his anger from us and we all thought a decisive confrontation was coming. [91]

Lapalme did not elaborate, but he had already revealed a great deal.

From mid-February to mid-April, Lévesque avoided speaking in public. His relations with the cabinet were undoubtedly very strained and he must have been called upon to justify himself before his colleagues. Considerable pressure must also have been brought to bear on the Liberal government by the private companies. But a year and a half earlier Lévesque had stated : "There are sixteen of us in the cabinet and all sixteen must agree on a decision. I therefore cannot say everything I think in public. But I will never say anything I do not believe in ; I would resign first." [92] On April 9, Lévesque addressed the members of the Canadian Club in Montreal. This was an important speech because it followed two months of silence and it leaves the distinct impression that the events of the preceding weeks had forced him to refine his thinking :

> I want to make one thing clear : as far as general objectives are concerned, all of us in Quebec are of one mind. The Liberal Party program that brought us to power was quite explicit and a substantial part of it has already been implemented, particularly in the fields of education and social welfare. However,

a lot remains to be done and, with regard to natural resources, I have made public some policies which, in my opinion, are in keeping with the spirit of the Liberal program, the overall goal of all modern economic policies, namely, growth, continuous growth, and also that social goal which should be so vitally important to us in Quebec — the development and advancement of the French-Canadian nation in particular. [. . .]

What we intend to have from now on — we are, I think, in the midst of making a substantial effort in this direction and the people, I am sure, would not have us go back to the old ways — what we want, and what we are going to have more and more, is a responsible government, which discharges its responsibilities and uses all the means at its disposal, including economic ones, to enhance the prosperity of its citizens to the fullest extent possible. I think this is quite a straightforward position and I cannot see that there is anything extremist about it. [. . .] Some people are scandalized at the slightest mention of the word [nationalization] or at least make a desperate effort to appear scandalized, as if revolution was just around the corner ! They do so either to sway public opinion in their favor or else simply because they do not understand, and have never understood, the true meaning and the true aim of our traditional democratic institutions. I do not have, I have never had, nor will I ever have any intention of proposing any measure that springs from a totalitarian view of government. But we have been used to the idea of weak government for so long that any attempt to restore its normal powers produces a reaction of panic, whether real or pretended, from many timid souls as well as from the privileged few. [. . .]

The basic problem throughout the world today is growth. [. . .] Let us consider for a moment how certain elementary principles of growth apply to our situation here and now. Our province must grow and it must do so in a way that benefits the majority of the population. This means — and let us be very clear and very frank about this — in a way that continually and increasingly benefits the French-Canadian nation, which has and will only ever have one physical base to call its own : the Province of Quebec. Our job is to see that this majority receives what is rightfully theirs, something they have never had in the past (which is partly their own fault), and to see that they and their children have a better future. Our job is to achieve this goal by utilizing our society's existing economic institutions and by making any necessary adjustments to them. We intend, as is our duty, to plan our growth in this

180

way because obviously no one else is going to do it for us. [. . .] Certain people have said that I am a left-winger whose goal is to abolish freedom and individual initiative. This is completely ridiculous. Nothing is more important in our society than freedom ; but freedom must never be used, as it too often has been, as a smokescreen behind which the interests of the majority are systematically sacrificed to the exclusive and excessive interests of a privileged few. Very simply, our task as the elected representatives of the majority is to see that neither the government nor society ever become the tool or plaything of any minority again. Indeed, I am quite sure that if we were ever to slip backwards like that we would deserve the carefully disguised and well-earned *contempt* of those few who might profit from our weakness and our corruption. The majority, I hope, would quickly rebel.

With this perspective on the problem, Lévesque came

inevitably to the calm conclusion, after studying the whole question for nearly two years with the best minds available, that in the present situation hydro-electric power is not being utilized to the advantage of the province's whole population as it should be. [. . .] One thing must be clearly understood : nationalization is not an end in itself but quite simply (1) the only solution in the public interest to the urgent problem of the operation and rational development of our hydro-electric resources and to the problem of the disparities in the cost of electric power ; and (2) one of our most important tools in the proper planning of our economic growth.

He ended by touching on the question of the relationship between the two language groups :

Quebec is becoming somewhat impatient and is especially tired of the tendency in some quarters to perpetuate the traditional image of her as a nice, old-fashioned province. She is fed up with social and political claptrap and the willing acceptance of her own short-comings. She definitely will not tolerate the selfish and irresponsible arrogance of those who will not ever attempt to understand her feelings. I think this impatience will become a permanent feature of our lives — as a Québécois and a Canadian, I sincerely hope it does. [93]

This was Lévesque's conception of the Quebec government and the role it ought to play. In retrospect, it is obvious that his conception was not really shared by some of his cabinet colleagues.

Indeed, one wonders if there was not some fundamental misunderstanding about this role from the very beginning, in 1960, which would explain the sudden loss of nerve and resolution on the part of certain ministers. Some of them regarded Lévesque's conduct over nationalization as "an abuse of ministerial responsibility," yet only needed to be convinced that his proposals had economic merits. Others, however, were much more deeply opposed. Lesage, for one, was intransigent in his opposition, in spite of Lévesque's speech to the Canadian Club. Lapalme later revealed that the premier remained "a bitter opponent of nationalization to the last minute." Journalist Jean-V. Dufresne went so far as to claim that Lesage had promised Shawinigan president Fuller that nationalization would never take place. [94] One thing was certain though : the premier never said a word on the subject.

Journalists Dominique Clift and Richard Daignault noted just at this time that, curiously enough, Lévesque — unlike Jean Lesage, Paul Gérin-Lajoie, and most of the other cabinet ministers — was not actually taking a firm stand. "Where is he headed ? What are his aims ? His ambitions ? No one but Lévesque knows for sure." [95] On May 3, the Minister of Natural Resources reiterated his position that Quebec's resources must become the property of the people of Quebec, provided that the shareholders were given a fair deal. A majority of the cabinet called on Lesage to silence Lévesque. Lapalme wrote :

> With Lévesque absent from a cabinet meeting, Lesage was persuaded by his colleagues to promise that he would put an end to the Liberal prima donna's campaign. But Lévesque walked in at noon — after we had been at work since 9:00 am — and the arrival of the member for Laurier stopped the flow of angry words from the man who was supposed to give him a dressing-down. There were a lot of rumors flying around at the time. Was it true that one evening a verbal battle bordering on a scuffle had broken out in front of a dozen startled witnesses in a suite at the Chateau Frontenac ? I wasn't there but the next day the whole town was talking about it. Lesage and Lévesque had apparently had a huge shouting match. [96]

On June 2, at the convention of the Federation of Saint-Jean-Baptiste Societies, and again on June 17, at the inaugural banquet of the second "French Week" in Cornwall, Lévesque repeated that it would be foolish to let the private hydro-electric empires become

July 1962. The Carillon power dam, on the Ottawa River, is in the background.

any more entrenched in Quebec. Soon a rumor was circulating that the Minister of Natural Resources was about to resign. His intention allegedly was to form a new political party with nationalist goals, whose leadership would include three Quebec "progessives," Jean Marchand, Jean Drapeau, and Jean-Jacques Bertrand.

Lévesque, however, finally succeeded in winning over a key political figure to his side — Georges-Emile Lapalme. "My final conversion," wrote the former Liberal Party leader,

> took place in the government plane one sunny morning when the visibility was about 100 miles and you could see from Granby to Mont Tremblant. Lévesque was talking away. Of

course, he's always talking, no matter where he is, but that morning, far from the applause and the excitement of the crowd, he managed, without even realizing it, to convince me that his reasoning and his figures were sound. [97]

But Lesage, the majority of the cabinet, and the directors of the Quebec Liberal Federation (QLF) were all adamant : nationalization simply was not acceptable. They had reached a stalemate and drastic measures were needed. "Just who was it," asked Lapalme,

> who had the idea that the government team and the Liberal Federation brass should go on a retreat ? It wasn't Lesage and it wasn't me ; an element of mystery surrounded the decision. In any event, someone suggested we do a complete overhaul of our basic policy and take a fresh look at the "adventure" René Lévesque was trying to thrust on us. [98]

On September 3 and 4, members of the Liberal Party, cabinet ministers, and directors of the Federation gathered at Lac-à-l'Epaule in the Parc des Laurentides.

So much has been said and written about Lac-à-l'Epaule that the name itself has become a household word, a synonym for a retreat or the act of washing "dirty laundry" in private. For a long time the Liberal meeting was shrouded in mystery because everyone involved was sworn to secrecy. Nevertheless, certain scraps of information have come to light over the years and have allowed us to reconstruct what happened during those two days spent in the middle of the forest.

Lapalme tells us that only on the afternoon of the second day did the nationalization of electricity come up for discussion. Lévesque confirmed this statement :

> That's true, up to a point. That is, we didn't come to the heart of the matter until the afternoon of the second day, but the subject was already in the air and people were chatting about it in small groups. The cabinet was there, along with two or three representatives from the Liberal Federation, the president, and a couple of others. The Lac-à-l'Epaule meeting had obviously been convened to settle the question once and for all. The question had created quite a lot of tension in the preceding months, so we had to be careful how we approached it. On the first day they had a party for us, at which there was a general lining-up of positions. We sounded each other out ; we chatted in corners. You found out where you stood. And it ended up with certain individuals acting as spokesmen

184

— two of us, for the most part : Marler spoke against the idea and I spoke for it. The rest of the cabinet was asking "Well, where do we go from here ?" Lesage presided of course. Yes, it was on the second day, around late morning or early afternoon, that it all began to happen. It was a long and difficult afternoon, a kind of confrontation between two different ideologies. The way people changed their minds back and forth was something to behold. A number of those present were quite upset ; then there were others who ... well, anyway. [99]

Did Lévesque look back on it as a painful experience ? "As far as the atmosphere that day was concerned, yes, to some extent. As far as the results were concerned, no. But I'd rather not discuss what the atmosphere was like." However, Lévesque talked about this atmosphere with journalists Pierre de Bellefeuille and Jean-Pierre Bergeron :

The dispute over nationalization had brought to a head a lot of the things that had troubled the cabinet during our first two years. There are always two wings — let's call them left and right for want of a better term — two wings in every government, even when the party concerned is an older one. In other words, two years of wrangling over many issues had divided the cabinet into two wings from the moment we started to implement the program. There were shadings of opinion between the two extremes, but the extremes were there in the cabinet nonetheless. Because of the months of public debate that preceded the cabinet's decision, the electricity question had deepened these differences of opinion to the extent that they became extremely painful, especially when you consider that at one point the government's very life was at stake. I remember before the decision was made at Lac-à-l'Epaule, there were at least two or three cases of ministers who argued, resigned, made a stormy exit, then came back, argued some more, had whispered consultations, and so on. It was two days of total insanity ! [100]

But the moment of reconciliation had arrived. Lévesque was asked to explain the why's and wherefore's of nationalizing the power companies. His cabinet colleagues then grilled him. Lapalme wrote :

An atmosphere of stuffiness, discomfort, and frustration prevailed. The two-day confinement, the heavy lunch with cocktails and wine, the real problems lurking behind the less important issues raised, the precautions some took to avoid provoking the Premier's anger, the feeling that the fate of both the government and individual ministers hung in the balance — all these different factors came together for one oppressive moment before giving way a little later to the moment of truth. [101]

It was a cabinet typical of the province itself, determined to carry out reforms but quickly reverting to conservatism, courageous and fearful, searching for a way to give private enterprise a good deal while at the same time expanding the government's powers.

After the question period, the premier asked the Attorney General : "Georges, do you agree with René's position ? If so what would you say to an immediate election on the matter, if everybody else agrees ?" Lapalme's support of both nationalization and an immediate election made all the difference. "It was Lapalme himself," Lévesque explained,

who had the idea of making it an election issue. Everybody soon came around to his way of thinking and suddenly it all fell into place. The idea hit most of us like a thunderbolt, but we quickly said to ourselves, without further reflection, "Yes, that makes sense." I thought, "This'll give us a damn good chance to campaign on economic issues, something that's never happened in Quebec." Some of the others perhaps thought that it would give new life to the party. I don't know if that's what they thought or not — maybe they did. I guess the idea was in the air, because it was a popular subject for discussion. [102]

Once the decision to hold an election had been made, no significant political events took place until the opening of the campaign. The elections were set for November 14 ; the Liberals' campaign slogan was "Maintenant ou jamais ! Maîtres chez nous." [Now or never ! Masters of our own house.] The Liberal program asked the people of Quebec to support the nationalization of electricity for a number of very different reasons, but it was above all touted as "the key to our economic liberation." The publicity went even further. "The nationalization of electricity is the crucial step ; it will mean the end of our colonial status and the real beginning of economic independence !"

On September 30, at a Liberal Federation banquet, Lapalme and Lévesque praised Lesage for his courage in putting the govern-

186

October 1962. The Minister of Natural Resources becomes a journalist again in order to explain to the public why the electric power companies must be nationalized. On his left is Robert Baillargeon, president of the Richelieu Club of Montreal.

ment's very existence on the line over this issue. The Minister of Natural Resources added :

> The Liberal solution is not a smokescreen but a rare example in our history of reasoned and reasonable courage. One of nationalization's advantages is that it will not only place the economic destiny of Quebec in the hands of its people but also relieve a bit of the bitterness present in French Canada's growing impatience.

187

Although Premier Lesage had been a fierce opponent of nationalization until the last minute, he swung into the campaign enthusiastically. Lévesque said of him later : "Jean Lesage could be very accommodating and this was a valuable quality to have. Once the agreement was made, as in the case of the hydro-electric issue, he took up the cause as vigorously as anyone else, perhaps more so. In this case, one thing is certain — his campaign was sensational." Meanwhile the journalists who were following the Premier noted that he was using the expression *"Etat du Québec"* [State of Quebec] more and more often.

Opposition leader Daniel Johnson was puzzled ; he could not decide what position to adopt. Was nationalization a good thing or not ? In the end, he promised that if his party was elected he would launch a public information campaign and then hold a referendum on nationalization. The member for Bagot questioned the figure of 600 million dollars which the Minister of Natural Resources had calculated would be the cost of this measure. Johnson thought the cost would probably exceed a billion dollars.

René Lévesque was busy. A film made with the help of Maurice Leroux showed him with a pointer, a blackboard, and a map trying to convince the people that nationalization made good sense. About one hundred copies were printed and distributed. One journalist who saw the film wrote : "He talks. You try to fight him off in your mind because you want to disagree. But he wins. The present system is like 'a straw bolt — it's completely crazy,' as he says more than once. While such expressions would sound strange coming from a career politician, they do not sound out of place at all in the mouth of a René Lévesque talking nationalization." [103] The Minister of Natural Resources told the members of the Montreal Richelieu Club that "even if we might be forced to make some small sacrifices right now, nationalization would be profitable in the long run." To the rumor spread by the *Gazette* that the Lesage government would eventually nationalize the paper and mining industries, Lévesque replied that the Liberal Party did not intend to commit itself to a general policy of nationalization. In Shawinigan, he stated that nationalization would pay for itself and leave enough surplus revenue after the first year to adjust excessively high rates without the need for indirect taxes. In Saint-Félicien, he promised to leave politics "if, after the nationalization of the power companies, the price of electricity does not drop in those areas where it is too high without at the same time producing a corresponding hike in other areas." In Beauport, he stated that nationalization would open the door to heavy industry, particularly iron and steel concerns.

Nationalization was not a panacea and Lévesque stressed that it would be dishonest to claim that it was. "But," he said, "it will be the first step in our liberation." He touched on a wider theme when he addressed the English-speaking students of Sir George Williams University : "The French Canadians have been the most patient people in the world. They shouldn't have to apologize now for wanting their place in the sun."

Generally, Lévesque's audiences paid close attention to what he had to say. But in the Gaspé his reception was more like a celebration. Journalist Pierre O'Neil followed him on his journey back home :

> *"L'homme qui se tient deboutte"* [The straight-shooter], as they call him here and in Quebec City, is a real hero to the people of the Gaspé. They come from all over to hear him. I travelled with one man, the father of seven children, who was hitchhiking to a spot forty-five miles down the road to sit in on Lévesque's "parliament." The Minister of Natural Resources is at home in the Gaspé ; everywhere he goes he's greeted with a friendly slap on the back. In Chandler, the minister received a thunderous welcome from the audience. [104]

But the Minister of Natural Resources was not always welcomed so warmly. The vice-president of the Lincoln National Life Insurance Company of Fort Wayne, Indiana, a certain Mr. McDiarmid, pictured Lévesque in these terms : "What you have here is a politician who talks as if he were Robespierre and acts as if the aristocrats were all about to be guillotined." [105] J. M. Bourbonnais, writing in the Montreal weekly *La Presqu'île,* compared Lévesque to Castro : "The Cubans thought they would become their own masters by expelling the Americans and their capital, but instead of winning their liberty they lost it. Now they live in misery and constant fear of an invasion, a new revolution, or Fidel Castro's firing squad. René Lévesque's dialectics are not unlike those of Cuba's bearded leader." [106] It would have been surprising not to see Robert Rumilly enter the fray : *Nouvelles Illustrées* asked for his observations on the election and printed them in its November 3 issue. Before advising his readers to spurn resolutely "the Lesage government, led by René Lévesque," because it is "too apt to lead us into socialism," the historian attempted to illustrate the misdeeds of socialism around the world :

> There is no need for me to point out that socialism and communism have always resulted in police states, economic catastrophe, and the oppression of the individual. In China, they have even gone so far as to experiment with "communes" : everything is held in common, including the land and agricultural implements ; even children are taken from their families and entrusted to the care of the state. The result has been the most terrible famine and the worst suffering ever experienced in the country's history. The Chinese are fleeing this hell by the thousands to Hong Kong or Formosa, just as the East Germans risk their lives to reach West Berlin. Rumania, which was once the breadbasket of Europe and sold its wheat to other countries, is now obliged under its socialist government to import this commodity. It has in fact recently completed a large purchase from France.

For a leading politician, an election campaign in Quebec means thousands of miles of travel and dozens of meetings, as Lapalme knew all too well : "Having known and lived through that human phenomenon played on a vast stage in terms of space, time, size, and numbers, I am completely carried away when I read in *L'Express* about the miniscule distances travelled by French politicians during a general election." [107] As a Liberal celebrity, Lévesque was obliged to travel the length and breadth of Quebec, yet he also had to look after his own election campaign in Montreal-Laurier where every Saturday he met with his constituents, as he had been doing for two years. A few days before the election, it was predicted that he would have an easier time of it than in 1960. His opponents, Mario Beaulieu of the Union Nationale and Hertel Larocque, an independent, were complete unknowns. And the "liquor licence police" were no longer around.

On November 11, Lesage scored an important victory in his televised debate with Daniel Johnson. While the Liberal leader was strengthened by the support of his colleagues and appeared confident, the Union Nationale chief did not come across well on television. The Liberal campaign ended the next day on this note of triumph. Lévesque was pleased with the six weeks spent talking to the people of Quebec :

> I was of course obliged to play a major part in the campaign, and what I really liked about it was that we spent something

like six weeks, non-stop, explaining a crucial economic program at the blackboard and on TV. That had never happened before. I had a really heavy schedule during the campaign because I had to defend the program. My job was to take the hydro-electric scheme out of the political arena, explain it, answer questions from Chambers of Commerce and all kinds of audiences, using figures to back up my answers — here is the way we'll do this, for such-and-such a reason, etc. I found it all an amazing experience. I think that whenever some big economic project is under consideration — whether during an election campaign or when it is first introduced — it should be discussed in public, because this adds to people's political maturity and God knows we need more of that ! [108]

On November 14, the people of Quebec said "yes" to the nationalization of electricity. The Liberal Party swept to victory in sixty-two ridings, eleven more than in 1960, while the Union Nationale won only thirty-two seats. For René Lévesque, the decision made at Lac-à-l'Epaule, and crowned by the Liberal success at the polls, was one of the greatest joys of his political career : "The Lac-à-l'Epaule decision and the election result, which amounted to a ratification of that decision, gave me a feeling of accomplishment, of satisfaction, of having seen something through. It was definitely one of the most interesting things that happened while I was in office." [109]

Although for a long time he was the only minister who believed that it was practical and necessary to nationalize Quebec's private power companies, Lévesque eventually managed to convince a majority of the ministers that this economic measure was valid, but only at the risk of an irrevocable split in the party. He told Pierre Berton on May 30, 1963, that he would "probably" have resigned if the Liberals had not accepted nationalization. [110] Then there was the trial by election during which Lévesque laid his future on the line and forced the rest of the party to do likewise. If the Liberals had been defeated, the Minister of Natural Resources would almost certainly have had to leave the party. But victory was theirs, and on May 1, 1963, Hydro-Quebec took possession of the power companies covered by the nationalization scheme, at a cost of 604 million dollars.

Reinforced by their second election victory in two years, the Liberals seemed to have nothing but smooth sailing ahead of them. But appearances were deceiving. Since 1960, the party had been a coalition of the most diverse political elements in Quebec : proponents of even more radical state intervention rubbed elbows with those who supported the principle of a completely free hand for private enterprise. Even before his one-man crusade for nationalization, Lévesque had provoked wrangling over his attacks against patronage and campaign fund abuse. The issue of nationalization had sharply polarized opinion in the party ranks and there was no guarantee that the November 14 election victory would heal the wounds inflicted at Lac-à-l'Epaule — things had perhaps gone too far by then. Moreover, the highly touted Liberal teamwork may have been more a dream than a reality. Perhaps Lapalme had this in the back of his mind when he wrote in his memoirs an account of how matters stood in July 1963 :

> Jean Lesage's greatest achievement in that three-year period was to hold together the disparate elements which made up his cabinet. But although there may have been unity, there was no real solidarity, the kind of solidarity which brought us together every day at noon and in the evening when I was the leader of our small Opposition group. Each minister led his own separate life : some had bought or rented houses, others had apartments. [. . .] In the evening there was often no one except myself in the ministers' dining room. We only really saw one another once a week at cabinet meetings, where there was naturally no time to be sociable. After '62 the united front began to fall apart ; it's probably fair to say that everyone was going his own way at that point. Paul Gérin-Lajoie turned his back on the rest of us and begun building the incredibly costly empire whose foundations have now collapsed. * René Lévesque, with his perfect disdain for discipline, tried our patience by continually promoting himself on radio and television ; Cultural Affairs was relegated to empty talk if not completely ignored in favor of a new highway or a culvert which had to be paid for — no one ever dreamed of scrounging the money from the Ministry of Education. [111]

Although these comments on Gérin-Lajoie and Lévesque must be considered in perspective, they are significant because they demonstrate that by July 1963 one of the top men in the Liberal Party was fed up with being in office. Lévesque, for his part, was

---

* Gérin-Lajoie was Minister of Education in the Lesage cabinet ; the "empire" referred to was the vast educational reform program for which Gérin-Lajoie was responsible.

still enthusiastic, as Robert McKenzie reported in the *Gazette* : "He retained the same engaging impetuosity, the same rumpled clothes, and the same air of occasional schoolboyish naiveté that had made him such an engaging television personality." [112] The November 1962 election may not have reduced tensions within the Liberal cabinet, but Lévesque still praised Lesage for his achievements. Without his tact, the Liberal government, the government of the "quiet revolution," would probably have been paralyzed by internal conflict. The premier may have only been postponing the inevitable, but in the meantime Quebec made tremendous progress under his administration. The Minister of Natural Resources expressed his admiration of the premier in these terms :

> We have to do justice to Jean Lesage. He had two or three qualities which, in my opinion, made him a great prime minister at the provincial level. First of all, he was one of the hardest working guys I've ever known. I've never seen anyone who spent so much time methodically going through his paperwork, day in and day out, nearly always managing to keep on top of what was happening in every ministry. It was important for the guy in charge of such a restless crew to do that. Secondly, he understood things quickly. At a certain point he perhaps turned this very quality from a virtue into a vice and became too sure of himself. But he was always quick on the draw. Finally, he had another strength which was also a weakness, that is, he was fundamentally a nationalist. He used to recall with great pride the days of Chubby Power * in Ottawa when he was a young MP and a member of what they called Quebec's "Little Chicago," the gang of young Turks from Quebec. His involvement was quite serious ; he was a real Québécois at heart. On the other hand, when it came to formulating policy — I'm not talking about the day-to-day running of the government, but about formulating policy, what specific measures to take, what bills to pass, etc. — he was a guy who basically didn't have any strong convictions. Which meant that he changed his mind to suit the circumstances. With these qualities and what I'd call a lack of established convictions, he was always having to deal with pressure from those in the cabinet who really did feel strongly about something. This might have been Gérin-Lajoie in Education, Kierans in his department, me in

---

* Charles Gavan Power, born in 1888. Lawyer and federal Liberal MP for Quebec-South from 1917 to 1957. He served as Postmaster General and Minister of National Defence and was later appointed to the Senate.

my department, or Laporte in his, once he held an important portfolio. Lesage was vulnerable to pressure of that kind, which wasn't necessarily a bad thing. You could say it was a bad thing because of course from time to time there were some setbacks, just as there were some triumphs. But it wasn't necessarily a bad thing in itself. [113]

What Future for Quebec ?

While popular support for the Liberals had opened the door to nationalization, the government had been preoccupied since June 1960 with more urgent problems. They had repaired the cracked foundations of their house and then put it in order. The various measures designed to eliminate the misuse of public funds were part of this process, what Lévesque called "attempts to bring order out of our intricate jungle." * Even the nationalization of electricity can be considered a necessary housecleaning measure of this kind because it had no immediate impact on other sectors of the Quebec economy. The same could be said of the long campaign to make education more accessible to the public.

In January 1963, after thirty months of Liberal government, it became apparent that no matter how necessary and worthwhile these measures had been, they had only scratched the surface. Should they rest on their laurels and be content to administer the province without a long-range reform policy ? Should the Quebec government be confined to the role of regional administration, only slightly above the level of municipal administration ? Lesage and Lévesque spoke of the Quebec government as the principal "lever" of the Québécois and the "fulcrum" of all French-speaking Canadians. To what extent had this ideal become a reality ?

Obviously the work of the Liberal government only represented a beginning. They had to prepare a more extensive program or else give up their struggle to make Quebec more self-assertive. Although Lévesque and his team in Natural Resources fully expected to go much further than they had, Quebec lacked long-range goals. What was to be done with this part of the world ? From then on it was up to the people of Quebec to define their goals ; the government, for its part, could respond by intervening in the economy and urging private enterprise to co-operate with its directives. This is a process some have called social planning ; others call it a social contract.

---

* In English in the original.

March 1963. Lévesque, Quebec's Minister of Natural Resources, boards the plane for Paris to solicit financing from French industrialists for an iron and steel works.

Lévesque had been a firm believer in planning since 1961. Although an Economic Advisory Council was already in existence and had produced a number of studies, Quebec had still made little progress in this field. So from 1963 on, the Minister of Natural Resources took up the cause of comprehensive planning for Quebec. On January 28, he said :

In the last year quite a few things have become clear. First

195

of all with regard to the overall problem of guiding economic activity, it's obvious that the antiquated doctrine of laissez-faire, which has nearly ceased to exist in practice, has lost its hold over men's minds once and for all. It's remarkable to see how the word "planning," which not so long ago was quietly derided by a lot of people, is now in very common use in our society. Only the real antediluvian still refuses to incorporate the word into his everyday vocabulary. We've now reached the point where the word grates on our nerves because we are growing more and more impatient to see it become a reality and produce concrete results. This is a healthy kind of impatience, yet we must not give in to it too readily. An economic system which has been under the exclusive and basically anarchic domination of private interests for so long cannot democratically reach agreement overnight on the application of a recipe which would demand acceptance of a comprehensive analysis, tight co-ordination of all resources in order to maximize returns, and the inevitable subordination, if not the sacrifice, of the particular to the general good. Because it is only a recipe, we'd have to expect that a lot of cooks would want to discuss how to best prepare the program. There would also be a fierce struggle between those who believed in it too strongly as an end in itself rather than a means and those who believed in it only to the extent that it would serve their own interests.

After introducing his subject with these observations, the Minister outlined his concept of planning :

Whatever proportions are finally decided on in preparing this recipe for economic planning, there are at least two ingredients whose inclusion is necessary if such a plan is not to become a kind of national fraud : (1) the economy itself must be a means of achieving the objective of every civilized society, namely, the enhancement of man's dignity through labor sufficiently well paid to guarantee the basic well-being everyone has a right to expect ; (2) the constraints of planning must not be simply imposed from the top but consented to by the majority so that they are the result of the most representative democratic participation in the formulation and implementation of society's goals. [114]

In short, the Minister of Natural Resources had great faith in planning. With the hydro-electric scheme a reality, he saw the establishment of a provincial iron and steel industry, and the cre-

196

Something in common. Lévesque and political opponent Daniel Johnson are on the set of the CBC television program Votre choix *to enjoy singer Félix Leclerc, their choice for the first featured artist in the series.*

ation of a general investment corporation, as well as an even more advanced educational program, as important elements in a comprehensive plan or, as he put it, a "great collective project." But planning would not be easy for Quebec within the federal context, if it was possible at all. In a study of regional development under the federal system, Roland Parenteau drew a sharp contrast between the concepts of "nation" and "region" in this regard. [115]

In the summer of 1962, Lévesque had told journalist Jean O'Neil :

> I've always been proud of being a French Canadian. We've had to take a lot of crap, and a lot of that has been our own fault. At the present time, nothing fascinates me more than what is happening to five or six million French Canadians, but that doesn't prevent me from looking at the whole situation

objectively when necessary. The important thing is not to take any more crap. [116]

This statement, which was picked up by a number of commentators, including Gérard Bergeron and Robert McKenzie, is a good illustration of Lévesque's nationalism, a kind of lucid pride which is both personal and collective. In 1963, he was understandably mistrustful of Canadian federalism, as he probably always will be, though he was prepared to put up with it as long as it did not become an obstacle to the development of *"la québécitude"* ["Quebecness"].

Although the Liberal government in Quebec City still had no comprehensive plan, it wanted the federal government to make certain concessions which would enable it to pursue its goals. These short-term objectives were limited to specific areas. In the areas of social welfare and education, both provincial jurisdictions, Quebec was faced with a heavy financial burden which called for the appropriation of revenues that, according to the constitution of 1867, came under federal control. The federal government would therefore be called upon to turn over these funds to Quebec. Lesage was in full agreement with this principle. On April 5, 1963, he asked Ottawa to turn over, within one year, 25 percent of the province's personal income tax revenue, 25 per cent of its corporation tax, and 100 per cent of the revenue from succession duties. Quebec also gave Ottawa notice of its intention to withdraw from certain shared-cost projects.

The Quebec government wanted to dispose of its own revenues as it saw fit and to recoup a portion of the taxes paid to Ottawa by the people of Quebec. It also wanted to be free of any obligation to the federal government with regard to the implementation of either its short-term goals or its overall plan for the future. But the politicians of Quebec perhaps did not yet fully realize the implications of such a position. Clearly the logical conclusion of the "planning" principle was to call into question the federal government's activities in some of its own jurisdictions. Even if the Quebec government had not done so at the time, such a policy would have inevitably called into question the appropriation of revenues originating in Quebec (for example, personal income taxes paid to Ottawa) for the use of "National" Defence. This was only a step away from outright rejection of federalism as it then stood and the assertion of full, unqualified sovereignty for Quebec.

198

As of 1963, Lévesque's attacks against Canadian federalism ✓
became more and more frequent. They were prompted by his na-
tionalistic feelings and a specific desire to have Quebec recover
the powers and the revenues she deserved. On March 23, he told
the *Financial Post* that he belonged to the school of thought that
saw Canada as a union of two nations rather than ten provinces.
Moreover, he expressed strong opposition to Prime Minister Lester
B. Pearson's nuclear arms policy and the role of National Defence
in general. "By acquiring nuclear arms, we would be spending a
lot of money for junk. Let's face it : if a shooting war broke out,
it wouldn't matter what Canada's weapons were. The war would
be waged over our heads and we would have no say about it. [. . .]
We need a good home guard. I'm serious about that." [117] Here was a
provincial minister who, though he was not yet demanding the
right to criticize federal policy, was well on the way to doing so.

Two months later Lévesque dropped a bombshell in Toronto with
the following statement : "To be honestly a Canadian, I shouldn't
have to feel like a native leaving his reservation every time I leave ✓
Quebec. Outside Quebec, I don't find two great cultures. I feel like
a foreigner. First and foremost, I am a Québécois, and second —
with a rather growing sense of doubt — a Canadian." Describing
the constitution of 1867 as "a 96-year-old sacred cow," he said
that it had to be modified "to make Quebeckers truly masters in
their own house." [118] The minister was ready to live with Confederation on condition that Quebec was allowed to do as she pleased
without federal interference.

In the same issue of the *Toronto Star,* political scientist Peter
Regenstreif quoted these remarks made in an interview by Quebec's
Minister of Natural Resources : "Confederation isn't sacred, you
know. It is just a bargain made 100 years ago. It has become a
bad bargain. Sometimes the only thing you can do with a bad
bargain is to get out of it. And that can be done democratically." [119]
A week later Lévesque speculated further in a speech to social
workers from the Quebec City area :

> From nearly every point of view, Quebec is at a great turning
> point in her history. Within this federation called Canada, the
> choice of options at our disposal is less and less suited to our
> needs. More and more you hear people talking about the yoke
> around Quebec's neck. In theory, a federal arrangement like
> ours should be beneficial in every possible way to all parties
> concerned. In Canada, one of these parties is the French-

Canadian nation, and federalism had so far failed to provide the minimum conditions necessary for it to grow and develop normally as it should have. This state of affairs is unacceptable and must be changed. [120]

This was the crux of René Lévesque's political position in June 1963. Confederation was not "sacred," but he was prepared to give it the benefit of the doubt as long as it provided Quebec with all that she needed to flourish. Apart from that, he was not willing to make any concessions to the federal arrangement.

English-Canadian journalists wrote that "French Canadians feel they are not accepted as equal partners on the national level." When asked what clauses he would change in the 1867 charter, Lévesque replied that he did not know for sure and expressed the fear that discussions might be reduced to a question of semantics. The problem, he pointed out, was much more fundamental : Quebec was struggling to make up for lost time. Lévesque believed in the virtues of planning as a means of realizing Quebec's "social contract," but since this contract had yet to be defined, Quebec was unable to describe its basic principles to English Canadians. Lévesque was sure of only one thing : having committed herself to this process, Quebec as a collective entity would have to exercise her capacities to the limit and bulldoze through all political and economic obstacles.

Claude Ryan, the new publisher of *Le Devoir,* found the attitude adopted by the Minister of Natural Resources disturbing :

> Mr. Lévesque has reached the stage where he must articulate in his own mind more clearly and coherently the political and economic goals he wishes to pursue. Problems relating to the management of our economic future and the future of Confederation are serious enough to warrant not just a candid and spontaneous approach, but also a conceptual framework whose implications have been carefully weighed. Mr. Lévesque has not yet made the transition from acting on impulse to sober thought. The man has become too important, too full of promises, to remain indefinitely standing in the doorway threatening to proclaim his anger to the outside world if he is not given a hearing inside the house. [121]

The Minister of Natural Resources had come to some firm conclusions about Quebec and, as he had promised the public, he continued to word within Confederation. On July 5, 1963,

1963. With customary flamboyance, Michel Chartrand temporarily steals the limelight at a public meeting called by Lévesque.

Le Devoir printed an interview with Lévesque by Jean-Marc Léger. In the opening sentences of the interview, Lévesque laid his cards on the table. He affirmed his belief in Quebec as a nation, but a nation without sovereign status :

> Everything we do in the near future must take into account two basic facts. First, French Canada is a genuine nation and contains all the elements essential to nationhood ; its sense of unity, its human and material resources, equipment, and talent are comparable or superior to those of many other peoples around the world. Secondly, however, we are not a sovereign people, politically speaking. There's no point going into the

201

question of whether we could or could not be : right now we aren't. We are therefore an authentic nation, but a nation without sovereignty. We must work with these realities and make these two poles our starting point.

Lévesque went on the explain to Léger that Quebec's two most important problems were to give priority to education and to achieve economic self-determination. There was no reason why living under a federal system should prevent Quebec from solving these problems.

Of course the federal system also creates an area of overlapping jurisdictions whose nature and boundaries must be jointly defined and redefined when the need arises, without any presumptive assertion of authority on the part of the federal government. This is a difficult and extremely delicate task, reflecting the grandeur and misery of a federation in which two nations purport to live in harmony, but it must be done. If we keep running away from this task, then either the minority nation will be smothered or else the federation will be in danger of falling apart. To sum up, if Canada hopes to thrive, then the legislative, fiscal, and administrative means available to this nation-state called Quebec and its overall role within the federal system must be allowed to develop to the fullest extent possible within that system. This is the most important priority and federal priorities must take second place.

Lévesque again disputed the allotment of large amounts of federal funds to National Defence :

Let me give an example, in passing, of what I consider to be absolute and secondary priorities. Suppose that the Minister of Defence, a federal official, spends a billion and a half dollars, whether wisely or unwisely, while at the same time — and this could be happening right now — education and other large-scale public programs falling within the provincial sphere have to wait with their tongues hanging out. Those funds appropriated for defence must be cut drastically and the provinces must be granted, through various channels, the funds necessary for their own development, because provincial priorities must always come before those of the federal government.

The minister considered the recovery of direct taxes from Ottawa as a more important fiscal priority than the channeling of investment

202

in Quebec or the redirection and utilization of new sources of capital.

On September 27, Lévesque addressed a student audience at the University of Sherbrooke and warned the federal government that Lesage's "25-25-100" ultimatum only represented a bare minimum : "We will certainly make much greater demands in the future," he noted. [122] A month later he again ranked redistribution of tax revenues as one of Quebec nationalism's major priorities : "If that isn't possible," he said, "our only choice would be to secede .... It wouldn't be the end of the world. What is Canada ? It's only a *gamble* * taken one hundred years ago. In a situation where our very existence is threatened, we're not going to resign ourselves to extinction." [123] The next day he told journalist Bruce West that an independent Quebec would be viable. "Why not ? We are approaching a population of six millions and have tremendous natural resources. Surely we could fare as well as some of the smaller Scandinavian countries, for instance." West added : "I asked him whether Quebec ever gave any consideration to the terms of the British North America Act when it considered secession. 'Constitutional niceties won't mean much when the majority in this province makes up its mind,' he said." [124]

For the Minister of Natural Resources, the three most important decisions the Lesage government would have to make in early 1964 concerned an iron and steel works, the pension plan, and Bill 60, a proposal to create a Quebec ministry of education. But planning — "a recipe for avoiding waste, inefficiency, and inertia" — was slow in coming, not only in Quebec but also in English Canada and in the majority of Western countries. Lévesque explained : "The fact is that it is difficult, painful, and laborious to master this kind of modern economic measure because most governments concerned have never attempted it to such an extent." [125] The Economic Advisory Council, which had been counselling the government on several major projects since 1961, promised to present a three-year plan at the beginning of 1965, to be followed by a second three-year plan and two five-year plans. [126] In April 1964, the Minister of Natural Resources revealed his basic position regarding an economic policy for the State of Quebec. There had to be an end to economic colonialism and decisions had to be made in Quebec, by the people of Quebec, "keeping in mind the goals we will have set

---

* In English in the original.

for ourselves." Since 1960, the government had become aware of how important its role was in the economy and the Liberals had realized the fundamental significance of the economic factor in all major decisions — political, legislative, and otherwise. "We need an overview, a uniting force, which the government can provide in the form of a Policy with a capital 'P,' that is, something which has the audacity and far-sightedness to answer our needs and achieve the goals we have just mentioned : greater knowledge and expertise." If such a plan was to be useful it must reject dogma and simply offer a technique ; it must also avoid losing itself in ramifications incomprehensible to the public. It was imperative that the public be well informed so that the constraints necessary to a comprehensive state economic policy could be reconciled with democracy. Finally Lévesque referred to "a sense of urgency without panic, without a resort to the makeshift." "We must take as much time as is necessary," he said, "but no more. This is why we need the pressure of public opinion to hurry along decisions which are ready to be made, because every year we lose now is like losing four twenty-five years ago." [127]

The Minister continued his critique of Confederation before a Laval University student audience :

> The present system is unnatural. It's a jungle in which a certain monster — the federal administration — has grown out of all proportion, while the provinces are simply pushed aside. Nevertheless, men are more important than laws. In what area are the biggest public investments made ? Nearly all of them are in the destructive and deadly area of shared-cost projects. All the federal government has done for the individual in the past fifteen years has in fact been under provincial jurisdiction. [128]

Confederation seen as a jungle ... In less than two years the minister had been heard to use the word "jungle" on forty-odd occasions in relation to the Canadian political system, hydro-electric power, Quebec's forests, monetary affairs, education, agriculture — all these were jungles through which Lévesque had been trying to see the light.

But as far as the political system was concerned, Lévesque was losing his illusions. Speaking to the predominantly English-speaking Young Liberal Association of Notre-Dame-de-Grâce riding in Montreal, he promised English Canadians that he would not talk to them any more about two cultures and two languages until he had found a satisfactory solution. "There are too many factors involved which make the situation confused, so, until the day comes when I have reached some understanding, this evening is the last time I will try to communicate with English Canadians on the subject. It is impossible for me to tell you what English Canada should do for Quebec ; you will have to discover for yourselves what is happening in Quebec, what French Canada is like, what its essential features are, what makes it tick." [129] To those who contested the legitimacy of a decision made by the people of Quebec concerning their future, Lévesque replied : "French Canada is a nation, and a nation has the right to decide its own fate. Independence is only one of three positive options open to Quebec and it is up to us to decide whether it is the right course to take." [130]

Whatever might happen to Quebec, the rights of the non-French-speaking minority would be respected, at least as far as Lévesque was concerned : "No matter what happens in the Quebec of the future, French Canadians would only destroy themselves if they sought to destroy the non-French-speaking population. It is extremist folly to speak of the damned English or the damned Jews. If they live in Québec, they have the same rights as we have and no matter what the Québec we live in, they are and always will be our fellow-citizens." [131]

Lévesque then came one step closer to the solution he sought for Quebec :

> Quebec is suffocating within the confines of an outmoded, obsolete Confederation, and the status quo is untenable now that Quebec has finished merely surviving and knows it can live a full life. Therefore, either Quebec will become an associate state within Canada, with a status guaranteeing it the economic, political, and cultural powers necessary for its growth as a nation, or else Quebec will become independent, free to choose its own destiny within the limits, of course, imposed by the interdependence of nations in the twentieth century. [132]

Pierre Laporte, Paul Gérin-Lajoie, and Jean Drapeau expressed their agreement with the Minister of Natural Resources. Was Quebec headed towards a consensus on the issue of its political future ?

Far from it. The idea of a new federalism was becoming a Tower of Babel, a confusion of competing terms. People began to play with new federalist concepts : co-operative federalism, united federalism, bi-national federalism, functionalist federalism, two languages — one nation, two languages — two nations, one language — several cultures, one culture — several languages, two languages — two cultures, two languages — several cultures, a just society, Quebec first, and, one of the last to surface, profitable federalism. The politicians sometimes deliberately led the public astray with their semantic intricacies.

During 1964, certain Canadian journalists believed they had been entrusted with a mission to save Confederation. There were times when it seemed as if *Le Devoir's* publisher, Claude Ryan, thought that the survival of Confederation depended on his opinions and the correspondence he exchanged with certain editors of the important Toronto newspapers, if not on the friendly relations between Henri Bourassa's daily * and certain influential English-Canadian dailies. As well as allowing historian Ramsay Cook and politician Douglas Fisher to write regularly in his columns, Ryan reprinted editorials from English papers. In his editorial of December 31, 1964, entitled "The Canadian dialogue in 1964," Ryan took stock of the situation :

> The man writing these lines was intimately involved with Canadian life in 1964. He travelled from one ocean to the other far more frequently than the demands of his job required. He spoke to more than a hundred different audiences. He kept a watchful eye on the national press. He kept up a voluminous correspondence with Canadians in every province on questions relating to the future of the country. He strove at the same time to keep in touch with his own milieu. Out of all these experiences one impression stands out so clearly that only those who wish to remain blind to the truth could ignore it : despite much ignorance, there does exist on both sides a real desire for reconciliation and understanding.

Claude Ryan's unconditionally federalist position was far from representative of any consensus among the people of Quebec and alienated many young people during the sixties. At one time it was even said that Ryan had betrayed the tradition of *Le Devoir*.

In the meantime, Lévesque continued his search for a viable solution. The Lévis College student newspaper wrote : "Taking as a starting point his previous proposals concerning an associate State or special provincial status, Mr. Lévesque remarked that 'the goal we must achieve is the most complete social and political

---

* *Le Devoir* was founded by Bourassa in 1910.

independence possible and an interdependence we will have to respect from an economic viewpoint'." [133] Needless to say, this statement made the headlines in all the Quebec dailies.

Meanwhile, young militants who were prepared to use violent means had been setting off bombs. The first wave of bombings took place in 1963 ; the second in 1964. In May 1964, in an address to students at Sainte-Marie College, Lévesque rejected the use of violence in any form, but the newspapers paraphrased one particular sentence incorrectly : "He told the students," reported the *Vancouver Sun*, "the use of guns and dynamite is immoral and these methods could be used only when no other means was available to obtain independence." [134] Two weeks later, afraid that some people might get the wrong impression from this report, he clarified his position :

> Quebec is, and must continue to be, a democratic society. It provides us with freedom of thought and speech, a freely elected government, and a complete legislative apparatus. Any person or group can advocate political or social changes, however radical they may be or may appear to be to certain people, and can use legitimate channels to gather support. In this context, physical violence and terrorist tactics are criminal and stupid. Their use reveals both a lack of courage and a lack of common sense. When you fight for your ideas in a democratic society, you need courage and determination to express yourself openly, to take the barbs and the bouquets, and to keep on going. These qualities are unnecessary if you strike at people blindly in the dark with nothing but brute force. All that needs is a somewhat degraded sense of human dignity, a contempt for human life, and a weakness of spirit typical of those who have so little faith in their ideas that they are afraid to fight for them democratically. We find this very weakness of spirit in those who on the one hand claim to be promoting Quebec's development and on the other are doing everything possible to poison the atmosphere and interfere with Quebec's social and economic progress. Fortunately, they amount to only a very small group of unbalanced persons who command no real support. In fact, I believe they are basically outsiders. They have read about terrorism elsewhere without any knowledge of the situation that produced it, a situation that has absolutely nothing in common with our own. They are therefore isolated and in reality do not communicate with anyone important nor with

anyone outside their circle. If what they did was not so dangerous, they would deserve pity more than anything else. [135]

On December 5, Lévesque reiterated a message on one of his favorite subjects :

> The task for *real democrats* is to see that the people become more and more knowledgeable and informed about their own interests. Freedom is being well-informed ; everything else flows from that. The task before us is to keep people informed, without confusing freedom with destructive irresponsibility. The principal tools of the real democrat are freedom of expression and freedom to inform. These two freedoms do not stem from one particular dogma or received idea ; they presuppose free trade in all ideas, old and new, all of which have their place in the evolution of political thought. They also presuppose that the right to demonstrate will be jealously protected since it is often the only means an unpopular and perhaps prophetic minority can employ to make itself heard. But given the present climate in Quebec, nothing justifies the use of violence and terrorism. [136]

People began to analyse the René Lévesque phenomenon. Jacques Godbout, a writer and filmmaker, wrote :

> Neither he, nor we, nor I, whether taxi-driver, farmer, dentist, or writer, really knew him then as we watched that program *Point de Mire* fly by on Tuesday evenings. Simply, and with unfailing honesty, this professorial type with the husky voice explained the world and its perils to us, while at the same time calming our worst fears by reminding us each time that men have always exploited other men and that no one is a saint. [. . .] Our first lay professor, seducing us from the screen without our ever noticing. Although he thought of himself as a popularizing journalist, he had become the first citizen to communicate intelligently with his fellow-citizens. René Lévesque was a myth long before he realized it. [. . .] René Lévesque, our latest and most modern myth, comes from a long line of heroes : after all, we've made Papineau a household word. What will happen to Lévesque ? A magnificent burial or a revolution ? [137]

A Quebec Ministry of Education was created in March 1964 ; the year ended with the presentation of the Parent Report, which set out the tasks ahead for the Ministry. Although we have been

208

placing great emphasis on Lévesque's position with respect to the future of Quebec and Canada, this does not imply that the Minister of Natural Resources was not interested in the Lesage government's major policies. On the contrary : when the time came, he made his position public. The same applied to his attendance in the Legislative Assembly : "When I had to be there," he said, "I was there."

By 1965, Lévesque was no longer mincing his words. At the beginning of February, after employees of the *Régie des alcools du Québec* [RAQ — Quebec Liquor Board] had been out on strike for two months, Premier Lesage simply advised the strikers to return to work, promising them that he would make a generous settlement afterwards. Lévesque, the last speaker to take the floor in the Legislative Assembly during the debate on the work stoppage, said :

> I am a union man by nature and by experience. The union is the voice of the salaried worker — he has no other refuge. Now if, God forbid, there ever happened to be an emergency fund for the RAQ strikers, I would contribute to it without any misgivings, even though I belong on what is known in such disputes as the management side. I simply see no conflict of interest there. These people have their union and must preserve it because their union gives them strength and dignity. I am convinced that this is true.

He then told his fellow deputies about an encounter with two of the strikers. They asked him : "Listen, we've got our backs to the wall, it's nine weeks or something like that now. What do you think we should do ?" Lévesque replied :

> First of all, don't give up. You have a union. For better or worse, you're unionized. You made the choice yourselves and you chose the union. This involves certain difficulties and obviously means accepting some painful responsibilities on occasion, such as the one you've taken on now by going on strike. Stick it out to the end ! If you don't give in you will gain strength and be respected as you have never been respected before. This strike has been hard on you but it's got to end soon, and because of it you will become — even though you didn't choose to be, it just happened that way — you will become pioneers in the difficult art which the government and its civil servants have to learn, namely, the art of living together. You will receive benefits you can be proud of for once, because instead of having accepted patronizing handouts as in the old days, you'll feel like you've damned well earned them. [138]

Few people failed to notice the contradiction between Lesage's position and Lévesque's. His "don't give up" became famous ; it was a slogan heard in many other strikes, especially those involving salaried employees of the Quebec government. Why had Lévesque repudiated Lesage's position ? Lévesque replied : "People have unfortunately forgotten that I once said, 'as long as I remain in politics (on the terms I have chosen), I can't say everything I think. But the moment I have to go against what I think, I'll go elsewhere'." [139]

His second attack was directed against the McGill University administration, which had just announced a 100-dollar increase in tuition fees. Speaking to 3000 McGill students, who had gathered to protest the increase, the Minister of Natural Resources said :

> Free education at all levels including university has always been a goal of the Quebec government, and any rise in students' fees represents a step backwards in terms of this overall goal. [. . .] Higher education is a fundamental right which must be guaranteed to all those who have talent ; moreover, it is a crucial investment for any civilized society. The Quebec government believes that education, as well as health and other vital needs, are basic rights which must be rescued, when the means permit, from the dense jungle of bank accounts and private interests. [140]

Here was another "jungle" where Lévesque felt a great deal of ground could be cleared.

His most bitter attack that year was directed against Noranda Mines. While touring several Quebec mining sites to meet union workers, the Minister of Natural Resources spoke on Saturday evening, March 27, in Rouyn, right in the heart of the Noranda "kingdom." "You had better learn how to behave in a civilized fashion while there is still time," he warned the mining companies, "or else society will be obliged to find structures other than the traditional ones used to run the mining industry." [141] Noranda Mines quickly issued a communiqué from Toronto, stating that his proposals were foolish. [142]

Two days later, at Sept-Iles, Lévesque clarified his position :

> The mining companies deserve fair treatment on condition that they play the game according to the rules : (1) accept the legislative framework ; (2) respect the normal demands of a collective, local revenue ; (3) give every possible encourage-

ment to social progress ; (4) maintain respect for the local population with regard to their skills, culture, language, and way of seeing things. [143]

But Noranda Mines did not care for his advice. In another communiqué, unsigned this time, and addressed to the Minister, the company alleged that his criticisms were vague and unfounded and that he had become the pawn of the United Steelworkers of America. [144] Lévesque continued the battle of words :

> Even if it were true that I was the pawn of the Steelworkers, I'd rather be the pawn of organized labor in Quebec than the pawn of Noranda Mines, which is what previous governments were. Noranda Mines treats Quebec society with utter contempt. Their policy is to crush the workers using every means possible, infiltrate the unions, sabotage the negotiating teams, and systematically refuse the workers what was conceded everywhere else ten years ago. [145]

Premier Lesage began to worry. Could these attacks against Noranda Mines, like those against the hydro-electric companies, mark the beginning of a campaign by the Minister of Natural Resources which would eventually lead to the nationalization of the mines ? It is likely that the directors of Noranda Mines approached Lesage and asked him to silence his Minister. Journalists Daignault and Clift reported :

> The speech made during a press tour of Quebec's mines developed into headlines of the kind that make business circles break into a cold sweat. Returning to Quebec City, Levesque met a stony-faced Premier Lesage. "I want proof of the charges you've made," snapped the Premier. It is understood Levesque put a number of people to work on a full report for the Premier covering employer-employee relations in all of Noranda's plants. [146]

Quebec's premier could be sure of one thing : his Minister of Natural Resources did not intend to proceed with a nationalization of the mines. Nevertheless, he wanted to "dot his i's," as he told Noranda president John R. Bradfield, who had requested "a private meeting to settle our differences." Lévesque wrote back :

> This debate does not concern me personally nor, dare I say, does it even involve questions related solely to mining. Two basic issues are at stake : first, your Company has shown very

211

little respect, if any, for the cultural climate of Quebec ; second, your company has consistently fought against the very existence of real trade unionism among its employees in Quebec. The civilized thing to do would be to recognize these facts and take strong measures to correct them. [...] As for the question of unions, your company has made its position quite clear. A special amendment to the labor code was needed before you would recognize the right to an optional union deduction from the wages of your Quebec employees. Yet this is a basic and unprovocative measure which had been voluntarily accepted by nearly all industries and mining concerns. [...] In order to discuss economic questions firmly and intelligently with a union, you must first concede that it has its place in the economy, that it represents a real and useful force with goals which in themselves are just as valuable and important as those of the business enterprise concerned. What sense would there be in three-way co-operation if the idea was only to unite industry and government against the unions ? [...] We have to tell the story as we see it. Needless to say, if this general summary of the situation does not in your opinion accord with the facts, we are ready to dot our i's in more detail. [147]

The second volume of the Report of the Interministerial Study Group on the Quebec Pension Plan contains the following statement :

We frequently allow ourselves to be carried away by misleading statistics and to describe Quebec's economy in terms of superlatives. But the moment we put aside our illusions, it is hard not to be struck by the analogy between the structure of Quebec's economy and that of the underdeveloped countries. Quebec has a two-sided economy : one side is strong, based on the development of natural resources according to the economic evolution of the whole continent and typified by mammoth business enterprises ... and the other is inordinately small, scarcely influenced at all by the first and primarily based on the satisfaction of local needs. [148]

Lévesque could not accept an attitude suggestive of the conflict between Rhodesia's leaders and its native population. In any event, it was unnecessary for him to provide Noranda Mines with further details since the company president had decided to keep silent after receiving the letter from the Minister of Natural Resources.

During 1965, Lévesque's attacks on the Canadian political system became less frequent. Did he prefer to let the Laurendeau-Dunton

Royal Commission, whose initial findings were released in February, speak for him ? "Canada is experiencing the greatest crisis in its history," *Le Devoir* reported. "The result will either be a rupture or a rearrangement of the conditions governing its existence. The situation is all the more serious because a certain proportion of the Canadian people are not even aware that the problem exists. [. . .] Today's conflict is no longer the traditional conflict between a majority and a minority. It is a conflict between two majorities : the English-speaking majority in Canada and the French-speaking majority in Quebec." [149] In May, Lévesque reiterated his profession of faith as a Québécois : "If they want Quebec to give up her culture and her institutions it will be over my dead body. We've taken a long time to get started but we're on the way, and Quebec's evolution can't be stopped now." [150] The next day he stated that the brief submitted by the *Presse étudiante nationale* [PEN — National Student Press] to the Quebec Constitutional Committee, recommending political independence for Quebec in conjunction with economic partnership, was most impressive and well prepared : "It is one of the very few briefs I have kept for myself. The solution put forward by PEN is quite valid and very practical." [151]

Lévesque had never taken much interest in discussions on the Canadian constitution, whereas Lesage and Paul Gérin-Lajoie had considered them very important. They supported the formula for repatriation and amendment of the constitution drawn up by Canadian politicians Davie Fulton and Guy Favreau. The intransigent stand taken by Lesage, who referred to those critical of the formula as "ignoramuses," raised cries of protest in nationalist quarters. Various individuals, social groups, and patriotic organizations believed that the formula was too rigid and sold Quebec's rights too cheaply. In March, Lesage asked two of his ministers, Pierre Laporte and René Lévesque, to fill in for the absent Paul Gérin-Lajoie and defend the Fulton-Favreau formula before a student audience at the University of Montreal.

Pierre Laporte, Minister of Cultural Affairs and Municipal Affairs, went about his task enthusiastically. "The Fulton-Favreau formula will protect Quebec from any unilateral action, and this represents an improvement over the present situation." But Lévesque, including himself among the "ignoramuses" on this matter, was more cautious :

The formula I have accepted appears to me to be neither the

213

guarantee of a new era, nor a yoke, nor a defeat, nor a surrender. It is a legal device for translating the *status quo* and, like all legal devices, it lags behind social realities. It is a kind of guarantee of survival, in itself an outmoded concept. The victory has come too late, but it is not a defeat.

Then he expressed his distrust of the legal debates.

We must be careful to avoid throwing ourselves headlong into *the wrong battle at the wrong time at the wrong place.* * [. . .] Quebec has evolved more slowly than the other provinces for many reasons. But for the Québécois, as for any other people, maturity means asserting their right to self-determination. They recognize that the real question behind the legal niceties is : how should we exercise this right and up to what point is it in our interest to do so ? No one today would attempt to block a majority decision by the people of Quebec on the question of their future. French Canadians are aware that they have a real homeland in Quebec. Our apprenticeship in self-determination has given us a taste for liberty. Whether our society progresses or lags behind depends entirely on us from now on. [. . .] A dynamic reality can't be restricted by legal phrases. Those who are playing up the dangers of this formula probably don't understand the realities of Quebec. [152]

It was up to Jacques-Yvan Morin, professor of constitutional law at the University of Montreal, to answer the two Liberal ministers. He quickly demonstrated that the Fulton-Favreau formula would make the colonial yoke weigh even more heavily on French Canada. He therefore recommended that it be rejected, a proposal that easily won the student audience over to his side. This encounter was of no great significance, except that "it was the first time René Lévesque admitted defeat in front of a student audience." One journalist wrote : "What seemed most significant about this debate was that for the first time a group of students expressed considerable disagreement with the Minister. [. . .] 'Opportunist !' shouted someone sitting near us. 'What's happened to him ?' asked another." [153]

Here is Lévesque's version of the encounter recorded eight years later :

Paul Gérin-Lajoie had gone to Europe; in the meantime, Lesage

---

* In English in the original.

had taken his place and at one particular cabinet meeting adopted what amounted to a more extreme position. That created quite a lot of tension, because his position was more extreme than that of the cabinet. During this period, the government position was uncertain, and before we had reached a firm decision on the subject the meeting came up. The University of Montreal students had made quite a fuss over it. Laporte and I were literally ordered by the cabinet and Lesage to defend Lesage's position, at least for the time being. It took me three quarters of an hour or an hour to decide. I said, "OK, I'll go." Meanwhile I was thinking to myself, "Politically it's not very important. It's just more legalities, more of these never-ending legal formulas. In fact Quebec's future will be decided by what the people want." In some ways that decision of mine helped set the pattern for my future political orientation. Anyway, I agreed to go and got myself soundly beaten in the discussion. But the funniest thing about it was that after I got outside I ran into Claude Ryan, who asked me, "Could you give me a lift? The weather's terrible. Do you have your car?" I said, "Yes, I've got my car; come on." At one point Ryan said to me in his usual fashion, "Yes, it was an interesting evening. But I think you'd be wise to pay more attention to constitutional questions. They could become more important than you seemed to think this evening." I laughed and said to him, "No need to tell me that. I've just realized it myself." [154]

In any event, pressure from both the public and the cabinet prompted Premier Lesage to suspend his campaign on behalf of the Fulton-Favreau formula late in March 1965.

The Defeat of the Liberal Government

The Liberal government remained productive even though it had been in office for five years. Early in the fall session of 1965, the Assembly passed laws establishing a pension plan, an investment fund for the pension plan, a collective bargaining agreement for government employees, a royal commission inquiry into agriculture, and a publicly funded mining exploration company (SOQUEM). But if in fact the Liberal team had existed at all, it existed no longer.

Mr. Lesage seems more firmly in control of his party than he was in the fall of 1964. But at the same time, never since

215

1960 has he been so splendidly isolated in his role as leader of the government. On the questions of the Fulton-Favreau formula, SIDBEC, * and the public service legislation, Mr. Lesage has had to defend his position virtually single-handedly. Men like Lévesque, Kierans, and Gérin-Lajoie have hardly opened their mouths. [155]

Furthermore, Lesage was becoming more and more mistrustful of Lévesque. One journalist wrote : "Because Lesage took personal charge of the launching of SIDBEC and the pension plan, Lévesque ended up more or less deprived of the chance to take a radical stand on these two questions which are so crucial to Quebec's future." [156] The party leaders clearly felt that the opinions expressed by the Minister of Natural Resources were often too radical.

But there was another question to be answered : was the government perhaps running out of steam ? Quebec's premier could not agree with this assessment.

> Today we are still moving at the same pace, the same rhythm, that is to say, at a gallop, but as might be expected, people have become used to this rhythm and so it has lost its novelty. That's the truth of the matter. The iron and steel project, the General Investment Corporation, the various volumes of the Parent Report which will bring about a complete transformation of our educational system — all this only lasts a day now in the newspapers. In 1960, people followed our every move and the most unimportant details were seen as part of the revolution taking place in Quebec. [157]

Was it just a matter of habit ? Perhaps, but if the public had grown accustomed to the government's pace, the government in turn had grown accustomed to the exercise of power. "It's quite strange," said René Lévesque.

> I get the impression that we missed the boat somewhat at the very beginning, simply because we weren't ready and perhaps because we weren't really aware how serious were the needs and frustrations people had been carrying around for such a long time. If we had realized just how much potential for change existed in Quebec in '60 and '61, at the beginning, we could have had something resembling a revolution, without

---

* Sidérurgie du Québec, a corporation created by the Quebec government in 1964 to initiate development of a comprehensive steel industry in the province.

destroying anything ; we would have found a way to tear down completely many of the bad habits and structures in Quebec. People were prepared to accept this. If they became less and less so, it was because we began to slow down and because the Liberal Party lapsed into the old vice of patronage, especially the patronage of powerful private interests, and the abuse of campaign funding. Things slowed down and people got fed up. Personally I've never believed in the attitude which says "at the end of three or four years you have to slow down because people are tired out." It wasn't so much that people were tired ; it was just that there were too many WORDS and, in many fields, not enough ACCOMPLISHMENTS and REFORMS. * That's what finally killed the government. It lost its drive ; it was weighed down by a good deal of corruption and plain bad ways of doing business which had reappeared with surprising rapidity. What's bred in the bone will out in the flesh, as they say. [158]

Because of the increasingly important role played by the campaign coffers in behind-the-scenes dealings, the party was forced to soft-pedal its reform program. This factor must also be considered in evaluating public disenchantment. And there was still another. Claude Ryan had alluded to the Quebec premier's "splendid isolation," and there was no denying that Lesage appeared more and more isolated, a fact which did not seem to worry him. His appeal to the Liquor Board strikers and his reference to opponents of the Fulton-Favreau formula as "ignoramuses" had shocked many people. The press, the unions, and the intellectual community were becoming increasingly critical of his party.

The premier, for his part, was running out of patience. In April, a young Quebec terrorist hanged himself in Bordeaux Jail with a strap taken from his artificial leg. The newspapers gave this event heavy coverage, prompting the following reply from Jean Lesage :

> I believe you are placing an undue emphasis on the most trivial matters. Let's talk this over frankly. Try to raise your sights a little higher and see things in proper perspective : the constitution, yes ; the federal-provincial conference, yes ; a guy who hangs himself in Bordeaux no — even with a strap from his wooden leg. Somebody is always trying to stir things up because some guy hanged himself in Bordeaux : we've had

---

* Emphasis mine. [Author's note.]

217

enough of that. There was a big fuss made when a farmer from Chafoura * hanged himself, even though at that time there was no television or radio. It was terrible : he hanged himself because his wife had been unfaithful to him. That was a lot more serious than this other business. Stop trying to make headlines out of trivial events and fillers. [159]

On June 12, the Quebec Premier launched a violent attack against the "separatist dreamers." He called them a variety of unflattering names : dangerous dreamers, disdainful theoreticians, weirdos, overgrown children, tinkers without a craft, certified schemers, doctrinarians, panacea-mongers. Many people who were still unconverted to the idea of sovereignty for Quebec were offended by Lesage's remarks. Claude Ryan wrote : "What is unpleasant about Mr. Lesage's manner is the egotistical way he lays claim to a monopoly on good sense, realism, and responsibility." [160] The premier's splendid isolation could therefore also be seen as sheer egotism.

Some of the reasons for the Liberals' political decline have become clear : lack of public interest, the campaign coffers, and the attitude of the premier. But there was one other extremely important element, the still unanswered question people had been asking for two years : after the introduction of measures designed to help Quebec back on its feet, what was the next step ? Where was Quebec headed ? Lévesque pointed out that there had been too many words and often not enough accomplishments and reforms. And what about the plan ? It had been under discussion for two years and each year it was promised for the following year. What was behind this apparent inability to produce a plan ? Lack of competence, lack of information, negligence on the part of the Economic Advisory Council, lack of political support, federal interference in Quebec's affairs ?

In March 1966, the Economic Advisory Council, which had still not been able to furnish a plan for Quebec, outlined the numerous obstacles that stood in the way of such a plan :

> Some of these difficulties included a dearth of information and research in the economic sphere, a lack of economic programming methods as well as personnel with experience in planning, and a climate unconducive to close co-operation between government, employers, and unions. Obstacles of an institutional

---

* Lesage's reference to "Chafoura" is an ironic jibe at his journalistic opponents ; there is no such place.

nature soon became apparent. There was an obvious lack in Quebec of structures or mechanisms designed to co-ordinate the activities of social groups, businesses, and governments, not to mention the activities of the various Quebec ministries themselves. The division of economic responsibilities between the federal government and the Quebec government placed another limitation on planning within the provincial jurisdiction. [. . .] Furthermore, economic analysis revealed problems inherent within the Canadian economy as a whole, but which were particularly serious in Quebec itself. It was necessary to acknowledge that economic activity sprang up in Quebec almost exclusively because of free enterprise, which to a large degree was run from decision centres located outside the province and evolved in step with foreign interests rather than the internal workings of the economy.

A few lines later, the Economic Advisory Council compared Quebec to certain European countries and referred again to the economic conditions peculiar to a federal system :

It would have been necessary to take into account all of Quebec's economic problems in order to have understood at the beginning of 1964 why it was impossible to formulate quickly a plan adapted to the needs of Quebec based on an established model such as the French Plan or the Dutch Plan. Economic conditions and goals in a territory with open borders, such as a province, differ completely from those in an independent, unified, and self-sufficient state. [161]

For whatever reasons, it is still not possible to judge the truth of all these remarks. One thing is certain : the Economic Advisory Council was painting a picture of a situation which Lévesque might have described as a "jungle" and it was admitting its inability to achieve any progress in this area after five years' work. Quebec was therefore doomed for the time being to remain at the talking stage and fall short of real accomplishments. The Johnson government would later rely on the use of rhetoric at the international level to cover up the short-sightedness of its policies at home. It was like seeing Madeleine de Verchères fight her battle all over again : the handful of settlers cleverly setting up a number of hats around the stockade and keeping up a steady fire to make the Indians outside think they were outnumbered. But the illusion was short-lived : the Bertrand and Bourassa administrations preferred to throw the gates wide open and let the Indians in.

On October 14, 1965, Premier Lesage shuffled his cabinet. Eric Kierans and René Lévesque left ministries whose main concerns were economic to take charge of the Ministry of Health and the Ministry of Family and Social Welfare respectively. If the two men were disappointed, they did not let their disappointment show, and at first they seemed enthusiastic about their new posts. Only much later did Lévesque reveal that they had both nearly left the government.

> In '65, when Kierans and I changed portfolios, we got out of the economic side of things because nothing was going very well any more. At that point we nearly cleared out altogether. I remember — and I think the same was true for Kierans — that it was guys we'd worked with like Michel Bélanger and others who convinced us to stay because there were still things to do. We were pretty fed up !

When asked if this had anything to do with difficulties involving the federal government, Lévesque replied :

> Sure ! That and everything else too. Basically the government had lost its drive. In some respects it had fallen into the old routine, and it became more and more difficult as time went on to see projects through to their conclusion. [162]

The day of the swearing-in, Kierans and Lévesque announced that they were going to work as a team in the area of social welfare. The Minister of Family and Social Welfare explained that certain urgent measures had to be introduced as quickly as possible : medicare for the poor, a universal health insurance scheme, and the formulation of a comprehensive social welfare policy. The new minister intended to be guided in large part by the report of the Social Welfare Study Group, prepared by J.-Emile Boucher, Marcel Bélanger, and Claude Morin, and presented to the Quebec government in June 1963. "I have read and re-read it, studied it from every angle," said Lévesque. "It must be implemented as soon as possible, more or less as it stands." When asked how long it would take him to implement his new social welfare policy, the minister replied : "I'll take however long is necessary.... Look at the nationalization of electricity, that went faster than I thought it would." [163] In an interview Lévesque added :

> Kierans and I formed a team that was intended to last at least two years. We said to ourselves : "Over the next two years

October 1965. The new Minister of Family and Social Welfare takes the oath of office.

we're going to try to marry Health and Social Welfare." We wanted to do something like what Castonguay did, but not so quickly, because there was a whole series of things to coordinate in that area which had to be approached with great care and tact. We were interested in seeing what we could do. [164]

During the first quarter of 1966, Lévesque's public statements became more and more personal. Despite his promise to English Canadians to refrain from speaking to them about language and culture as long as his own opinions were undecided, he spoke to four hundred McGill University students on January 24. The *Gazette* quoted from his speech : "Many businesses here, he said, seem to be arrogant and ignorant of the fact that 80 per cent of the population is French. He warned them to be civilized and respect the French position *while there is still time.*" [165] The minister felt that certain English-speaking businessmen had an almost Rhodesian attitude to the French-speaking majority. A month later he said :

221

"The awakened French Canada is not against any group or its rights, only against the entrenched privileges of a dominant minority. Quebec's awakening is a positive phenomenon that is not only tolerant but deeply respectful of minority rights. Not privileges, but rights." [166]

In Sainte-Foy, he advised a group of seventeen- to twenty-year-old students

> not to join any political organizations before completing university, since that would be a sign of premature old age ; you have no business latching on to fixed or fanatical ideas or to uncompromising attitudes. You should keep your mind open to something besides the passions of the moment. [...] I am evolving continually ...and I think politicians and citizens alike should do so. [...] In the field of human endeavor, I reject the idea of dogma. If I were dogmatic, by definition that would mean that I had stopped thinking. Which is what reassures me about being attacked by both the Quebec Socialist Party and the extreme right-wing magazine *Aujourd'hui-Québec,* since being 100 per cent socialist is crazy if it means twisting reality to make it fit the dogma, and creating soulless, complicated bureaucratic machines like the ones in the USSR, which only oppress the people. [167]

At a conference on poverty in Montreal, he returned to this subject : "Being a realist is sometimes difficult, but it's more effective than preaching high-minded unattainable ideals." [168]

Kierans and Lévesque had given themselves two years to get things in order in the field of social welfare. But their partnership did not last that long, because in April 1966 Jean Lesage announced a general election for June 5. On April 18, a journalist asked Lévesque for his comments on this decision. "I only want it to be over as quickly as possible," he replied. He explained that the situation before an election was always the same. "Once you know it's coming, everybody turns up in the House and does less and less work and makes more and more election promises." [169]

The Liberal Party had a head start simply because no one could imagine the late Maurice Duplessis' party returning to power. Two nationalist parties, *le Rassemblement pour l'indépendance nationale* [RIN — Rally for National Independence] and *le Ralliement national* [RN — Nationalist Rally], were ready to do battle with the Liberals and the Union Nationale, whose election slogan was *"Egalité ou indépendance"* [Equality or Independence].

222

1965. The Lévesque-Kierans team faces the press.

The Liberal strategists organized the campaign around their leader, Jean Lesage ; the team that had contested the two previous elections was no more to be seen. The new approach to this campaign was in keeping with the evolution the Liberal Party had undergone. As Claude Ryan observed : "This election will not mark a great moment in our political life, as did the elections of 1936, 1944, and 1960. It will be more the administrative kind, one that will reflect the relative competence of the various teams rather than any fundamental ideas." [170]

Certain public opinion polls were predicting a Liberal win, but only by a slight margin, until a few days before the election, when it was announced that the two major parties were neck and neck. But the Quebec press showed the Liberals in a less favorable light than the principal opposition party, the Union Nationale. The image offered of the *Rassemblement pour l'indépendance nationale* was particularly favorable, whereas a number of undesirable features in the *Ralliement national* had been played up. [171]

The result of the June 5 election was a tremendous upset : the
Union Nationale was returned to power. The Liberals had managed
to elect only fifty deputies, while the Union Nationale under Daniel
Johnson had elected fifty-six. When we look for an explanation
of this defeat, which in retrospect seemed inevitable, no single factor
stands out above the rest. Did it have to do with "the fresh new
image presented by the Union Nationale"? Or perhaps the harsh
demands of the Liberal reform program, which left thousands of
discontented people in its wake and "aroused profound anxieties
in large sections of the population"? Was it the presence of the
RIN which, in thirteen ridings, made up the difference between the
Liberals and the Union Nationale? Did the electorate want to teach
Jean Lesage a lesson in humility? And what about the behavior
of the Quebec press, which had supported the Union Nationale?
Robert Cliche believed that the defeat was due to the "lack of
public participation in the reforms introduced by the Liberal Party
in several areas." The publisher of *Le Devoir* wrote : "The Liberals
were the principal architects of their own defeat : they were too
sure of themselves and at the same time incapable of masking or
repairing the numerous flaws that had appeared here and there in
their machine before it was too late. They succumbed once again to
their usual weakness — complacency." The disaster might also
have been the result of outdated electoral boundaries. The returns
in fact showed that the Union Nationale had won with 41.2 per
cent of the popular vote, whereas the Liberal Party had come second with 47 per cent. On the evening of election day, Lévesque
admitted that "if the party's goals have been and still are valid, then
the government failed in its efforts to explain them clearly to the
people." [172] A few days later, speaking on a CBC program, he
lamented the fact that Quebec could only move ahead in fits and
starts and was incapable of sustaining "a steady rhythm of progress." He added : "Perhaps it will some day." [173]

Seven years later, Lévesque described how he felt the day after
the election :

> First of all, I wasn't surprised by the result because we had
> watched the campaign go to pieces very quickly. Lesage's
> entourage had the fatal idea of mounting a Gaullist-style cam-
> paign — they had used the term before but they didn't ap-
> preciate the implications — in other words, to centre everything
> around one man. It was the first campaign not centred around
> the team. This time Lesage went campaigning all by himself,

occasionally with Claude Wagner, but usually by himself. That quickly undercut our whole image. In retrospect, of course, you can find other reasons —ᵧ the weariness of six years in office, etc. But I remember as I came back from a tour of the Lower St. Lawrence and the Gaspé having the feeling that everything had gone wrong. That was around mid-May, at least two or three weeks before the election. Putting together the reactions of those covering other regions, keeping an eye on what was going on around me, reading the papers and the polls which said 55 or 56 seats or something like that, I said to myself : "If they're right, that's fine, because things could be a lot worse." You sensed there was no way to regain the ground we had lost. Lesage had really made too many mistakes and he was too much the centre of attention to be able to put us back on the right track. So I wasn't surprised the evening of June 5. Disappointed ? A little, because, strangely enough, I'm a bad administrator when it comes to my own affairs, but I liked being in the government, being part of the decision-making apparatus, the administrative apparatus. Moreover, Johnson had to admit when he took charge that the department had been well administered. He couldn't find anything wrong ; it was in good shape because I liked the work. So the evening of June 5 there was a certain disappointment in giving up the reins just when the team Kierans and I had formed was about to get off the ground. From the political point of view, on the other hand, there was no great disappointment because you could feel it coming for some time. [174]

Was the disappointment mitigated because the government's defeat allowed Lévesque to follow his own course ? "No, that isn't what came to mind at first," he replied. "I felt the mixed reaction I've just been describing that evening or the next day. Then there was a new challenge on top of that — working in the Opposition. I hadn't known what it was like, since I had gone straight into the government without any previous experience."

The Opposition was certainly formidable ; many said of the Johnson government that it had the strongest opposition ever seen in the history of Confederation. Journalist Vincent Prince wrote :

In fact, one wonders if Quebec will ever have an opposition of this stature again. [. . .] Mr. Lesage will give the new Premier his greatest cause for concern by pestering him from all sides at once. But there are others as well. The new Minister of Education will not be holding all the trumps when he clashes

225

with Mr. Paul Gérin-Lajoie, who not only knows the workings of this department but was also the man behind all the educational reforms. He is well known, moreover, for being a hard worker. And what can we say about Mr. René Lévesque, who even when he sat on the Speaker's right, could be trusted to have strong opinions of his own ? [. . .] Then there is Mr. Pierre Laporte, who showed while in office that he was a good administrator and a skilful parliamentarian. [. . .] The same can be said of Mr. Eric Kierans, the financier who quickly learned the art of politics and government. The other former ministers — Gérard-D. Lévesque, Claude Wagner, Lucien Cliche, Alcide Courcy, Gaston Binette, Bernard Pinard, Claire Kirkland-Casgrain, Richard Hyde, and Emilien Lafrance — will not always be easily satisfied either. [175]

However, there were more disappointments to come. Not only did Quebec lose the government that had fostered the quiet revolution, but the strong opposition expected of the Liberals never materialized. Why ? According to Lévesque :

It soon became obvious that the exercise of power had exhausted some of us, and many had reputations they just couldn't live up to any more. Paul Gérin-Lajoie was one of the few who didn't seem to be played out. Many were completely exhausted and ended up empty shells, although, to tell the truth, some of them had always been that way. You always get people like that in a government, but their true colors show more readily as opposition members because if you're no longer the Honorable Minister with important things to do, then it's really obvious. But what weakened us most the first year was the wrangling which soon cropped up over our future course. A whole group of us felt there wasn't much point in continuing the political struggle just to get back into power some day and find ourselves at the helm of the same old sinking ship. [176]

After the 1966 elections, the Liberals held held several *post-mortem* meetings.

First of all, tradition demanded the meeting of the defeated cabinet. Then there were the meetings with what was known as the Liberal Federation, which had recently become quite active after having been pretty much shelved during the government's last days in office. But in the course of getting ourselves together after the defeat, it suddenly became important to talk to the guys who had been neglected before. [177]

The last meetings were concerned with the party's future direction. "We obviously couldn't help wondering where we were headed in the next four years," said Lévesque. "Or in other words, how we could get ready for the next stage."

Lévesque was happy to let events take their course, since he was rediscovering a certain freedom. On July 26, he stated in an interview with the *Gazette* : "I have the impression it could be fascinating." The interviewers added : "Especially after six years of that damned thing — power — which he compared with being caught in a narrow corridor and having to move straight ahead without stopping to explore behind any of the doors." The ex-minister continued : "Now I'm at the end of the corridor and there are 25 doors waiting, now I can stop and think about things, like the political role of television." And indeed in July and August he launched a series of violent attacks against privately-owned radio and television stations. At the beginning of September, he expressed the opinion that the social measures being taken in Quebec on the whole were like "a kind of patchwork quilt, with the pieces stuck together according to luck at the polls and election promises, socio-economic conditions, and occasional political pressures." How could this situation be untangled ? By settling the jurisdictional disputes between Quebec and Ottawa, another jungle in which "even a mother cat would be unable to find her little ones," and by the progressive elimination of the virtual monopoly exercised by private charity and the churches. [178] This statement was enough to make the secretary-general of the Quebec Liberal Federation, Henri-A. Dutil, fly into a rage. Dutil asserted that the QLF had received "just treatment" at the hands of the private broadcasters and said he could not condone Lévesque's position concerning private charity and the virtual monopoly of the churches.

In the political sphere, Lévesque was more and more convinced that Quebec was a colony, "an underdeveloped society, undereducated, colonized, lacking in character and pride, though, paradoxically, well fed and comfortable, lulled by the élite and its puppet kings into the kind of utter mediocrity that could be fatal to it, exalting its culture yet destroying its language at the same time." [179] In October, he stated : "The brute fact we must accept is that economically we are a colony. And only by taking control of our economic life, which the state alone is capable of letting us do, can we guarantee the survival and development of our language and our French culture." [180] But many of those who, like Lévesque,

227

were busy mulling over plans for the Liberal Party's future did not share this opinion. Lévesque explained the situation to journalist Jacques Guay :

> After the 1966 defeat a group formed around Lapalme, the "Club Saint-Denis" gang. We held post-mortems until we were blue in the face. We enjoyed ourselves, but we kept wondering, "where are we headed ?" We had to take our next leap forward. "What status do we want for Quebec ?" Some of them were getting cold feet and even questioning the *"Maîtres chez nous"* position. They felt that that slogan, which had helped us win in 1962, caused our defeat in 1966. Since we couldn't all agree, we decided to shelve the constitutional question and we went back to the problem of campaign contributions. [181]

The Liberal Federation held a convention in Montreal from November 18 to 20. Three Liberals — Kierans, Casgrain, and Brière — made representations to the Federation leadership concerning democratization of the party finances. They wanted to put into effect a resolution adopted at the 1963 convention which called for "the creation of a steering committee which would delegate to certain parliamentary members and party officials the responsibility for working out collection procedures and administering all party funds in co-operation with the party leader." Lévesque did not hesitate to lend his support to the trio and took a strong stand on campaign contributions.

> The major parties who have formed governments in Quebec use financing methods that are relics of an outmoded feudal system, incompatible with democracy and extremely dangerous to the public interest. The leader of the party, who appoints the campaign fund collectors, traditionally retains sole responsibility for collecting and administering party funds, while the elected members and party workers are kept in the dark. When the parties took their turn at governing, secretly financed by a handful of men unaccountable to anyone but themselves, for a long time they went so far as to barter Quebec's natural resources for campaign contributions ; this in addition to the system of kickbacks, selling permits, etc. [182]

On this same occasion the member from Laurier gave as an example Mitchell Sharp's "mysterious and disturbing" decision to postpone implementation of a federal health insurance scheme. "How much did the insurance and pharmaceutical companies contribute to the campaign coffers ?" asked Lévesque.

Summer 1972. The Parti Québécois leader astride a pony at a picnic in Saint-Léonard.

While the convention was in full swing, the CBC broadcast an interview obtained by journalist Teddy Chevalot with Irénée Lapierre, retiring president of the Liberal Federation. He stated that Eric Kierans was "a tool of René Lévesque" and that Lévesque himself "was no longer of any use to the Liberal Party." He then added : "I would go even further and say that he's no longer useful to any political party." [183] His remarks caused a great uproar at the convention on its last day of business and he was forced to withdraw them. Of the three who wanted to be elected in order to clean up the party finances, Eric Kierans was the only who succeeded — Casgrain and Brière were defeated by Bernard Pinard and Jean Morin. The reformists therefore won a moral victory, but the Lapierre incident aroused bitter feelings and the party left the convention more divided than ever.

It quickly became apparent that the presence of Eric Kierans at the head of the Liberal Federation administration would not be a sufficiently strong antidote to what Lévesque called "the most destructive, the most corrosive poison that can attack parliamentary institutions" — the abuse of campaign funds. But the deputy for Laurier went his own way. He wanted to move beyond the talking stage to answer the question "Where is Quebec headed ?" and to convince the people of Quebec — after convincing the Liberal Party itself — of the need for a plan. "A plan," he said,

> is the itinerary of a society. A plan could be implemented without delay in Quebec if the government really put its mind to it. Even though Quebec now has a government that is conservative and therefore basically against planning, it would still work because Quebec is experiencing a turning point. The people of the province are beginning to discover their real needs, their life-and-death concerns, while the established élites resist the necessary changes at every turn and work their overriding influence upon the major parties. A plan means that the state must take the upper hand completely, and act as motor, co-ordinator, and prime mover ; at the same time it must lay all its resources on the line, from beginning to end. A plan requires that men, especially politicians, comprehend the general good and possess a consuming devotion to it. This means a government made up of politicians who have no connections with private interests, who are obsessed with the general good. For the time may come when electoral considerations have to be sacrificed in the interests of planning. [184]

And why place such great importance on economic factors ?

> If we master our economy, it will serve us well and vice versa.
> [. . .] If we want our existence to have some direction, we must
> bring the economy of Quebec under our control in an orderly
> manner or else our best efforts will be in vain. [185]

And what would happen if Quebec did not finally manage to
formulate a plan ? Lévesque's answer : "If we do not manage to
draw up this itinerary for ourselves, then we are in danger of
floundering around until discouragement sets, in and eventually,
given the kind of age we live in, of undergoing the same slow
disintegration that seems to be the fate of all those smaller nations
who are incapable of self-development." [186] For five years Lévesque
had believed in the merits of planning and in the necessity for the
state to solve fundamental economic problems. "Only the State of
Quebec is capable of accomplishing this by encouraging the people
of Quebec to fight for their own interests."

In February 1967, he made a speaking tour of the western
provinces. "In Vancouver he stated that the situation in Quebec is
the same as in Rhodesia — 'a privileged minority governs a deprived majority. The only difference between Quebec and Rhodesia
is the color of our skin'." [187] And he warned English Canada :
"Either Quebec gets a new deal or eventually it will get out. [188] In
Saint-Jean-d'Iberville, he stated that "the least Quebec should do
would be to fight to get a *new association* with the rest of the
country." [189]

Lévesque's opinions concerning Quebec's place on the North
American political checkerboard were becoming more and more
precise. He was still a deputy and a member of the Liberal Party
despite his disagreements with the party leadership, and he wanted
to renew the debate on the party's future course, which had been
suspended before the convention of November 1966. On April 1
and 2, twenty "progressive Liberals," as they were called, held a
special meeting at a Mont-Tremblant hotel. Those present included
Eric Kierans, René Lévesque, Paul Gérin-Lajoie, François Aquin,
Yves Michaud, Claire Kirkland-Casgrain, Jean-Paul Lefebvre, Robert Bourassa, and Gilles Houde. [190] All had been preoccupied with
the evolution of the party's political philosophy since the convention in November. Lévesque's position was unequivocally nation-
alistic ; others, like Gérin-Lajoie, Bourassa, and Lefebvre, were
undecided. [191]

231

Lévesque gleaned little from the meeting in the Laurentians, though he came to realize that the majority of the Liberal deputies did not share his feeling that there was an urgent need to settle the constitutional question. Laurent Laplante, editorial writer for *L'Action,* wrote : "From now on it's up to Mr. Lévesque to state clearly under what conditions he is prepared to remain in the Liberal Party." [192] Lévesque gathered around him like-minded members of both the Liberal Federation and the Laurier Riding Liberal Association in order to hammer out a new party philosophy. Claude Ryan was watching him evolve :

> Whenever Mr. René Lévesque makes public his private anguish over the political future of Quebec, there is something in his manner of doing so that is both unusual and captivating. [. . .] Mr. Lévesque remains a very special kind of man. He risked everything for the Liberal Party in 1960. He was one of the chief architects of the renaissance for which his party was responsible between 1960 and 1966. Even while in office, he has always managed to preserve his independent attitude, a certain quality at once very personal and very detached which has made him, and continues to make him, a very special sort of person. Mr. Lévesque has often got away with doing and saying things that would not be forgiven in a Gérin-Lajoie or even a Kierans. [193]

Another Liberal Party convention was scheduled for the fall of 1967. The leaders of the Party and the Federation were concerned about the solutions which might be put forward by the Lévesque group. As of June, the Liberal Party executive had decided that the "six key subjects accorded top priority in the convention debates" would not include the constitutional question, which was not, they felt, of much interest to the public. Lévesque found this decision "hard to believe" :

> The Quebec Liberal Party is in danger of being irrevocably betrayed. For several years this party presided over the unprecedented rejuvenation of Quebec and of her government in particular. It is only reasonable to expect this process to continue accelerating, because it is still very new and its forward progress cannot and must not be stopped. It is equally reasonable to expect this process of accelerated development to arouse a certain amount of anxiety : after all, the whole business has had more than its share of sorcerer's apprentices. But what we

232

cannot allow is to have Quebec betrayed by the virtual renun-
ciation of all our most valuable accomplishments to date. I
think the public expects us, and rightly so, to show some
courage and confront the question "where is Quebec headed ?"
then to discuss matters openly and flexibly so that everyone will
have a clear understanding of the situation. In that way we
will know where we stand and can shake hands on it, no matter
whether we continue on together or not. [194]

The party leaders then changed their minds and decided to include
the constitutional question on the convention agenda after all, giving
it "top priority among the top priority subjects."

The day of reckoning was near. Lévesque had been working out
a new political philosophy with the help of Robert Bourassa, a
young accountant and Liberal member for Mercier. What exactly
was this newly elected deputy's role ? Lévesque said,

Robert played the game — how sincere he was I don't know.
What was going through his head at the time ? I don't know.
But for the crucial two or three months before the month
preceding the convention — from, say, early summer or late
spring to September — Bourassa was part of our group. There
was Brière, Boivin, Beaulé, a few dozen people altogether, of
whom about one dozen were really active, as well as — I'll
never forget this — nearly the whole Laurier Riding Liberal
Association who had rallied to the cause, thrown in their support, and been kept informed all the way, including, among
others, Gérard Bélanger, who was president of the Association
at that point. Robert Bourassa played his part along with the
rest of us. I remember he not only studied the project and
helped with the work, but it was in his basement — and this
is a fact — on the eve of the last day, that we completed the
final revision of the rough draft I had prepared. I had been
given the job of writing up a resolution, though it was in fact
more like a manifesto. He found excuses that evening, mostly
financial and so on, terribly last-minute excuses, for not sticking
with us. That's how he dropped us, although he had been with
us all through the crucial period right until that evening. It
was quite a surprise — and I'd prefer not to elaborate on that
— to see him drop out at the last minute. There was only one
other guy who quit, but he had perfectly good reasons. He was
employed by an English firm and he had young children ; he
had no money ; and he was sure he'd have been fired if he
signed our document. So his decision was completely under-

standable, but in Bourassa's case, it was hard to understand, because he wasn't in the same position. [195]

Immediately upon announcing the decision to include the constitutional question on the convention agenda, the party asked Paul Gérin-Lajoie, president of the Political Commission's Constitutional Affairs Committee, to prepare a report on the subject and submit it to the committee members before the convention began. Eric Kierans, president of the QLF, made a public statement to the effect that there could not be two constitutional positions within the party. The message was clear : the party intended to make short work of the Lévesque "problem."

Chapter 4 — References

1. Pierre de Bellefeuille and Jean-Pierre Bergeron, *La Révolution Tranquille*. A series of 13 one-hour documentaries produced for CBC radio. Second program, 17 June, 1972.
2. *Le Devoir,* 13 January, 1959.
3. *Le Devoir,* 14 February, 1959.
4. De Bellefeuille and Bergeron.
5. Ibid.
6. Georges-Emile Lapalme, *Le vent de l'oubli* (Leméac, 1970), pp. 281-282. Vol. 2 of his memoirs (3 vols.).
7. Interview with R.L., 9 May, 1973.
8. Ibid.
9. Ibid.
10. Jacques Guay, "Comment René Lévesque est devenu indépendantiste," *Le Maclean,* February 1969.
11. Ken Johnstone, "The Man in the Middle of Quebec's New Deal," *Maclean's* 18 November, 1961, p. 43. The author quotes the French translation, "René Lévesque à la conquête de l'économie," *Le Maclean,* December 1961, p. 65.
12. André Gilbert, Pierre Larivière, and Jacques Patenaude, "Vingt ans de journalisme, Mouvement-Souveraineté-Association, Espoir-Difficultés-Avenir," *Défi,* n.d., p. 5. (Probably published between January and April, 1968.)
13. Lapalme, *Le vent de l'oubli,* pp. 286-287.
14. Ibid., p. 286.
15. Interview with R.L., 9 May, 1973.
16. *La Presse,* 7 May, 1960.
17. See Jean-Louis Roy, *Les programmes électoraux du Québec,* 2 vols. (Leméac, 1970-71), 2:378-388.
18. *La Presse,* 16 May, 1960.
19. *Le Devoir,* 21 May, 1960.
20. *Montréal-Matin,* 26 May, 1960.

21. *Le Devoir,* 27 May, 1960.
22. *Le Devoir,* 29 May, 1960.
23. André Laurendeau, *Le Devoir,* 31 May, 1960.
24. *Le Devoir,* 31 May, 1960.
25. *Le Soleil,* 31 May, 1960.
26. *Notre Temps,* 4 June, 1960.
27. *L'Evénement-Journal,* 7 June, 1960.
28. *Le Guide du Nord,* 9 June, 1960.
29. *Montréal-Matin,* 9 June, 1960.
30. *La Presse,* 9 June, 1960.
31. *La Presse,* 10 June, 1960.
32. *La Voix de l'Est,* 11 June, 1960.
33. *La Tribune,* 11 June, 1960.
34. *Le Devoir,* 13 June, 1960.
35. *Le Devoir,* 16 June, 1960.
36. Ibid.
37. Ibid.
38. Lapalme, *Le vent de l'oubli,* pp. 287-288.
39. *Le Devoir,* 16 June, 1960.
40. *Notre Temps,* 18 June, 1960.
41. *Le Devoir,* 20 June, 1960.
42. Ibid.
43. Ibid.
44. *Le Devoir,* 21 June, 1960.
45. Ibid.
46. Ibid.
47. Gérard Filion, *Le Devoir,* 21 June, 1960.
48. *Le Devoir,* 22 June, 1960.
49. Jean and Marcel Hamelin, *Les moeurs électorales dans le Québec, de 1791 à nos jours* (Editions du Jour, 1962), p. 116.
50. Gérard Filion, *Le Devoir,* 23 June, 1960.
51. Jean Hamelin and André Garon, "La vie politique au Québec de 1956 à 1966," in *Quatre élections provinciales au Québec,* ed. Vincent Lemieux (Presses de l'Université Laval, 1969), p. 14.
52. Quoted by de Bellefeuille and Bergeron.
53. Gérard Bergeron, *Ne bougez plus! Portraits de 40 de nos politiciens* (Editions du Jour, 1968), p. 151.
54. Jean O'Neil, "René Lévesque, un intérêt dévorant : le Canada français," *Le magazine de La Presse,* 7 July, 1962, p. 4.
55. Interview with R.L., 9 May, 1973.
56. *L'Action catholique,* 6 July, 1960.
57. Georges-Emile Lapalme, *Le paradis du pouvoir* (Leméac, 1973), p. 39. Vol. 3 of his memoirs (3 vols.).
58. *L'Action catholique,* 19 August, 1960.
59. *La Presse,* 20 September, 1960.
60. Francine Vachon, unpublished interview with Lévesque (Montreal, 5 October, 1971).
61. *L'Action catholique,* 19 October, 1960.
62. *Le Soleil,* 19 October, 1960.
63. Lapalme, *Le paradis du pouvoir,* p. 51.
64. Interview with R.L., 9 May, 1973.
65. *La Tribune,* 29 November, 1960.
66. Fernand Séguin, interview with Georges-Emile Lapalme on CBC television's *Le Sel de la Semaine,* 18 November, 1968.

67. *Le Soleil*, 1 February, 1961.
68. *Le Soleil*, 3 March, 1961.
69. *L'Action catholique*, 20 April, 1961.
70. *L'Action catholique* and *Le Devoir*, 19 June, 1961.
71. *Le Devoir*, 27 June, 1961.
72. *L'Action catholique*, 9 June, 1961.
73. *La Tribune*, 22 September, 1961.
74. *La Presse*, 13 May, 1961.
75. *La Réforme*, 2 December, 1961.
76. *Le Nordet*, 6 December, 1961.
77. *Le Devoir*, 31 October, 1961.
78. *Le Nouveau Journal*, 28 November, 1961.
79. René Lévesque. Text of his address, 26 October, 1961, pp. 15-16.
80. *Le Devoir, Le Nouveau Journal, Le Soleil,* and *La Presse,* 18 November, 1961.
81. *Montréal-Matin,* 10 November, 1961.
82. *Le Devoir,* 4 December, 1961.
83. *L'Action catholique,* 13 December, 1961.
84. Quoted by Peter Gzowski, "Portrait of an Intellectual in Action," *Maclean's,* 24 February, 1962, p. 30. The author quotes the French translation, "Un capitaliste socialisant : Pierre-Elliott Trudeau," *Le Maclean,* March 1962, p. 55.
85. *La Presse,* 12 February, 1962.
86. René Lévesque. Outline of his address at the opening of Electricity Week, 12 February, 1962, p. 5.
87. Interview with R.L., 9 May, 1973.
88. *La Tribune,* 14 February, 1962.
89. Vincent Prince, *La Presse,* 14 February, 1962.
90. René Lévesque, *L'électricité dans le Québec.* Text of statement distributed to the press, 15 February, 1962, p. 8.
91. Lapalme, *Le paradis du pouvoir,* p. 165.
92. *La Presse,* 19 October, 1960.
93. René Lévesque. Text of his address to the Canadian Club, Montreal, 9 April, 1962, p. 8.
94. Jean-V. Dufresne, "La bataille de l'électricité," *Le Maclean,* November 1962, p. 84.
95. Dominique Clift and Richard Daignault, *La Presse,* 17 April, 1962.
96. Lapalme, *Le paradis du pouvoir,* pp. 166-167
97. *Le Soleil,* 19 October, 1960, p. 169.
98. Ibid., p. 170.
99. Interview with R.L., 9 May, 1973.
100. De Bellefeuille and Bergeron, 1 July, 1972.
101. Lapalme, *Le Paradis du pouvoir,* pp. 173-174.
102. Interview with R.L., 9 May, 1973.
103. Réal Pelletier, *Le Devoir,* 23 October, 1962.
104. Pierre O'Neil, *La Presse,* 8 November, 1962.
105. Quoted by Richard Daignault and Dominique Clift, *La Presse,* 12 November, 1962.
106. J.M. Bourbonnais, *La Presqu'île,* 11 October, 1962.
107. Lapalme, *Le paradis du pouvoir,* p. 185.
108. Interview with R.L., 9 May, 1973.
109. Ibid.
110. *La Presse,* 31 May, 1963.
111. Lapalme, *Le paradis du pouvoir,* p. 226.

112. Robert McKenzie, *Montreal Gazette,* 11 January, 1963.
113. Interview with R.L., 9 May, 1973.
114. René Lévesque. Text of his address to the convention of electricity co-operatives, 28 January, 1963.
115. Roland Parenteau, "Les problèmes du développement régional dans un état fédératif : l'expérience canadienne," *Revue d'économie politique,* March-April 1963.
116. Jean O'Neil, "René Lévesque, un intérêt dévorant," p. 12.
117. *Financial Post,* 23 March, 1963.
118. *Toronto Star,* 1 June, 1963.
119. Ibid.
120. *L'Action catholique,* 7 June, 1963.
121. Claude Ryan, *Le Devoir,* 29 June. 1963.
122. *La Tribune,* 28 September, 1963.
123. *La Presse,* 29 October, 1963.
124. *Toronto Globe and Mail,* 31 October, 1963.
125. *Le Soleil,* 5 December, 1963.
126. *Financial Post,* 22 February, 1964.
127. René Lévesque, "La politique économique de l'Etat du Québec," *L'Action nationale,* September 1964, pp. 44-75.
128. *La Presse,* 16 January, 1964.
129. *La Presse,* 7 March, 1964.
130. *Montréal-Matin,* 24 March, 1964.
131. *Montréal Gazette,* 7 April, 1964.
132. *Le Devoir,* 17 May, 1964.
133. *L'Echo,* December 1964.
134. *Vancouver Sun,* 12 May, 1964.
135. *Le Devoir,* 1 June, 1964.
136. *Le Devoir,* 7 December, 1964.
137. Jacques Godbout, "Faut-il tuer le mythe René Lévesque ?" *Le Maclean,* November 1964.
138. *Le Devoir,* 4 February, 1965.
139. Quoted by Pierre Léger, "Qu'on me juge sur ce que je fais, le reste n'est que déshabillage," *Photo-Journal,* 19 May, 1965.
140. *Le Devoir,* 23 March, 1965.
141. *Le Devoir,* 29 March, 1965.
142. *La Presse,* 30 March, 1965.
143. *Le Soleil,* 30 March, 1965.
144. *Le Soleil,* 2 April, 1965.
145. *Le Devoir,* 5 April, 1965.
146. Richard Daignault and Dominique Clift, *Ottawa Journal,* 30 April, 1965.
147. *Le Devoir,* 1 May, 1965.
148. Quoted by James Bamber, "Lévesque contre la Noranda," *Le Maclean,* November 1965.
149. *Le Devoir,* 26 February, 1965.
150. *Le Soleil,* 17 May, 1965.
151. *Le Devoir,* 18 May, 1965.
152. *Le Quartier Latin,* 25 March, 1965.
153. *Le Devoir,* 19 March, 1965.
154. Interview with R.L., 9 May, 1973.
155. *Le Devoir,* 10 August, 1965.
156. Richard Daignault, "Où en est René Lévesque ?" *Le Maclean,* September 1965.

157. Denis Vaugeois, *Canada-Québec : Synthèse historique* (Editions du Renouveau Pédagogique, 1968), p. 555.
158. Vachon.
159. *Le Devoir,* 24 April, 1965.
160. *Le Devoir,* 14 June, 1965.
161. Quoted by James Iain Gow, *Administration publique québécoise* (Beauchemin, 1970), pp. 40 and 42.
162. Interview with R.L., 9 May, 1973.
163. *Le Devoir,* 20 November, 1965.
164. Interview with R.L., 9 May, 1973.
165. *Montreal Gazeztte,* 25 January, 1966.
166. *Montreal Star,* 28 February, 1966.
167. *L'Evénement,* 11 March, 1966.
168. *Le Devoir,* 18 April, 1966.
169. *L'Action,* 19 April, 1966.
170. Claude Ryan, *Le Devoir,* 21 May, 1966.
171. Results of a survey carried out by Guy Bourassa and Francine Dépatie, *Le Devoir,* 19 October, 1966.
172. *Le Devoir,* 8 June, 1966.
173. *Le Devoir,* 23 June, 1966.
174. Interview with R.L., 9 May, 1973.
175. Vincent Prince, *Le Devoir,* 7 June, 1966.
176. Interview with R.L., 9 May, 1973.
177. Vachon.
178. *Le Devoir,* 6 September, 1966.
179. *Le Devoir,* 1 October, 1966.
180. *La Presse,* 4 October, 1966.
181. Guay, p. 26.
182. *La Presse,* 14 November, 1966.
183. *Le Devoir,* 21 November, 1966.
184. *Le Nouvelliste,* 9 November, 1966.
185. *La Voix de l'Est,* 28 November, 1966.
186. *Le Devoir,* 29 November, 1966.
187. *Le Devoir,* 22 February, 1967.
188. *Montreal Star,* 20 February, 1967.
189. *Montreal Star,* 4 March, 1967.
190. *La Tribune,* 4 April, 1967.
191. *Toronto Globe and Mail,* 8 April, 1967.
192. Laurent Laplante, *L'Action,* 8 April, 1967.
193. Claude Ryan, *Le Devoir,* 9 May, 1967.
194. *Le Devoir,* 12 August, 1967.
195. Interview with R.L., 9 May, 1973.

5

A Choice for Quebec

By September 18, the thinking that Lévesque had been engaged in concerning "the basic prerequisites for the economic, social, and cultural progress of the people of Quebec, as well as for their political development," had culminated in the following statement :

> From a purely revisionist point of view, our demands would seem to surpass both the best intentions displayed by the "other majority" and the very capacity of the regime to make concessions without an explosion.
>
> If we are talking only of revision, they will tell us, our demands would lead to excessive weakening of that centralized state which English Canada needs for its own security and progress as much as we need our own State of Quebec. And they would be right.
>
> And further, they could ask us — with understandable insistence — what in the world our political representatives would be doing in Ottawa taking part in debates and administrative acts whose authority and effectiveness we intend so largely to eliminate within Quebec.
>
> If Quebec were to begin negotiations to revise the present frame of reference, and persisted in this course, [. . .] we would soon fall back on the old defensive struggle, the enfeebling skirmishes that make one forget where the real battle is, the half-victories that are celebrated between two defeats, the relapse in to divisive federal-provincial electoral folly, the sorry

239

consolations of verbal nationalism and, above all, ABOVE ALL ELSE — this must be said, and repeated, and shouted if need be — above all the incredible "split-level" squandering of energy, which certainly is for us the most disastrous aspect of the present regime.

After making this diagnosis, the member for Laurier attempted to answer the eternal question "What does Quebec want ?" : *

What should we conclude from a cool look at the crucial crossroads that we have now reached ? Clearly that we must rid ourselves completely of a completely obsolete federal regime.

And begin anew. [. . .]

For our own good, we must dare to seize for ourselves complete liberty in Quebec, the right to all the essential components of independence, *i.e.,* the complete mastery of every last area of basic collective decision-making.

This means that Quebec must become sovereign as soon as possible.

Thus we finally would have within our grasp the security of our collective "being" which is so vital to us, a security which otherwise must remain uncertain and incomplete. [. . .]

In short, this is not for us simply the only solution to the present Canadian impasse ; it also is the one and only common goal inspiring enough to bring us together with the kind of strength and unity we shall need to confront all possible futures — the supreme challenge of continuous progress within a society that has taken control of its own destiny.

[. . .] there is no reason why we, as future neighbours, should not voluntarily remain associates and partners in a common enterprise ; which would conform to the second great trend of our times : the new economic groups, customs unions, common markets, etc.

Here we are talking about something which already exists, for it is composed of the bonds, the complementary activities, the many forms of economic co-operation within which we have learned to live. Nothing says that we must throw these things away ; on the contrary, there is every reason to maintain the framework. [. . .]

To sum up, we propose a system that would allow our two majorities to extricate themselves from an archaic federal framework in which our two very distinct "personalities" paralyse each other by dint of pretending to have a third personality common to both. [1]

---

* In English in the original.

Here at last was a clear, concise formulation of Lévesque's political ideas. The Liberal Party convention was to be held October 13-15, and in the meantime Lévesque had to convince the party members of the merits of his thesis. But the party leaders reacted quickly. Eric Kierans stated : "René Lévesque's proposal will go down to defeat. The Liberal Party will not accept his call for an independent Quebec." Jean Lesage warned party members that the convention organizers would not give "priority to the Lévesque resolution." Paul Gérin-Lajoie reserved judgment and said in a more conciliatory manner : "I am struck by the calm objective tone of this document."

Pierre Bourgault, the president of the *Rassemblement pour l'indépendance nationale,* asked Lévesque to join the RIN. Claude Ryan wrote :

> One always had the feeling that, deep down inside, this man harbored a seething mass of convictions, desires, perceptions, and dreams which he could not bring himself to reveal in all their nakedness. Mr. Lévesque has finally thrown off his stifling inhibitions. Monday evening he became the public leader with a clearly defined position that Quebec political opinion has travelled a long and painful road to discover. [2]

The party leaders withhold their support

Lévesque's chief ally at the 1966 convention, Eric Kierans, not content to reply in only a few lines, wrote an article entitled, "What would become of a separate Quebec from the economic point of view ?" The answer, he claimed, was simple : "The separation of Quebec from the rest of Canada would hurl the people of Quebec into misery, poverty, and unemployment." His first proof was this : "At the present time, nearly 35 per cent of the funds paid out by the federal government to the provinces goes to Quebec. Taxpayers in Quebec contribute only 25 per cent of these payments. Independence would cost us dearly in this province because we receive more than we pay out." [3] In retrospect, these figures, which were used as an argument against Lévesque's thesis, are surprising. On September 30, 1970, a study undertaken by the Quebec Ministry of Intergovernmental Affairs — *Quebec's Share of Federal Government Expenses and Revenues from 1960-61 to 1967-68* — was made public. It concluded :

From 1960-61 to 1967-68, the amount Quebec received in federal expenditures did not exceed her contributions to these expenditures. More precisely, Quebec received from the federal governments only what it paid for and made no profit over and above its contribution. [. . .] Through the revenues its citizens and institutions pay to the federal government, Quebec in a way pays for its own equalization.

With the convention opening just hours away, the Liberal Party was divided by squabbling and agitation. Lesage said he supported Gérin-Lajoie's report. Henri-A. Dutil, ex-secretary of the QLF, accused Lévesque of wanting to install "an extreme left-wing régime" in Quebec. Eric Kierans said that "it was time to sweep separatism out of the Liberal Party and Quebec once and for all." Party leader Lesage asserted his authority and warned the member for Laurier that he would have to "submit or resign" if his proposal was rejected by the convention. Jean-Luc Pépin, a federal Liberal cabinet minister, compared Lévesque's document to the "political essays of the Age of Enlightenment" and added : "I have no quarrel with the Age of Enlightenment or the French Revolution. I would only point out that they led to the Terror, Napoleon's disctatorship, and, above all, the Restoration." Even before the convention opened, deputies Kierans, Wagner, Lefebvre, Courcy, Lechasseur, Hyde, Goldbloom, Brown, Blank, and Kirkland-Casgrain had all rejected Lévesque's thesis.

Journalist Gilles Daoust noted : "Incidentally, several observers have expressed surprise at the fact that debate on the Lévesque thesis was not reserved for the convention itself. Had the party leadership not made it clear that any resolution could normally be submitted to the convention in general for consideration ?" [4] Lévesque himself, author of the "sovereignty-association" thesis, stated : "We had hoped to have at least a decent, honest, democratic hearing, but it's obvious that our hearing will be a travesty." Editorial writer Laurent Laplante, acknowledging what seemed inevitable, wrote : "By throwing Mr. Lévesque overboard, the Liberal Party has bought itself a big, beautiful, brand new rudder, but has lost its motor." [5]

The Liberal convention opened on the evening of Friday, October 13. In his welcoming address, the president of the Liberal Federation, Eric Kierans, suggested in thinly veiled terms that Lévesque and his supporters should leave the party if their proposal was rejected. Then the organizers asked the delegates to vote

242

on procedural rules. For both the Constitutional Affairs Committee meeting on Saturday afternoon and the plenary session in the evening, the organizers proposed a vote by show of hands. Their suggestion was accepted by the convention.

Lévesque knew very well that such a procedure would be prejudicial, if not fatal, to his case. At six o'clock, Saturday evening, after four long hours of deliberation by the Constitutional Affairs Committee, Lévesque announced his resignation from the Liberal Party.

> When Mr. Lévesque coolly and calmly announced his decision, a wave of emotion swept the convention floor. For four or five seconds there was a pause, just long enough for Mr. Lévesque to step down from the podium. Then a group of about sixty loyal supporters thronged around him to offer their congratulations, applauding loudly. The journalists standing nearby could see he was on the verge of tears. But he quickly composed himself and left the hall followed by a large number of people. [6]

Why six o'clock ? "It couldn't have gone past midnight," Lévesque pointed out, "because the motion would have been jammed in between a lot of others and pushed through the machine. The vote would have been a real farce. We lost the vote Friday evening when a secret ballot was rejected." [7]

Although Lesage claimed that Lévesque's departure had left the party "stronger than ever," Robert Bourassa, the member for Mercier, felt that it represented "a great loss to the party," and that Lévesque would be "a difficult man to replace." He added : "The party will no longer be insured against lapses into bourgeois complacency." [8] Columnist André Langevin was disgusted by this turn of events :

> What a wonderfully democratic convention this was, muzzled from the outset by an imposed dogma. As they faced the convention, the heretics, who took a heretical stand on more than just the constitutional question, realized that their departure had been expected for a long time. Their proposal was not merely condemned in advance but dismissed out of hand. There was no need to agree with Mr. Lévesque's thesis in order to feel humiliated by the financial scare argument perpetrated by Mr. Eric Kierans, one of the few prominent English Canadians who seemed to have made Quebec their cause. [9]

On November 1, 1967, Lévesque told a Laval University student audience that a former economic advisor to the Quebec government, Jacques Parizeau, had helped put the finishing touches on the economic section of the manifesto. Parizeau confirmed this. *Le Devoir* reported :

> He said that he had not helped with the writing of the manifesto itself, which he learned about only a few hours before its publication. But he talked with Mr. Lévesque for several hours in the following few days while the former Liberal cabinet minister was preparing an economic appendix to the document. He added that Mr. Lévesque used several of the ideas that had come up in their conversations and pointed out that he had engaged in similar exchanges over the preceding ten years with several Quebec politicians who wanted to discuss certain questions with him. [10]

Time to quit or found a new party ?

Laurier was the first riding association to give its support to Lévesque. More than fifty dissatisfied Liberals resigned from the association and the party to form the Laurier-Lévesque Association, with Gérard Bélanger as president. Although the member for Laurier was very pleased with this development, he was wary of any precipitous or makeshift organization on the provincial level : "We want to avoid any premature manoeuvre, which could only have a divisive influence." [11] Starting in November, Lévesque made a speaking tour of Quebec to explain his thesis and visited Shawinigan, Sorel, Sherbrooke, Granby, Quebec City. In Three Rivers he was welcomed at the Notre-Dame Hall by eight hundred union workers, who had been "won over to his thesis beforehand, to judge by the applause he received." Journalist Michel Roy tried to find out what was behind his success here : "This is the first time," he wrote, "that a politician who has opted for independence has been so well received by a group of union workers." Roy asked Jean Gérin-Lajoie, the Quebec director of the United Steelworkers of America and vice-president of the *Fédération du Travail du Québec* [FTQ — Quebec Labor Federation], Fernand Daoust, another vice-president of the FTQ, Jean-Marc Carle, director of external relations for the Steelworkers, and André L'Heureux, head of political education for the CSN [*Confédération des Syndicats Nationaux*] * whether they could explain Lévesque's warm welcome. The four union leaders,

* See note on p. 10.

April 1972. Publication of the Parti Québécois Manifesto. Lévesque is flanked by economist Jacques Parizeau, author of the section in the Manifesto dealing with economics, and Camille Laurin, the party's house leader.

three of whom were present at the meeting, put forward two reasons :

> First and foremost, Mr. Lévesque's own personality is the main reason for his success with the union workers, for they have always seen him in the vanguard of the fight for social justice. [. . .] Secondly, they point out that this meeting is very important insofar as it represents a "new phenomenon," one which would "certainly have to be watched closely in the future." To sum up, it is no longer possible to say that labor is massively and unanimously opposed to all formulas for sovereignty.

Jean Gérin-Lajoie added :

> It was the first time he had encountered any union workers since his resignation from the Liberal Party. They know the

conditions under which he left the Liberals and are pleased that he decided to break off relations with a bourgeois party. There are strong emotional undertones in this reception. The workers have a desire to get a fair share of what society has to offer ; they are often on the verge of revolt ; they feel that things are not exactly going well. Lévesque symbolizes in their eyes a hope for justice. [12]

Lévesque's supporters included a group of Liberals who had also resigned from the party. They included Gérard Bélanger, Rosaire Beaulé, vice-président of the QLF, Marc Brière, a candidate for party office defeated at the 1966 convention, Guy Pelletier, a Liberal candidate defeated in the riding of Témiscouata in 1966, Monique Marchand, a member of the party's Political Commission, Réginald Savoie, president of the Political Commission's Educational Committee, Jean-Roch Boivin, president of the convention's Commission on Manpower and Labor, Pothier Ferland, and Maurice Jobin. These ex-Liberals, along with four hundred delegates from the main economic regions of Quebec, gathered at the Dominican monastery in Montreal on November 18 and 19 to "shape and organize the support for the sovereignty-association thesis which has arisen in every part of Quebec."

Lévesque and the members of the interim steering committee spent virtually the entire first day of the convention from morning to night answering the hundreds of questions put to them by the delegates. The following day, a short-term strategy had to be decided on. It quickly became obvious that "sooner or later they will have to create a new political party." Although a number of the delegates wanted to see a party formed immediately, the convention chose to establish for the time being a limited form of association. It was given the somewhat awkward title *Mouvement souveraineté-association* [MSA — Sovereignty Association Movement]. Some wanted to call it *Mouvement Lévesque* [Lévesque Movement], *Option Lévesque* [Lévesque Option] or *Thèse Lévesque* [Lévesque Thesis], but Lévesque himself was strongly opposed to these suggestions : "We must not reduce the *sovereignty-association* constitutional option to a personality cult. It belongs to all of us, not just to me. I am only an instrument of the movement and that is all I want to be." [13]

At the press conference that followed, Lévesque stressed the convention's representative nature ("this is the first time I've seen a meeting in Quebec with such good representation") and the im-

246

portance of the many decisions it had made ; nevertheless, the work of the MSA had barely begun. Journalist Jean-V. Dufresne wrote :

> They must expand, make contacts, spread their ideas, convince people, plan ahead, read the various documents and the little paperback edition the committee chairman is getting ready for publication, discuss, prepare for Lévesque's tour, encourage those with natural leadership qualities to come forward, build up regional committees with strict attention paid to local differences in economic and social composition, keep abreast of local problems, etc. The great majority of the delegates felt that without all this effort creating a party would only lead to disaster. [14]

As soon as this first MSA working convention was over, Lévesque acknowledged that he still had no idea what the movement's program would be like, adding that whatever he said for the time being was nothing more than his personal opinion. Nevertheless, if it were entirely up to him, "the movement would have no dogmas to expound and should not rely on borrowed solutions. What we need is a popular movement organized by and for all the people. But one thing is clear : in Quebec the State is our driving force. The majority of those measures which have done the most to shape Quebec's evolution since 1960 were taken by the government." [15]

By accepting the leadership of this new political movement, Lévesque lost much of the personal freedom he had discovered after the Liberal defeat in June 1966. During the week following the meeting at the Dominican monastery, he spoke at Glendon College in Toronto, the Paul Sauvé Centre, the University of Sherbrooke, *l'École des Hautes Études Commerciales,* and Jean-de-Brébeuf College. English-Canadian journalist Ian Macdonald, who had been following Lévesque for some weeks, concluded that his enemies had counted their chickens before they had hatched :

> They buried René Lévesque much, much too soon. His slight, gaunt figure, topped by a creased face with caved-in cheeks, is hardly a symbol of health and strength, but Lévesque is very much alive with an intense, burning desire to shape Québec the way he feels it should be. [. . .] Lévesque is exactly the type to turn on the heat. While his opponents figure out ways to try to cool him off, look on Lévesque as one of Canada's livelier corpses. [16]

August 1972. A press conference held by the Parti Québécois.
On Lévesque's right is Marcel Léger and, on his left, Pierre Marois.

At the beginning of 1968, Lévesque stated that the MSA would only become a political party on two conditions, namely that it be financed by public contributions and that it reflect the aspirations of the people as a whole. "The people of Quebec," he said, "do not deserve the political parties they have now, with their secret funding and their corruption." The party would also have to represent the whole population. Months earlier Lévesque had told students at Montreal's Mont-Saint-Louis College : "You must understand that a majority of the people in this province are still very conservative in nature and that a party hoping to get into office must to some extent take them into account. [. . .] Because of the make-up of the population, a party can't get into office without granting these conservative elements some minimal representation." [17]

January 1968. Lévesque launches Option-Québec. *His much awaited book was a follow-up to the Sovereignty-Association Movement Manifesto (fall 1967).*

As part of the MSA campaign to publicize the issue of independence, Lévesque launched a book called *Option-Québec* on January 17, 1968. It was described as a "little sovereignty-association dictionary." On February 1, the author was to autograph copies of his book in a busy Montreal shopping mall. An English-speaking journalist wrote :

> The invitation said Place Ville Marie at "midi précises," but, characteristically, René Lévesque arrived at "midi quarante cinq précises." However, even though he was 45 minutes late he turned one corner of the shopping promenade into a sort of politico-literary happening. One hundred or more passersby and newsmen were jammed shoulder-to-shoulder in the corridor outside La Maison du Livre, all straining to catch a word or two from the province's most fascinating politician. [18]

The Association was moving ahead with giant strides. In some ways progress was perhaps too rapid. As the news came in that 37 per cent of Quebec's teachers were in favor of this political option, Lévesque stated : "It's been going five or ten times faster than we thought it would. By March or April '68 we expected to have working organizations in the principal economic areas, but we're already operating at the riding level." [19] Three weeks later the MSA leader said he was "pleased but worried" about the movement, "because it is growing at a rate that could create problems of over-extension and lack of proper preparation." [20] Lévesque feared another eventuality as well :

> There's always the chance you'll pick up a lot of useless hangers-on at the beginning. You have to be careful not to become a catch-all. Often the people who get in on a movement at the start include those who simply like to call attention to themselves : you know, the professional belly-achers and grumblers, the deadwood, the people nobody else wants, who say to themselves, "Any port in a storm." You have to take your time and size things up before you throw open the organization to people of that kind, because once inside they may try to take control and say to everyone else, "It's ours now." What we want is a popular party, not one that looks like an old party starting all over again. [21]

Nevertheless, the time seemed right to transform the movement into a political party. On February 29, a press release from the steering committee invited all registered members to attend a general meeting on April 20 and 21 at Maurice Richard Arena. In the course of the meeting, the members would be asked to vote on three important questions. First, "would it be preferable to found a political party or keep the group founded by Mr. René Lévesque as a movement ?" The steering committee's position on this question was to advise the membership to found a party. The agenda for the meeting also included discussion of the movement's future course and the basic outlines of its eventual program, as well as the structure and regulations of the organization. The following statement by Lévesque, which appeared in November 1963, explains what he thought a political party should be. It is important to remember, however, that he was speaking of the Liberal Party at the time :

> Basically I think it can be summed up in three words : demo-

April 1968. The public statements by Lévesque and François Aquin reveal that their positions are irreconcilable.

cratic, progressive, Québécois. "Democratic" first of all means that vested interests and cliques are excluded. The party must keep its doors wide open and welcome all those willing to support its program as well as those who value their freedom of expression and their right not to agree at all times on all questions. A democratic party is not a collection of automatons. It is a meeting ground for free citizens who will consent to the minimum amount of discipline necessary in any organization that really wants to accomplish something, rather than simply contenting itself with being a directionless forum. A democratic party is also one that belongs to its members and whose financing is entirely, with no hidden qualifications or mysteries, in their hands. "Progressive" is an adjective that applies to a party which is not afraid of change. Now more than ever we must accept social and economic change as normal and healthy. A progressive party not only accepts such change but must also have the courage to propose changes which seem desirable and to get them quietly under way as soon as it is in power. And it must continue to do so with the same thoughtful boldness as long as it is in power, or else it will sooner or later become a conservative party, which is equally respectable but not the same thing at all!... "Québécois" for me means first of all that we must accept straight off the equality of all Quebec citizens in the eyes of every institution and the law and be ready to defend this principle whenever necessary, regardless of cultural, religious, or even political affiliations. Every Québécois is and must remain a full-fledged citizen. This is an absolutely essential idea and one we must never forget, especially during troubled times such as those we are now experiencing. Furthermore, "Quebec" must signify *French* Canada in a collective sense. We are the Quebec nation and we comprise more than 80 per cent of the province's population. Others may feel at home almost anywhere, but we will never have another secure homeland to call our own except Quebec. A Quebec party must always be thinking of this, must work tirelessly for the national interests of French Canadians and every day, in every field, must strive to bring us closer to the time when we will be, once and for all, *maîtres chez nous.* [22]

Lévesque quit the Liberal Party precisely because, as a member, he was prevented from putting many of these beliefs into practice and because he undoubtedly wanted to see them realized in another political party.

The First Convention

The scene of the first MSA convention, which began April 20, 1968, was the Maurice Richard Arena. More than 1200 delegates participated in discussions centring around the cultural, social, economic, and political workshops where the basic elements of a preliminary political program touching on all these aspects of Quebec life were laid down. There was a lively discussion in one of the cultural workshops. The MSA's interim steering committee recommended to the delegates that they approve "a system of primary and secondary English-speaking schools which would be subsidized according to how many citizens declared that English was their mother tongue in a census to be held every five years." Although many approved this resolution, many others objected.

On the following day, Sunday, there was a plenary session. The resolution to transform the movement into a party was quickly approved. "It is resolved by the general assembly of the members of the Sovereignty Association Movement that a mandate be given the steering committee to enable the MSA to participate actively in the founding of a political party which will bring together all those sharing the same basic objectives." It was agreed that the founding convention would be held "within the six-month period after April 21." Then the resolution concerning an English-speaking school system came up for discussion again. François Aquin, a former Liberal deputy who had resigned in August 1967, was completely against any such subsidies, which he regarded as a matter of privilege. Lévesque, on the other hand, believed that this was an issue of basic rights and announced to the convention a few minutes before the vote : "I am free to leave when I like." [23] The implication was of course that he felt he would be obliged to leave the movement if the subsidies proposal was voted out. This led certain observers to condemn what seemed to them "imperialism." After a hostile exchange between Aquin and Lévesque, the chairman called for a vote and the convention supported Lévesque by 481 to 253 votes, with 51 abstentions.

Asked to comment on the results, Aquin replied that he would remain in the movement to pursue the fight for unilingualism. He had in fact joined the MSA in order to unite all the independence movements, the MSA, the *Rassemblement pour l'indépendance nationale* [RIN], and the *Ralliement national* [RN]. RIN president Pierre Bourgault began making monthly statements in November 1967 on the subject of union. He announced at that time that he and Lévesque had agreed to form a common front. The next day Lévesque denied there was any question of a common front with the RIN. [24] Then the RIN leader announced that he would meet with the MSA leader to discuss amalgamation ; Lévesque did not respond. Bourgault made another public statement to the effect that he would be willing to cede the leadership to Lévesque if the RIN joined the MSA ; still no response from Lévesque. Bourgault lost his temper and said Lévesque had a "colonial mentality." A few weeks later the RIN president said that negotiations with the MSA might come to an impasse over two problems : the school system and monetary union, two issues on which the thinking of the two parties was radically opposed.

Lévesque chose never to reply to Bourgault's statements and, moreover, scarcely ever referred to him when speaking of the amalgamation of the independence movements, for various reasons. The two men had arrived at their positions on independence by two very different routes — those of emotion and reason. The differences were sometimes so marked that it seemed the two men were not fighting for the same cause. For Lévesque, the language question was secondary in the sense that he expected it would work itself out as a natural consequence of independence. Bourgault, however, was determined to settle the language question through legislation. He supported independence for reasons of "dignity," while for Lévesque dignity would in a way come with growth. Lévesque had exercised power and knew that some concessions had to be made ; Bourgault had no such experience. Lévesque had described as "madness" a statement by Bourgault to the effect that, under certain conditions, the government of an independent Quebec would sink ships in the St. Lawrence Seaway.

Lévesque was therefore deeply mistrustful of Pierre Bourgault and also seemed to be trying to win time for the MSA. He wanted to avoid official amalgamation with the RIN because he considered the two groups very dissimilar. He was also pleased to be "out-flanked on the left." Pothier Ferland, one of his assistants, said as he left the April 1968 meetings :

> The results of the discussions on unilingualism have shown that the members of the Sovereignty Association Movement are not radicals. Now amalgamation can take place on a healthier basis, even though it may perhaps take more time. Furthermore, a small unaffiliated core of radicals will probably remain active outside the independence party. This will be helpful to the new party because the public will be able to distinguish more clearly between these *radicals* and the *moderates* who have joined together in Mr. René Lévesque's party. [. . .] Lévesque's victory has demonstrated the validity of "popular realism." The public will now have an easier time understanding the MSA and will not see it as an intransigent and vengeful movement. Amalgamation will also be easier if the radicals are eliminated at the outset. [25]

The author asked Lévesque the following question : "Pierre Bourgault kept trying to persuade you to amalgamate with the RIN. Not only did you not rise to the bait, but you also gave the impression later that you wouldn't have minded seeing a political party more radical than the MSA on the Quebec scene. Is this true ?" Lévesque replied :

> First of all, as far as that is concerned we founded the MSA at the Dominican monastery in November '67, if I remember correctly, and one of our basic intentions was to encourage an amalgamation of the independence groups and at the same time

to persuade the largest possible number of undecided nationalists to form a party. What we wanted to create was a sort of rallying ground. We avoided hemming it in with silly regulations ; instead we left it wide open so that people could come and go as they pleased. It was a kind of crossroads, much more a movement than a structured political party, which meant we could let others get interested and at the same time respond to certain demands, which I still think is legitimate. Despite the appeals of all sorts being issued by the RIN and other groups, we preferred to wait until the pressure of the situation led them to accept the idea of an amalgamation on equal terms. We didn't want amalgamation to take place under our control any more than we wanted it to take place under theirs. But I think the RIN, especially at the beginning, had something in mind like, "They're a small group who've just come on the scene, while we're already a party. So they're bound to come over to us." And I can understand their attitude. But if we'd gone along with them it would have been the kiss of death — the RIN had gone as far as they were ever going to go because of the attitudes they felt obliged to adopt. That was their business. But we wanted to create a new image, and this amalgamation would have been carried out in a new context. It was purely a question of strategy if you like. As far as seeing some advantage in a left-wing or extreme left-wing party is concerned, your observation is correct. The RIN really never was a left-wing party. Their brand of radicalism was much more verbal than actual. In fact, the program of the Parti Québécois, as it now stands and even as it was originally, is a good deal more progressive, if I can use that term, than the RIN's ever was. There may be less high-sounding verbiage, but there are far more concrete aims designed to promote change. I liked the idea then of having an RIN around, and I like the perennial presence nowadays of the pseudo-party run by Charles Gagnon and Company. * For two reasons. First of all, it marked us off very clearly as a fairly advanced centre-left party, more leftist I think than any party that has ever held power in the history of Quebec, yet moderate leftist all the same. That means people can see you're distinct from the extreme leftists who are always going on about forming a workers' party but aren't capable of actually doing so. I'd like to see them make up their minds, because from our point of view the political landscape

* Charles Gagnon (who was imprisoned with Pierre Vallières) often talked about forming a nationalist party which would truly represent the interests of the working class, but the party never materialized.

would be clearer and it would be easier for us to find our place in that landscape. It seems an inevitable part of future developments as well, because, whether we like it or not, Quebec is bound to end up as the kind of society in which the political game is played out over a wide range, running from left to right with the usual shades in between. However, I hope we don't go too far in that direction because if we get into a situation like the Fourth Republic in France, we'll look pretty foolish. But it seems only logical that the political spectrum should include all the major ideological positions. [26]

The upshot was that, when the April 1968 meeting was over, the MSA was far from ready to amalgamate with the RIN. In June, there was a federal election. Pierre Trudeau, the newly-elected leader of the federal Liberal Party, was regarded by many English Canadians as the man to curb the nationalism which had been stirring in Quebec for over ten years. On June 5, Robert F. Kennedy was assassinated in Los Angeles. During an election rally in Abitibi, a handful of nationalists created a disturbance and Trudeau then compared the "separatists" to "Kennedy's assassins," referring to them as "hate mongers." With the Saint-Jean-Baptiste holiday only a few days away, many Québécois were offended by Trudeau's deliberate attempt to stigmatize the nationalist movement. Lévesque made a point of telling Trudeau that "by using Kennedy's still warm body to instil fear in the people, he had shown himself to be the worst kind of demagogue." [27]

But there was more trouble ahead for the nationalists. Trudeau had received an invitation from the Saint-Jean-Baptiste Society of Montreal to attend the big parade scheduled for the night of June 24 in Montreal. The federal elections were to take place the next day. The Liberal Party leader accepted the invitation, but many nationalists believed that Trudeau should not be present since he was "a much-discussed candidate in the next day's elections." Pierre Bourgault invited the people of Quebec to demonstrate their disapproval publicly in the street. The whole business amounted to a confrontation between the two leaders.

On the evening of June 24 fighting broke out between nationalist demonstrators and police while Trudeau looked on from the balcony of Montreal's City Hall. The police enthusiastically threw themselves into their work. All the journalists present, including the television crews, remarked on the extremely violent tactics employed by the police. The newspaper *Montréal-Matin,* for example, described them as "acts of unbelievable brutality." The result was that 135 people were wounded and nearly 300 arrested, 81 of whom were minors. The chief of police and the mayor of Montreal said, of course, that they had only done their duty.

The next day, Pierre Trudeau and his party won the election in Quebec and throughout Canada. For René Lévesque, all those implicated in the Montreal disturbance were equally to blame, regardless of whether the chief underlying cause was the attitude of the police, the provocation created by the presence of the man who aspired to be prime minister of Canada, or the violent behavior of certain demonstrators. At a press conference he said :

> The MSA strongly condemns all forms of violence, whose only result can be to divide and weaken even further a small nation which has already been sufficiently downtrodden because of its position as a political minority, its economic backwardness, and its social inferiority. Too many people, often unfortunately including those very ones who should be setting an example, have been playing with violence like so many sorcerer's apprentices. The events that took place on June 24 in Montreal are unfortunate examples of this development. In the preceding few days, there were direct incitements to use violence as a means of political action. In this regard the MSA wishes to state unequivocally that it disapproves completely of these methods, which are facile and can only lead to anarchist adventures degrading to everyone concerned. For our part, we will continue at all costs to avoid this abyss which could engulf the future history of Quebec. Our cause will triumph by force of persuasion and the tireless determination it has inspired in us. The challenge we are extending, in spite of all the provocations, is addressed to this nation's rational faculties rather than its emotions. [. . .] A more immediate problem is the provocation that many people felt was created by the presence of a man, a much-discussed candidate in the following day's election, who placed himself above, not to say outside, the nation whose national day was being celebrated. The stupid thoughtlessness of those who invited him was surpassed only by the irresponsibility of certain others who launched a demonstration that was inevitably destined to get out of hand. [. . .] The police naturally had to maintain order ; but being badly equipped and quite untrained to meet the demands of such a situation, they quickly confused the maintenance of order with out-and-out repression. [. . .] As for the future, we

257

don't claim to have a cure for every ill, but it seems obvious to us that only by gaining their political freedom can the people of Quebec be assured of the collective security and dignity whose absence is the most fundamental cause of those temptations, including both violence and resignation, which some of us find difficult to resist. Only a people who are their own masters and who build by themselves the progress and justice they need are likely to avoid the two pitfalls of slow drowning in the *melting pot* * and wasteful pseudo-revolutionary rebelliousness. [28]

Lévesque would countenance no compromise with violence in Quebec. In this sense he was a real pacifist who wanted the MSA or the party which grew out of it to adopt a similar attitude ; and, as far as he was concerned, Pierre Bourgault and the RIN had nothing to offer them. Furthermore, during the press conference following the above statement, he confirmed that negotiations with the RIN on amalgamation had been suspended until July 6, when an expanded group of MSA delegates was scheduled to meet. The MSA considered that the RIN had just signed its own death warrant, and Lévesque wasted no time in putting an end to the negotiations.

On August 4, the leaders of the MSA and the *Ralliement national,* René Lévesque and Gilles Grégoire, announced that their two groups would join together to form a new political party in the fall. They had reached agreement on four basic goals : "To create through democratic means a sovereign, French-speaking State ; to develop not only electoral, but also economic, social, and cultural democracy ; to establish rigorous safeguards for the educational rights of the English-speaking minority ; and to negotiate an economic treaty in association with English Canada." [29] The president of the MSA went on to point out that negotiations with the RIN had broken down over the question of the English-speaking school system. François Aquin now had no choice but to resign, since his two basic tenets, amalgamation of all nationalist groups and rejection of any subsidized English-speaking school system, had been thrown out by the MSA and the RN. Not long afterwards he left the movement headed by Lévesque.

There were no more obstacles to prevent the transformation of the MSA into a political party. The group had undergone a trial

---

* In English in the original.

October 1969. The Parti Québécois convention in Montreal.

run of one year. The RN had stated its willingness to join forces with the MSA. There was detailed agreement on the educational rights of the English-speaking minority in a sovereign Quebec as well as on the question of violence. A preliminary political program had been drafted. All that remained was to found the party.

From October 12 to 14, 1968, 957 delegates representing every region of Quebec gathered at Laval University and the *Petit Colisée* in Quebec City to found the party. Lévesque was elected president, Gilles Grégoire, vice-president, and Fernand Paré, secretary and treasurer. Jean-Roch Boivin, Marc Lavallée, Gérard Bélanger, Claude Laurin, André Larocque, and Marc-André Bédard were the other members of the party's first executive committee. Rosaire Beaulé, one of the first members in the movement, summed up the delegates' feelings : "Exactly one year ago to the day, right here in Quebec City, a group of twenty people dramatically resigned from the Liberal Party. Today not twenty but twenty thousand Québécois have gathered around René Lévesque to further the cause of our collective liberation." [30]

The name chosen for the party was, according to Lévesque, "a very appealing name, perhaps too appealing" — "Parti Québécois." For the president, "this most appealing of names for a political party" represented a great challenge ; but there was more to the challenge than the name alone suggested. "We must find a way," Lévesque told the delegates,

> to prove, without becoming obscure or hopelessly idealistic, that a political party can be realistic without lapsing into opportunism, can truly belong to its members without becoming ineffective, can be a meeting ground for adult, responsible citizens without becoming an academic club, and can even retain the passion of a great cause without succumbing to fanaticism or unplanned agitation. [31]

It was now up to the party members to speak out and bring their case before the people . . . .

Chapter 5 — References

1. René Lévesque, *An Option for Quebec* (McClelland and Stewart, 1968), pp. 24-30. The author quotes the original French version, which first appeared in *Le Devoir,* on 19, 20, and 21 September, 1967, and was subsequently reprinted in *Option-Québec* (Editions de l'Homme 1968), pp. 35-42. From *An Option for Québec* by René Lévesque, reprinted by permission of the Canadian Publishers, McClelland and Stewart Limited, Toronto.
2. Claude Ryan, *Le Devoir,* 20 September, 1967.
3. *Le Devoir,* 2 October, 1967.
4. Gilles Daoust, *La Presse,* 13 October, 1967.

5. Laurent Laplante, *L'Action,* 14 October, 1967.
6. *Le Soleil,* 16 October, 1967.
7. *L'Action,* 16 October, 1967.
8. Quoted by François Trépanier, *La Presse,* 16 October, 1967.
9. André Langevin, "Kierans : l'ombre d'un gros batôn . . . ," *Le Maclean,* December 1967.
10. *Le Devoir,* 2 November, 1967.
11. Ibid.
12. Michel Roy, *Le Devoir,* 13 November, 1967.
13. *Le Soleil,* 20 November, 1967.
14. Jean-V. Dufresne, *Le Devoir,* 20 November, 1967.
15. *La Presse,* 20 November, 1967.
16. Ian Macdonald, *Vancouver Sun,* 7 December, 1967.
17. *Le Devoir,* 21 March, 1967.
18. *Montreal Star,* 2 February, 1968.
19. *La Patrie,* 14 January, 1968.
20. *Le Soleil,* 7 February, 1968.
21. André Gilbert, Pierre Larivière, and Jacques Patenaude, "Vingt ans de journalisme, Mouvement-Souveraineté-Association, Espoir-Difficultés-Avenir," *Défi,* n.d., p. 16. (Probably published between January and April 1968.)
22. *Point de Mire* (a publication of the Laurier Riding Liberal Association), 1 November, 1963, p. 5.
23. *Le Soleil,* 22 April, 1968.
24. *Le Devoir,* 15 November, 1967.
25. Quoted by *Le Soleil,* 22 April, 1968.
26. Interview with R.L., 9 May, 1973.
27. *La Parole,* 12 June, 1968.
28. *Le Devoir,* 29 June, 1968.
29. *La Presse,* 5 August, 1967.
30. *Le Carabin*, 17 October, 1968.
31. René Lévesque. From the text of his opening address to the MSA-RN convention, 11 October, 1968.

Postscript

We have come to the end of this study of René Lévesque, but he continues to fight for his cause. We could have followed him during the first few months of the Parti Québécois' existence, examined his attitudes to the events surrounding the passage of Bill 63, * described his first election campaign as leader of the "Sovereignty" party, depicted his strained features the evening of the election when he felt compelled to speak of "a great victory" despite the fact that his party had won only 6 per cent of the seats with 23 per cent of the popular vote, watched his astonishment when he learned that his three former colleagues Trudeau, Marchand, and Pelletier had decided to go so far as to invoke the War Measures Act and that Pierre Laporte had died, heard him decry the *La Presse* demonstration before it took place, † noted his reluctance to join the *Front commun* of May '72, ‡ and so forth.

The following comments from journalist Thomas Sloan speak for themselves :

> . . . René Lévesque has, from all indications, simply been obey-
> ing the imperatives of his own nature, an unusual combination
> of idealism, enthusiasm, impulsiveness, and intelligence. This
> has not been a conscious, calculating, play-actor's drive toward

---

* The legislation that guaranteed immigrants to the province the right to choose either English or French as the language of instruction for their children in the schools. Despite widespread demonstrations and highly organized opposition to the bill throughout the province, only four deputies — including Lévesque — voted against it.

† In the fall of 1971, employees of the Montreal daily *La Presse* went out on strike. Lévesque refused to sanction the demonstration that was to be held on their behalf in front of the *La Presse* offices because he feared there would be an outbreak of violence. As a result of the demonstration, one person was killed, 50 were injured and 300 arrested.

‡ The three most influential Quebec unions — the Quebec Labor Federation, the Confederation of National Trade Unions, and the Quebec Teachers' Corporation — called a general strike of public employees in May 1972. The courts ordered employees in essential services back to work ; the leaders of the three unions, who took a common stand urging them not to do so, were imprisoned.

April 1970. Lévesque leaving the Parti Québécois airplane at Ancienne Lorette airport.

power, but something more basic. Mr. Lévesque may not have an aversion to power, but he will probably have few hesitations about giving up its perquisites if he decides that he cannot, by means of power, attain his main objective : the building of an economically strong, socially progressive, and politically autonomous Quebec. [1]

Nor do these comments from psychiatrist Camille Laurin need any elaboration:

Ever since I began working with him, René Lévesque seems to me to have understood and empathized with the contradictions facing every Québécois, which compel him to strive for liberation and at the same time prevent him from achieving it. This is why he himself oscillates between the light and the dark, impatience and confidence, tenderness and severity, scolding

*29 April, 1970.
The Parti
Québécois leader
casts his vote
in the provincial
election.*

and the call to self-betterment, whenever he thinks to himself
or talks to others. This is why he plumbs his own depths when
in need of counsel during times of crisis. This is why he is a
symbol of contradiction in everyone's eyes, and an object of
recognition, hatred, and love. This is why, quite simply, destiny
could have chosen only him as the midwife of our liberty. [2]

The following lines by Gérard Bergeron could also serve as an
epilogue :

He will perhaps be the man responsible for our future reinte-
gration, the man who is already the polarizer and integrating
magnet for those under-, underdeveloped Americans, the
people of Quebec ! He has demonstrated beyond a doubt that
he is neither a hanger-on nor a joiner, nor the kind of man
who will temporarily give up his principles for political gain.

Such idealism combined with such a strong dose of pragmatism makes an explosive mixture : with all the compressing and kneading it has undergone, it is bound to blow up eventually ! [...] Anyone with this make-up could never be at ease with himself and must experience the same kind of subconscious trembling that afflicts an entire nation because it suffers the misfortune of being French Canadian in North America. During the course of his long, laborious struggle to carve out a meaningful place in space and time for this group, Lévesque has become something other and more than himself : he has become the very people he has tried to represent, with its rare moments of vivacity in between the long silences of still waters.[3]

Here are the observations of author, actor, and astrologer Guy Hoffman :

I am reminded of those who do not believe in astrology when I see how precisely the aspects in his chart tell the story of his success. In his make-up I find first of all a luminous, logical, powerful, and rare intelligence, which can only improve as time goes on. I see writ large the successful completion of the task undertaken with the help of gifts in science, the arts, writing, oratory (less clear), and, aided by strong intuition, a kind of sensitive and illuminating second sight. His weaknesses stem from an almost unhealthy modesty, a shyness which becomes less painful as he grows older, lurking fits of dangerous, impassioned, and nervous anger .... Harmful qualities, but ones he has tried to use to his advantage. All this means he could undertake anything, meet any challenge. To make the portrait absolutely precise, we should add that there is some anxiety and that the shy quality has turned to nervousness. [...] Throughout his life all his changes of course will be impressive and effective. The need to take the initiative will again contribute to his ability to undertake anything, to meet any challenge. All this is also shot through with sensuality, a sure guarantee of success !

And from the philosopher and actor Doris Lussier :

This man, whose prodigious intelligence and uncommon courage have thrust him into the vanguard of our political struggle, possesses, as far as I can see, all the qualities necessary to lead the people of Quebec. René Lévesque is a man with a clear understanding who sees what lies ahead ; these are the prerequisites of political wisdom. His genius consists in his having seen the problem of Quebec not just as an unrelated series of events but in its all-encompassing historical perspective, which is necessary in order to understand the true dimensions of the problem and therefore allow the judicious selection of the right solutions, so that we can resolve the problem at the level of our higher interests. He recognizes the practical aspects of the problem and the real difficulties involved, but this does not prevent him — as is unfortunately the case with so many other leaders — from seeing that what is at stake is nothing more nor less than the life or death of the nation. For French Quebec, today or tomorrow, it is *to be or not to be*.* 4

Former Union Nationale deputy Jérôme Proulx wrote :

René Lévesque's mystique reveals itself in a kind of popular symbolism which is struggling to liberate our collective unconscious. With his gift for debunking, he enumerates and identifies all the obsessive phantoms of Quebec mythology. By familiarizing the people with the object of their fear, he has made them aware that this phenomenon of hallucination is collective and has therefore worked out a pacifying therapy. René Lévesque talks on equal terms with his people : as he tracks down fear, he gives us an admirable description of what he is doing. And the very fact that he is a liberated colonial lends full weight to his authority. [. . .] The people of Quebec look at René Lévesque, that great victor over himself, as though he were a magic mirror, and find themselves feeling stronger and more confident. [. . .] This verbal machine says out loud what everyone keeps to himself. He reaches every stratum of society from the university to the farm because he expresses what is most profound, most hidden, and most genuinely Québécois. This process of identifying our most secret feelings is so effective that we feel almost ashamed to admire it. [. . .] René Lévesque's simplicity has destroyed the myth of the all-powerful superman thirsting for power. He draws his strength from a knowledge of his own limitations, a sense of personal conviction, and the hopes of an entire people. In contrast to the cult of personality, he presents an image of a man of good will burdened by fate with a heavy responsibility ; when he is acclaimed by a crowd, they do not cheer an idol but a man of flesh and blood to whom they can communicate their faith in the future. [. . .] This simplicity completely accounts for his charm and also serves to do away with the myth of the dandy : he has neither hairdresser, nor tailor, nor chauffeur ; there

---

* In English in the original.

February 1972. The auditorium of Montreal's Ecole polytechnique
— Lévesque criticizes the politicians in Ottawa.

is nothing narcissistic about him and he abhors flaunting himself
in any way. The only luxury he allows himself is to let himself
be himself. [...] The ghosts of a fallen *Establishment* * haunt
Quebec but to René Lévesque they are familiar faces. He
unmasks them, scrutinizes them, and exposes them. Could this
be the progressive stripping away of a collective fear ? [5]

This is how a CBC journalist described him in an interview with
the author :

I'll tell you the most revealing glimpse I ever had of René
Lévesque. It was the middle of the October crisis. Pierre
Laporte had been dead for a week. Every politician had at least

---

* In English in the original.

May 1973. A Parti Québécois fund-raising drive collected $800,000 and ended with a rally which drew 10,000 supporters.

two bodyguards looking after him. All of us, to a man, were stunned by those events. It was 9:30 in the evening and there was fog outside. Stanley Street was dark. I was just arriving to do my program. Suddenly, who did I see? This little man leaving the CBC where he had just spoken to the people of Quebec, with a cigarette in his mouth, no bodyguard, completely alone with all the responsibilities he had at the time. He crossed the street at an angle and disappeared into the fog, carrying the problems of the people of Quebec on his shoulders. [6]

It would be possible to write and write and write about this phenomenon unique in Quebec's history, a man who upon his entry into politics in 1960 had already lived a rich life. I have tried to do his life justice ; as for what lies ahead, who knows where his forward momentum will take him ? I have chosen to end our story at the point where it becomes more and more difficult to distinguish Lévesque's philosophy and orientation from that of the Parti Québécois.

Having referred to Réal Caouette and Pierre Trudeau as "unholy monsters," Gérard Bergeron added with regard to the leader of the Parti Québécois : "Lévesque, however, triggers a process of collective self-examination more in the style of Gilles Vigneault than the other two." I did not want to end this book without including the following private notes made by Lévesque on April 6, 1970, three weeks before the Quebec election, and initially obtained without his consent. These reflections, in which Lévesque does in fact occasionally sound more like Gilles Vigneault, reveal more about the man than the rest of this entire book. Like the song by Renée Claude and Stéphane Venne, they are entitled *Le début d'un temps nouveau* [The Beginning of a new era].

> We're finally coming down the home stretch. I'm writing this on April 6, the day after our incredible opening at the Maurice Richard Centre in the city's east end. It was built to hold 8000 people, but more than 12,000 people crushed each other (and us) to get in. Several thousand more outside, in the cold, a spring that still hasn't managed to shake off winter. Like Quebec, which has had trouble in recent years realizing that it is ready for a normal, healthy life.
>
> The struggle isn't over yet. But you get the feeling — you have to feel these things as much as know them, it seems to me — that it will all work out ; perhaps, by some miracle, starting this very month. You sense it in the people who couldn't get into the jam-packed arena : it's cold, but you get the impression that they find it warm anyway ; they're disappointed but not unhappy. They seem to have noticed in themselves a touch of the real spring which isn't far off and is trying its best to blossom forth.
>
> In this last mad dash, which for us is just the last lap on a track we've been tearing around for three years now, the sounds, the images intermingle. The 21 days left will be like a film gone haywire. It would be good to focus on the nice parts, the really fine stuff in this whirlwind of sequences, and not lose any of it. But we'll never do it.
>
> OVERCOATS RIGHT-SIDE OUT
>
> ... Those people who live on the North Shore I went to visit the day before yesterday. They got together in Sept-Iles,

Schefferville, Baie-Comeau, Hauterive, Port-Cartier, and Ga-gnon to charter an old DC-3 so they could all *fly up to* Montreal together for the evening. Going by way of Sherbrooke and, taking routes which also have to be felt to be believed, by way of Wolfe and Richmond counties.

At Port-Cartier, there was that Mr. Bujold, 80-odd years old. A dyed-in-the-wool Tory, I'll bet. But still young enough to meet the challenge of a new season— he didn't turn his old coat inside out, he simply threw it in the garbage . . . and he doesn't seem to be bothered by the cold ! The evening before in St-Hilaire, looking as young as the youngsters around him, there was an old Grit 84 years of age, a Mr. Boivin, sitting in the front row in a crowd of 1200 people . . . . Here and there you see people being brought together again, as always happens at important moments, good or bad, in any family, grandparents and grandchildren and those in between . . . . Could it be that we are really about to take off ?

LIFE AND DEATH

. . . In Sept-Iles, a worker who takes 20 of his precious accumulated days off to come on with us full-time until the end of the month . . . a month which is almost frightening on account of the overflowing tide of energy and devotion which have been summoned up spontaneously in every corner of Quebec. In Asbestos, the frustrated teacher who wonders how he can still keep his teaching job separated for 21 days from the civic duties which fire his enthusiasm after school hours . . . . Elsewhere, the guy who simply dropped his job altogether : "I'll go back and see them in May ; they told me they'd probably wait . . . ."

. . . In Montreal, one in the morning, a truck in front of the local fund-raising office. Sitting up front and unable to get out because of his rheumatism, the father carefully supervises the operation. His son fills up the letter bags which go out (if the mail is still running) to solicit from every corner of the province the funds which keep us going. Up top, his daughter finishes sealing them up with her team of volunteers. "We have to make it work," says the father, "that's all that counts. And there are more of us down at the house if need be . . . ."

Is it possible that this burst of enthusiasm which has affected thousands of Québécois, men and women of all ages and back-grounds, literally tearing their hearts out for no other reason than wanting finally to feel at home once and for all, is it

270

possible that it may all have been in vain by the end of April? It's almost a matter of life and death. Because, if that happens, you wonder how such enthusiasm could be rekindled in the foreseeable future (it would have to be the foreseeable future or never). Like summer ending in the month of May... It seems to me it can't be done again....

OLD EBB TIDES

But it's not over yet. Our Cassandras with their blue or red * campaign coffers, are on the loose.... Like so many mixed-up crows who've got the wrong season and try to make the leaves fall just as the sap is rising!

In the madness which has taken hold of them, they're prepared to do anything, even bring on a collective miscarriage. Of course, they don't really know what trouble they could cause. They don't feel anything anymore — their minds and their senses are overflowing, obsessed with the baubles of the old petty exercise of provincial power, the Blue in abject fear of losing them and the Red in a rage to win.... Poor, wretched power, but it supplies its devotees with pomp, prestige, and perquisites.

Mr. Pierre Laporte is bound to denounce us as bomb-throwers in the morning paper. Is it possible that the most orthodox *Establishment* * figures have been conniving with Mr. Caouette? He sees us heading for a bloodbath very soon, while a little later a certain Dumont sees written in the flaming sky a Communist *coup d'état* scheduled to take place on April 24 (or 25)! Well before the 29th, either they're going to die laughing or else we'll make Vietnam look like very small beer. There will always be St-Bruno Gilbertes † everywhere, declaiming, waiting, fulminating....

This is the final outburst of conditioned impotence and it cannot, must not, be anything more than verbal. Their voices get louder and louder, but only because they feel themselves slipping away. Like an exhausted, receding tide making its last furious assaults, sometimes so violent that standing on the beach you are surprised to find it is only the ebb tide after all....

---

* See note on p. 37.
† In English in the original.
‡ A reference to Gilberte Côté-Mercier, leader of the *Bérêts Blancs* (White Berets), an extremist politico-religious group which once organized a pilgrimage to Saint-Bruno after a woman reported seeing the Virgin Mary there.

Postscript — References

1. Thomas Sloan, *Quebec* : *The Not-So-Quiet Revolution* (Ryerson Press, 1965) p. 69. The author quotes the French translation, *Une révolution tranquille* ? (Hurtubise HMH, 1965), p. 98.
2. *Témoignage de Camille Laurin* : *Pourquoi je suis souverainiste* ? Published by the Parti Québécois, n.d., p. 56.
3. Gérard Bergeron, *Ne bougez plus! Portraits de 40 de nos politiciens* (Editions du Jour, 1968), p. 146.
4. Doris Lussier, "L'indépendance sans le séparatisme ou pourquoi je quitte le parti libéral," *Le Devoir*, 26 October, 1967.
5. Jérôme Proulx, *Le panier de crabes* (Editions Parti Pris, 1971), pp. 203-205.
6. Louis Martin, in a personal interview with the author.

1 2 3 4 5 LaF 79 78 77 76 75